III private perf.
artist assoc. w. parte. roles

The Performing Arts in Contemporary China

The
Performing Arts
in
Contemporary
China

Colin Mackerras

Routledge & Kegan Paul
London, Boston and Henley

First published in 1981
by Routledge & Kegan Paul Ltd
39 Store Street, London WC1E 7DD,
9 Park Street, Boston, Mass. 02108, USA, and
Broadway House, Newtown Road,
Henley-on-Thames, Oxon RG9 1EN
Set in 10/12pt Palatino by
Input Typesetting Ltd, London SW19 8DR
and printed in Great Britain by
Redwood Burn Ltd
Trowbridge & Esher

British Library Cataloguing in Publication Data

Mackerras, Colin
The performing arts in contemporary China.
1. Performing arts – China
1. Title
790.2'0951   PN2874   80-42215
ISBN 0–7100–0778–7

Contents

Preface   viii

1   Historical background   1

2   Performing arts policy in the history of China since Mao Zedong   38

3   The traditional forms of the performing arts since 1976   74

4   Theatre in its modern forms   107

5   The cinema   128

6   Music in the performing arts   154

7   Bringing performances to fruition   176

8   Conclusion   204

Appendix   Musical notation   215

Notes   217

Selected further English-language reading on Chinese performing arts since 1949   226

Selection of journals useful for the Chinese performing arts since 1976   228

Index   229

Illustrations

between pp. 118 and 119

1 and 2   Scenes from the Clapper Opera of Puzhou *Maishui (Selling Water)*

3   Scene from the Shaoxing opera *Liang Shanbo and Zhu Yingtai*

4   Scene from the *Shaoju Limao huan taizi (Exchange of the Heir-Apparent for a Leopard Cat)*

5   Scene from the Clapper Opera of Puzhou *Xu Ce paocheng (Xu Ce Runs on the City Wall)*

6, 7, 8 and 9   Scenes from the Shaoxing opera *Hongzhu nü (The Red Pearl Girl)*

10   Scene from the *Kunqu* drama *Nao tiangong (Havoc in Heaven)*

11   The famous Sichuanese actor Zhou Qihe

12   A *quyi* performance in Chengdu, Sichuan Province

13 and 14   Scenes from an acrobatics performance in Beijing

15   Scene from the modern *Pingju Chuigushou gaozhuang (The Actress Places an Accusation)*

16   The full cast of *The Actress Places an Accusation*

17   The author with cadres of the Literature and Arts section of the *Guangming Daily*

18   The final scene of the spoken play *Jiujiu ta (Save Her)*

19   Members of the cast of the spoken play *Qinggong waishi (Unofficial History of the Qing Court)*

20   Part of a Chinese orchestra

21   Children dance at a primary school

22   Nezha, hero of a cartoon film for children

23 Scene from the film *Erquan yingyue (Moon Reflected on the Second Springs)*

24 and 25 Scenes from the film *Xiaohua (Little Flower)*

26 Scene from the film *Languang shanguo zhihou (After the Blue Light Flashed)*

27 The famous actor Zhang Junqiu

28 Learning to do cartwheels at a training school

29 and 30 Training young actors and actresses

Preface

Probably no area of Chinese society was affected more by the overthrow of the 'gang of four' in October 1976 than culture. Among the categories of cultural life, the performing arts were affected as deeply as any. Jiang Qing, Mao Zedong's widow and the leading figure of the four, had been greatly interested in the performing arts and extremely influential in them. This is one reason why her departure from the political scene should carry such important implications for them.

The deep changes are the reason for writing this book. It aims to describe the transformations in all the multiple aspects of the performing arts and to set them against the development of Chinese society as a whole. It aims to illustrate and analyse the significance of the performing arts since the death of Mao Zedong and its corollary, the fall of the 'gang of four'.

To define what to include in 'the performing arts' is not easy. Clearly the stage arts such as opera, spoken plays, and dance cannot be omitted. Music is also a reasonably obvious candidate because it is 'performed' commonly on a stage or as a companion to the stage arts. A less clear-cut art-form is cinema. The creation of a film clearly demands 'performance', but its screening does not. I have decided to include it here for several reasons. One is the striking parallels between cinema and the other arts mentioned above. Another is the overwhelming numerical preponderance of the motion picture in terms of that fundamental ingredient of the performing arts, the audience.

The sources of information for the material in this book are of various kinds. The first is written and includes mainly the numerous relevant art journals published in the People's Republic of China, as well as various daily or periodic general newspapers, both from China and other countries. In addition, I have used a number of books on the Chinese performing arts, although it will be appreciated that the recent nature of the subject limits the number of relevant published books and makes periodicals much more important.

A second source is personal experience in China. In addition to living in China as a teacher just before and at the beginning of the Cultural Revolution – from August 1964 to September 1966 – I have revisited that country several times. From the point of view of this book the main occasions have been in January 1977, September and October 1978, and late December 1979 to the beginning of February 1980. On all occasions, especially the last two, I went frequently to the theatre and visited organisations relevant to the performing arts.

In writing on a contempory subject one is always confronted by the problem of keeping up to date. Since this book was completed Hua Guofeng has fallen and the 'gang of four' has gone on trial. Nevertheless, the overall direction of change, both in China and its performing arts, has remained constant. If one had to pick a single updating event relevant to the subject of this book, it would be the death of the famous film star Zhao Dan on 20 October 1980. Only two days earlier he had written an article in *People's Daily* asserting that if external controls from official bodies were too stringent they would ruin literature and art. The passing of so significant a figure forms a landmark in the cinema, while his last ideas are representative of trends in Chinese thinking on the arts today.

From 13 January to 2 February 1980 I was under the special sponsorship of the Union of Chinese Dramatists and should like to place on record my appreciation for the help its members gave me. They arranged many vitally important interviews and meetings for me, helped me with their own prodigious fund of information and experience, took me numerous times to the theatre and treated me with the utmost kindness.

Many others have assisted me in the writing of this book. They include the School of Modern Asian Studies, Griffith Uni-

Preface

versity, which provided financial help for the necessary research, Mrs Kay Allen, who typed the drafts, and Mrs Lisa Ho, who prepared the index.

On the other hand, I am alone responsible for the views expressed in this book, and for any shortcomings it may contain.

Colin Mackerras

1

Historical background

No form of art, nor any branch of the performing arts, can live outside the confines of its own society. By its very nature it must be rooted within a particular context – social, economic, historical or political. In the People's Republic of China (PRC) especially, the performing arts are to a significant degree welded tightly into the society that produces them. For these reasons it is necessary to consider the context and background of the contemporary Chinese performing arts in order to understand their aims and nature. Moreover, it will be appropriate to discuss the performing arts themselves parallel to the political, social and economic setting. This background chapter will cover the period from the establishment of the PRC in 1949 to the autumn of 1976, the year when Zhou Enlai and Mao Zedong died.

Since its foundation in 1949 the PRC has demonstrated a number of constant characteristics as well as aspects of change. Let us begin with those of continuity.

Some constant characteristics of the period 1949–76

One of the most pronounced features of the Chinese since 1949, and indeed before, is their strong sense of patriotism and nationalism. This latter concept, which can be defined as sense of nation and national identity, is an offshoot and result of the vaguer and broader idea of patriotism, simply love of country.

1

Neither is an uncommon phenomenon in the modern world but they are possibly even more pronounced in China than in most other countries. Partly because of the extent to which foreign peoples have attempted and succeeded in taking advantage of the Chinese over the past century and more before 1949, the Chinese have found it in their interests to develop rather clear ideas about the nature and uses of nationalism. It is virtually impossible to find a Chinese who would deny being patriotic and their feeling expresses itself in numerous ways. One of them is in the performing arts. The themes of films and plays shown in China since 1949 and before are shot through with love of, and loyalty to, China. The form may vary, resistance to one enemy invader or the desire to adhere to a national leader or economic target, but the sentiment is strong and all-pervading, as pronounced in the performing arts as in real life.

A related feature which has remained reasonably constant over the years since 1949 has been the strength of tradition and, at the same time, attempts to undermine this power. The Chinese Communist Party (CCP) has striven for social change, and has to a great extent achieved its aim, but it has done so within the knowledge that tradition has remained strong. There is something of a dilemma here for any government, especially a radical one, because the power of tradition is really nothing more than that of the Chinese past. Patriotism would suggest an affection for this past, a desire for social change would lead towards its transformation. The dilemma is a constant one in China. At some stages since 1949 the pressures to change tradition have been stronger than at others but at all times the conflict has remained. As we shall see, it has manifested itself nowhere more clearly than in the value placed on the traditional performing arts. At all times the Chinese have claimed to cherish their traditional culture, but the manner of interpretation, based on the requirements of revolutionary change, has sometimes come closer to contempt for the performing arts of the past than love for them.

Among the most important characteristics of traditional life was the numerical preponderance of the peasantry. This is still the case today, since more than four-fifths of the Chinese people live in villages and away from major cities. The types of houses, the structure of the places where the people live at the most grass-roots level, remain unchanged. The durability of the building materials has improved. The quantities of food have risen. The commune system has resulted in a change in the mechanism of government. Yet the texture of village life shows a great deal still that would have been recognisable centuries ago. It comes as no surprise that the problems of the peasantry have been one of the major interests of playwrights and actors since 1949, even though the extent has varied from time to time, often reflecting government policy, and rural themes do not overall occupy four-fifths of the repertoire of the performing arts.

Whether in the villages or cities, life in China has been dominated by a struggle to produce enough to go round; and production has remained an important theme in the theatre since 1949. China has always been a poor country, and remains so today. The degree of poverty may vary from region to region; it is more pronounced in the southwestern province of Guizhou or the northwestern drought areas of Gansu than in the lower Yangzi Valley, where Zhejiang and Jiangsu are possibly the best endowed provinces in China. Yet even in the most affluent areas it is impossible to escape the impression of great poverty and extremely simple living conditions. Though outright death by starvation does not occur today, as it used to on a horrific scale in the past, it remains a threat which no Chinese government can afford to ignore.

Mao Zedong turned this acknowledged poverty into a positive feature despite the suffering it had caused in the past.

China's 600 million people have two remarkable
peculiarities; they are, first of all, poor, and secondly,
blank. That may seem like a bad thing, but it is really a
good thing. Poor people want change, want to do things,
want revolution.[1]

Thus it is largely to overcome the problem of poverty that the Chinese have undertaken a revolution, radical social change, or, as Mao has defined it, 'an insurrection, an act of violence by which one class overthrows another'.[2]

3

From 1949 to 1976 China was undoubtedly a revolutionary nation in which the government and people strove to bring about radical change in society. The people in all parts of China professed an enthusiasm for revolutionary ideology. Within Chinese history this period is one which exhibits great changes from the past. Yet ironically we can still claim that interest in revolution and adherence to Marxist–Leninist philosophy were themselves constant features of those years. To this day the Chinese state and, in general, the Chinese people avow adherence to a revolutionary system of ideas which they describe as Marxism-Leninism-Mao Zedong thought. They claim Lenin to have developed the ideas of Marx, and Mao Zedong to have built on the combined ideas of Marx and Lenin.

Marxism is a materialist philosophy. Materialism means not the love of material things, but that it is matter and the material base which determine the nature and mode of operation of society. Matter is what produces those things which all people need, so the material base implies the means of production: land, factories and so on. Ownership of the means of production is the key to power, and it follows that those groups which own the means of production are the ruling classes. Those classes which possess very little nevertheless work; and because the owners make money from the labour of those who do not own the means of production, Marxists regard the latter as the exploited classes.

In this view of the world ideas, culture and the arts are the result of the material base of society, not the other way round. In other words, the ruling classes which own the means of production automatically devise ideas and cultural forms and content to suit their own interests and thus hold on to power. Whether deliberately or not, they attempt to persuade the labouring or exploited classes in society to accept ideas which will keep these groups of people in subjection.

Since it is ownership of the means of production which determines how people think, it follows that social forces of a similar kind determine how history develops. It also follows that it is classes and not individual people which are important in shaping history and society. No individual, however great,

4

can influence the course of history, unless as part of a class or social force.

Marxist philosophy argues that no change can take place without conflict. Contradictions are the motor of change in the sense that when classes or forces fight against each other they produce social transformation, and only through tension and conflict does change come about. This notion of dialectics is central not only to Marxism but also to Mao's thought, in which class struggle is of supreme importance. Mao saw this tension between the classes as something which could never be ignored. It is true that the emphasis which the government of China placed upon class struggle in the period between 1949 and 1976 was not entirely constant. Yet the idea was always in the fore-front, and even in those few years when it declined in import-ance, this slighter significance itself turned out to be a key feature of PRC development, as we shall see in the summary of China's post-1949 history below.

In the context of Chinese history the main exploited group engaged in this class struggle is the peasantry. Mao Zedong pursues his definition of revolution, quoted earlier, by saying:

> A rural revolution is a revolution by which the peasantry overthrows the power of the feudal landlord class. Without using the greatest force, the peasants cannot possibly overthrow the deep-rooted authority of the landlords which has lasted for thousands of years. The rural areas need a mighty revolutionary upsurge, for it alone can rouse the people in their millions to become a powerful force.[3]

Himself a peasant, although not a very poor one, Mao from the 1920s on regarded the peasantry as the main bulwark of his revolution. It is this class which, because of its poverty, is the most eager to bring about social change.

The major body within China espousing and propagating the doctrines of Marxism-Leninism-Mao Zedong thought has been the Chinese Communist Party. Founded in 1921, when it held its first Congress in Shanghai and later Hangzhou, this body has had a chequered and exciting history, but there has been no period since 1949, with the possible exception of the Cultural

Revolution, when its dominance has been seriously questioned. It has grown in size, from 1,210,000 in 1945,[4] to more than 35,000,000 in 1977,[5] the latter figure being nearly thirty times the former. China may claim to be less elite-ridden than in earlier days, yet the extreme authority of the CCP makes that body the most important of any elite which may exist in China.

Even though Marxism holds that it is not individuals but social forces which determine history and social development, yet there have been several personalities within the CCP so significant that one can claim them as dominating the history of the period from 1949 to 1976. The two most constant and important are undoubtedly Mao Zedong and Zhou Enlai. Mao was the Chairman of the CCP from 1935 until his death on 9 September 1976 and Chairman of the People's Republic of China from its establishment in October 1949 until April 1959. Zhou Enlai was the Minister of Foreign Affairs from 1949 until February 1958 and in effect dominated China's foreign policy all through the period 1949 to 1976. From the beginning of the PRC until his death on 8 January 1976 he was also the Premier of the Government Administrative Council and from September 1954 its successor the State Council. Because these two were the most permanently influential men in PRC history, their deaths in a very real sense signified the end of an era.

Mao's position as Chairman of the CCP and Zhou's as Premier of the State Council illustrate another constant feature about the period 1949 to 1976: the dual structure of administration in China. On the one hand there is a party which exercises supreme authority; on the other hand there is the state organisation which is administrative but also influential. Mao it was who dominated the Party, Zhou Enlai the State organisation. This is not to say that Zhou Enlai was not a member of the CCP; indeed his authority derived in part from his senior CCP membership. Nor can it be claimed that Mao Zedong held no authority in the State structure. In fact as Chairman of the PRC until 1959 he was its supreme executive. Yet it remains true that the influence of the two men was primarily seen respectively on the Party and the State level. Zhou Enlai was the man principally responsible for putting into effect the ideas of Mao. The Chinese today also respect Zhou Enlai as the man who helped Mao work out his ideas and in some cases restrained him from excesses.

The dual Party and State structure of administration in China is reflected not only at the national level but also at the provincial and lower. Each province, city and county has its Party and State administration. The dual structure is found at every level, from the highest to the lowest.

This consistent dual administration, and especially the Marxist concept that all society rests on a particular material base, suggest that China sees itself as an integrated society. It is in no sense fragmented into numerous parts. Hence, the performing arts which are the subject of this book must occupy a very definite place within the system. In brief, the performing arts are like culture and the arts in general in that they are part of the superstructure of society; that is to say, they rest upon the material base and are determined by it.

It is very important in a Marxist state – and indeed elsewhere – that the government should have means for projecting its messages to the people. The performing arts occupy a vital aspect of communications in China. This applies not only to particular policies, although these are certainly reflected in the performing arts, but also to overall attitudes, general ideas, a whole way of thinking.

The performing arts are important in all societies, not merely Marxist ones, because they contain images of good and bad which influence the way people cast their value judgments. Whether they want to or not, people identify with certain characters within dramas or films. A playwright has ways and means of encouraging the spectators to sympathise with a certain character, to dislike or distrust another. The features of the 'goodie' are those which the onlooker involuntarily regards as desirable, which he himself wishes to emulate. On the other hand, there are those characters whom the playwright can establish as being unworthy of sympathy and with characteristics which the onlooker may wish to avoid.

The Chinese are indeed conscious of how these images operate and the term 'image' is one found quite frequently in Chinese literature on the performing arts. It is the ability of the performing arts to influence the way people regard the world and what they consider to be good or desirable, and bad or undesirable, which makes them so important. In a country such as China the performing arts assume an importance even greater than in a Western society, because of the relative lack of the kind of media which dominate the richer countries of the world, such as television. As a matter of fact the performing arts since time immemorial have been China's principal sculptor of emotional images.

The performing arts are traditionally a mass form of art in China. Indeed, the ruling elite in the past tended to look askance at most types of drama even to the extent that it was a punishable crime for their children to witness any but the most carefully selected theatrical item.

Theatre and other performing arts have been the cultural form most closely related to the people's daily lives. Any special occasion was an excuse for a drama, festivals of all kinds, particular events and so on. Yet nobody really needed a special occasion as an excuse for drama. Wandering companies from time to time brought it to the villages. The people knew the stories and what the costumes meant, they identified with, despised or hated the particular characters being portrayed on the stage. The performing arts have thus always been reasonably tightly integrated into society. The present situation since 1949 whereby Marxism demands integration between society and the performing arts is actually nothing new in China.

Because the performing arts occupy so important a place in the communications between the government and the people it follows that the authorities have always been very keen, indeed have insisted, upon knowing what went on in the theatres. In the period 1949 to 1976 also, government control of the performing arts was a constant feature. The degree of the control varied to some extent but it never sank below a level which would be regarded as extremely high in most countries of the West.

The preceding pages have drawn attention to a number of characteristics in China which have remained reasonably constant between the years 1949 and 1976, including those which relate to society in general and to the performing arts in particular. Of course it would be possible also to list many others.

But in addition to continuities, there have been many features illustrating social or political change over the same period, and it is to these which we now turn.

History of the PRC and its performing arts to 1976

Because of the integration of Chinese society over the period 1949 to 1976, it is most appropriate to deal with the general history and that of the performing arts together.

The technical term in China for the accession of the People's Republic of China on 1 October 1949 is 'liberation', and the date's anniversaries are celebrated as National Day. The event was the result of long years of war, including civil war from 1946 to 1949, leading up to the victory of the CCP. There are many reasons for this success, and certainly they lie outside the scope of this book. The failing morale of the Guomindang (Nationalist Party), helped by galloping inflation, both factors due in part to the War against Japan (1937–45), and the high confidence of the CCP, assisted by its tight ideology and organisation, were certainly important factors. It is very striking that the CCP, unlike the Guomindang, had a clear policy on the performing arts: that they should assist in the process of educating the masses. The Communists went down among the people and they never hesitated to do what they could to bring their messages of liberation and struggle against the exploiting classes to the people. The CCP had little difficulty in persuading the peasants and the workers that they were being exploited. Dramas emphasising such themes certainly assisted its cause. In the light of the importance of the performing arts as a method of communication and the very conscious policy of the CCP in using them for propaganda and inspiration purposes, it is possible to argue that the performing arts played a role as one of the causes of its victory.[6]

The PRC to the Cultural Revolution

After the civil war had led to the CCP's triumph and the establishment of the PRC, the Party set about the task of strengthening its political power. Most observers put the 'period of consolidation' from 1949 to 1952, and within these years there were four major events or trends.

The first was the destruction of the power of the opposition classes through a series of campaigns. The major rural one was land reform. The political power of the landlords and of the big bourgeoisie rested upon their ownership of land and of the urban means of production respectively. Since China is a predominantly rural country in which over 80 per cent of the people are peasants, land reform was the more important of the two. In June 1950 the new government issued the Agrarian Reform Law of the PRC under which land was to be seized from the landlords and distributed among the peasants. As a matter of fact, the CCP had issued land laws even before it came to power in the whole of China, and for that reason land reform had to some extent been carried out in those parts of China where the CCP had earlier held sway. But the June 1950 law set the seal on a nationwide process of redistribution. Land reform was not a plain-sailing process. Passions were stirred up among the peasants based upon their generally quite genuine grievances revolving around their exploitation by the landlord class. Quite a few landlords were punished, or even killed. On the other hand, many were persuaded to repent of the way they had treated the peasants, or threw in their lot with the new government. What is important is that land reform meant the end of the political power of the landlords. Although they have continued to exist since 1952 when land reform was completed, they no longer matter in political terms in China.

The urban counterpart to land reform was a series of two campaigns directed principally against the comprador bourgeoisie, that is, the big bourgeoisie with close connections with foreign powers,[7] although it is true that the national bourgeoisie, or capitalists without foreign connections, were also to some extent affected. Just as land reform rendered the landlords politically impotent, so these two urban campaigns broke the power of the big bourgeoisie.

At the same time as it successfully strove to undermine the power of opposition classes, the new government attempted to change the family life of society, the second of the four major trends and events of the consolidation period. In particular, on 1 May 1950 it promulgated the Marriage Law of the PRC which laid down equality between the sexes, banned arranged marriages, concubinage, polygamy and interference in the remarriage of widows, and greatly facilitated divorce. In the countryside it had been more or less universal practice that the parents of a young person should decide whom he or she married and arrange the marriage, through the aid of a matchmaker, with the parents of the proposed spouse. Clearly women had suffered much more than men under the system because of their greater dependence upon their family, both before and after marriage. To uproot this system of arranged marriages and to promote equality between the sexes were not easy matters. They required radical attitudinal change on the part of both men and women, young and old, and were not brought about simply through the issuing of a law. It is not surprising to find a great deal of propaganda and emphasis upon the subject in the early years of the PRC. Moreover, the government has continued to apply pressures against arranged marriages and in favour of equality between the sexes in more recent years as well.

To lay down progressive marriage regulations was not something new to 1950; both the Guomindang and the CCP had promulgated such laws well before then. Yet this was the first time that a really serious attempt had been made to put such a law into effect on a nationwide basis. The comparative success of its implementation carried both political and economic, as well as social, implications. To apply the doctrine of equality between the sexes radically increased the political influence and participation of women at the expense of men. At the same time, the former function of the family as an economic unit of society was drastically undercut by the Marriage Law. The economic, and hence political, power of the great clans thus suffered a very serious blow.

The third trend or event in the first period after liberation was the attempt at economic reconstruction in the wake of the civil war. The new government took measures to reduce the staggeringly high rate of inflation, it started to get agriculture back on its feet and began to reorganise and expand industry.

It also got the railway network functioning again after the extreme disruption of years of war and civil war, and began the expansion of the transport system. Finally, it began the takeover of foreign enterprises.

In the field of foreign affairs, the period of consolidation was characterised by friendship with the Soviet Union and hostility towards the United States. With the former China signed a Treaty of Friendship, Alliance and Mutual Assistance on 14 February 1950. In October the same year, Chinese troops intervened in Korea in a war lasting until June 1953 against the United Nations armies led by the United States. China threw a great deal into that war both in terms of manpower and of material. Rightly or wrongly, China feared that it would be again occupied as it had so recently been by the Japanese; consequently the war exercised a somewhat greater impact on the Chinese people than on those of the United States or most other countries which took part. Certainly the Korean War made the Chinese very spy-conscious, a fact which helped stir up feelings of vengeance and fear in the process of land reform and the various other campaigns of the time.

In all the developments described the performing arts played an important role. The CCP government strove to carry on the policy which had operated in the liberated areas; to put over the communist message on a nationwide basis through drama and film and thus help in the consolidation of power. It set up a hierarchy to supervise theatre throughout the country. In particular, on 10 July 1950 its Ministry of Culture organised the Drama Reform Committee to help in the development of drama reform. What this meant was that the traditional theatre which had dominated the lives of Chinese people for so long was now to undergo change in order to propagate values appropriate to the era of the CCP rather than the traditional attitudes of the feudal period. The classical theatre certainly survived, indeed it even grew in health in the more stable conditions which prevailed now that the civil war was over. The old actors continued or began again to ply their trade. Probably the major change demanded in the reform of this revived tradition was to place a far stronger emphasis on modern and contemporary themes. Foremost among them in the first years was the Marriage Law. A typical story involved a young woman forced by her parents to marry somebody whom she did not love and who was entirely unsuitable. An appeal to the CCP brings on a struggle with her parents but success in marrying the young man of her choice, who is of course progressive politically. There is scope for considerable variety in stories of this kind.

China also made a real attempt to set up its own socialist film industry. Foreign films were restricted to those of the Soviet Union or other socialist countries. During the Korean War that conflict was by far the most popular topic in Chinese studios. Films – as well as dramas – dealt with the evil of the American imperialists in their war of aggression in Korea and in support for the Chinese troops. The government took concrete steps to see that the people in their millions saw such films. Performing arts of all kinds were contributing to the processes of land and marriage reform, were familiarising the people with the ideas of the new society, and helping them to appreciate or get used to it.

The period in PRC history following consolidation is that of the First Five Year Plan from 1953 to 1957. Co-operation with the Soviet Union grew increasingly strong in the early fifties and the First Five Year Plan clearly demonstrated adherence to the Soviet model in economic development. Strongest emphasis went to heavy industry, and to industry in general, growth in which was extremely fast during these years. Attention was also paid to agriculture. In 1955 the co-operativisation of land began. Under this programme most of the land which had been distributed among the peasants as a result of land reform was now placed into co-operatives where collective ownership of the land prevailed.

From a political point of view this was on the whole a period of great confidence. The Korean War was over and China enjoyed a few years of unparalleled peace. It had a strong ally and felt reasonably secure against powerful enemies such as the United States and Japan. The threat of a Guomindang return no doubt survived but it was somewhat less menacing than during the Korean War. This confidence in the success of the government's consolidation of power is reflected in the holding of the First National People's Congress in September 1954. The

National People's Congress is the highest organ of countrywide state political power in China, and it ratified and formalised the establishment of a permanent central government structure. Possibly the Congress's main task was to adopt the state constitution, which, in Article 1, laid down the PRC as 'a people's democratic state led by the working class and based on the alliance of workers and peasants'. Article 17 called on all state organs to 'rely on the masses of the people, constantly maintain close contact with them, heed their opinions, and accept their supervision'. The document is generally fairly liberal in tone and specifies a number of types of freedom, such as those of religion and association. The National People's Congress was followed, in September 1956, by the Eighth National Congress of the CCP, exemplifying the parallel development of the State and Party organs of power. It was the first since liberation, the seventh having taken place from April to June 1945 in Yan'an, and thus showed an atmosphere of considerable self-assurance.

Towards the end of the First Five Year Plan period came a series of political and cultural events which shook this confidence somewhat. The first was the Hundred Flowers Movement. In 1956 the CCP invited the people to speak their minds fully and freely, or 'to let a hundred flowers bloom', but fear of retaliation made initial reaction very slow. In April 1957 the Party again issued the invitation, with much stronger force. This time response was strong and immediate. A deluge of criticism came forth in all forms of media. In particular, May and early June 1957 is the period when the 'Democracy Wall' began in Beijing. Many of the criticisms concerned individuals in the CCP or the way the CCP operated. Some of them, however, attacked the socialist system itself, and this neither the Party nor the government could tolerate. From 8 June on China's main newspaper, *People's Daily*, called for a brake on the extent of criticism. It argued that the Hundred Flowers Movement was being used by rightists to try and overthrow the CCP.

The period of liberalism turned into the Anti-Rightist Campaign, aimed clearly against those whom the CCP and government regarded as hostile to themselves. Many such people had been in the forefront of the criticism during the Hundred Flowers. Large numbers of intellectuals, CCP members and cultural

14

figures were sent to the countryside to undertake 'corrective labour'. The impact on morale is not hard to guess, because the Party had promised during the Hundred Flowers that the invitation to criticise was not simply a plot to expose its enemies, but now it turned against those who had taken the Party at its word. Many of those sent to the countryside during the Anti-Rightist Campaign were not pardoned until 1979.

For the performing arts the years of the First Five Year Plan saw continuing reform, and conferences were held to discuss the associated problems, including how one should portray heroes, religious figures and villains in the traditional opera. In accordance with the co-operativisation of land and similar events in other economic sectors, the performing arts also saw a degree of nationalisation. Many opera companies which had been privately run before liberation were taken over by the State, including fifteen in Tianjin and sixty-nine in Shanghai in January 1956. The government also established its own new opera companies, the most important example being the major Beijing Opera Company of China on 10 January 1955. The cinema industry expanded, with a number of new studios set up. To make a film from an opera was certainly not new – the revolutionary opera *Baimao nü (The White-Haired Girl)* had been filmed in 1950 – but the years 1953 to 1957 saw important attention given to operas, especially traditional operas, by cinema directors. The Shaoxing opera *Liang Shanbo yu Zhu Yingtai (Liang Shanbo and Zhu Yingtai)*, a classical love story issued as a film in 1953, is a particularly well known case in point. A two-part colour film was made in 1955 from the stage artistry of the Beijing Opera's, and indeed China's, best and most popular actor Mei Lanfang.

The Hundred Flowers Movement produced a significant impact on all performing arts, including theatre and cinema. The scope of available items reached its greatest breadth since 1949. In the field of drama the Ministry of Culture issued a directive on 17 May 1957 relaxing all prohibitions on particular pieces, which said in part: 'from now on, as far as dramatic items banned in the past are concerned . . . the theatre companies and artists of every region should take care of them by themselves according to prevailing local conditions.' [8] However, just

15

as the Hundred Flowers period did not last long in the overall development of China, so the period of liberalisation was very short-lived in the performing arts. From the onset of the Anti-Rightist Campaign the range of dramas performed and films shown narrowed substantially, and previous bans returned.

In China's overall development the Anti-Rightist Campaign merged into the Great Leap Forward in 1958. This was a period of ambitious economic development along a clearly Maoist model. China turned its back on the Soviet model of economic development it had employed in the First Five Year Plan, and chose a path in which ideological motivation and the mobilisation of the masses took a much greater role than hitherto. Part of the new mode of development was the establishment, in 1958, of the rural people's communes, which attempted to integrate agricultural and industrial production, education, the arts, administration and militia in a single social unit. The CCP claimed that the communes were a spontaneous development. Whether this was true or not, it is clear that the trend towards rural communisation on the basis of the co-operatives gathered momentum very quickly.

The Great Leap Forward was the first time that a truly radical mode of economic development had been attempted in China. It created an impact on relations with the Soviet Union, which resented the suggestion that China's social system might now be more advanced even than the parent of socialist societies. It was one of several factors causing early strain between China and the Soviet Union. There were also clear implications in the Great Leap Forward for the leadership of China. The fact is that influential sections of the CCP violently opposed Mao's Great Leap strategy. So great did the tensions become that the Great Leap Forward was quickly abandoned and Mao's influence began to decline. In April 1959 the National People's Congress appointed Liu Shaoqi to replace him as Chairman of the PRC, while letting him retain the post of Chairman of the CCP. Although the Chinese government tried to avoid the appearance that Liu's appointment was in fact a dismissal for Mao, it is almost certain that Mao regarded it as a rebuff. Liu's authority expanded at Mao's expense and the two became bitter rivals.

Economically the aftermath of the Great Leap Forward was

a very lean era. The earlier enthusiasm of the Great Leap Forward turned very sour as harvest yields fell drastically and food
shortages began to occur. The reasons for these are not entirely
clear. The Chinese themselves claimed that they were due mainly to extremely serious natural disasters; 1960 in particular saw
the worst combination of drought and flood that China had
seen for a century. Others, however, have claimed that administrative mismanagement was a much more important cause. In
the summer of 1960, right in the middle of these difficult years,
the Soviet Union withdrew its technicians and experts for
reasons related to the continuing and accelerating decline in
relations with China. Their departure merely exacerbated the
very difficult economic conditions prevailing in China at that
time. Liu Shaoqi's government responded with economic policies dramatically opposed to those of the Great Leap. Free mar-
kets revived in the countryside, private plots expanded in the
communes, the profit motive and material incentives returned
stronger than ever, the participation of the masses in decision-
making declined, and the status of the expert technician and
the manager rose.

One of the slogans of the Great Leap Forward period was
'walking on two legs'. This was subject to a number of different
interpretations, in the most directly economic field meaning a
parallel and similar emphasis on both industry and agriculture.
In the field of the performing arts it meant a stress both on the
traditional and modern drama. In effect this meant a continuing
revival of traditional operas, provided their theme was patriotic
and focused sympathy on the peasant and other masses as
against the feudal ruling classes, and a new and heavy accent
on dramas with modern and contemporary themes. As so often
in China the policy of 'walking on two legs' was introduced by
a major conference on drama which the Ministry of Culture
held from 13 June to 14 July 1958. Its resolution stated:

At the same time as we make modern drama items the
core, push ahead the Great Leap Forward in theatre work
in an all-round way, and strongly develop modern drama
items, we should continue earnestly to dig up and arrange
traditional items, and also rehearse new historical items.

17

On the basis of fully developing the superior traditional art,
we should create new socialist dramas, and strongly serve
the workers, peasants and soldiers, and the socialist
revolution and socialist construction.[9]

As the Great Leap Forward and its enthusiasm for mass mobilisation waned, so also did that for modern dramas with
propaganda themes; and from 1959 on the traditional leg carried
ever greater weight, while the modern limped more and more
weakly. It may be that this tendency was at least in part con-
nected with the Sino-Soviet dispute which gathered momentum
from the time of the Soviet withdrawal of experts in 1960. A
reaction against a European power and the influence which it
had exercised upon Chinese society may have helped towards
a reassertion of the traditional Chinese theatre, a form of art
which the Chinese could really see as their own and which had
suffered almost no foreign influence. The climax of the trend
towards imbalance in the two legs was a partial return to the
liberalism of 1957. In March 1962, a National Conference for the
Creation of Spoken Plays and Operas was held in Guangzhou.
Attended by over 200 playwrights, opera composers and others,
it gave strong encouragement to the policies of 'letting a
hundred flowers bloom' and a concomitant relaxation of Party
control over literature and the arts.

Over the years 1958 to 1962 cinema followed trends similar to
those in drama. In the early period the industry did its best to
produce large numbers of films on the current Great Leap, as
well as on CCP and prerevolutionary historical themes. But in
the early 1960s, fewer films came out and they tended to centre
far more round the past. A good illustrative example is the film
on the novel *Honglou meng (A Dream of Red Mansions)* which
appeared in 1962.

It comes as no surprise that Mao, whose influence had suffered so greatly as a result of the rejection of the policies of the
Great Leap, was not happy with the way in which China was
developing in the early 1960s. At a plenary session of the CCP's
Central Committee held in September 1962, he attempted to
reverse policy towards the idea of mass mobilisation and participation. Mao's slogan of the plenum was 'never forget class

struggle'. Characteristically interpreting events in class terms, he was indicating his fear that Liu's economic and cultural policies were resulting in the regrowth not only of capitalism but also of the power of the bourgeoisie. Tendencies, he suggested, must be changed, or a capitalist restoration would soon supervene. The years 1963 to 1965 did in fact see the persistence of Liu's policies, but pressures mounted with ever greater intensity to reverse them. One could sum up that this was the period when Liu Shaoqi's economic influence reached its height but when ideological preparation was gathering force for the Cultural Revolution.

In the countryside the main sign of the coming change was the Socialist Education Movement, which aimed to eliminate corruptions of various kinds among rural cadres. In addition to stamping out a resurgence of outright offences, such as bribery and nepotism, it sought to reduce the power of cadres to make them blend better with the masses as equals, not to stand over them as masters, and not to seek privilege. Both Mao and Liu supported the movement, but each tried to give it his own particular stamp and to increase the influence of his respective ideals in the countryside. The other major preparation for the Cultural Revolution was in the field of foreign affairs. The early 1960s saw an intensification of the split with the Soviet Union in which charges and counter-charges were laid by both sides. A split developed so bitter that it went far beyond the realm of ideology, where it had begun; it came to rest firmly in the field of national interest and made each side see the other as a threat to itself. This mutual perception put real poison into the Sino-Soviet relationship.

Possibly the sharpening struggle that preceded the Cultural Revolution was nowhere better crystallised than in the performing arts. One faction, led by Peng Zhen the Mayor of Beijing and others, believed that the traditional operas should be maintained in strength. On the other side were those who believed that the drama should be completely revolutionised to project heroic proletarian images to the people; the traditional opera should be totally suspended, at least for a while, so that the modern operas could secure the first place on the stage and in the affections of the Chinese people. This group was led above all by the wife of Mao Zedong, former filmstar Jiang Qing, and the radical Mayor of Shanghai Ke Qingshi.

It was in 1963 that Mao's wife began to assert herself politically by trying to exert influence in the cultural sphere, apparently with the blessing of Mao himself. In the first place, when the heads of the CCP's cultural bureaux met in April 1963 to discuss the content of dramas and literary works in China, Jiang Qing had a circular distributed 'on suspending the performance of ghost plays', in which it was clearly proposed that traditional operas of all kinds should be prohibited.

The same year Jiang Qing began visiting Beijing's most reputable Beijing Opera companies, controlled by Peng Zhen, and did her best to persuade the actors that modern operas on directly up-to-date themes and with contemporary characters would be more appropriate to the socialist period than traditional. She is reported to have told them on one occasion:

> You eat grain grown by the peasants, you wear clothes made by the workers, you live in houses built by the workers, the People's Liberation Army is the frontline of our national defence, yet you do not represent them on the stage. I'd like to ask what is the class stand of artists. Where is the 'conscience' of artists that you constantly talk about.[10]

Jiang Qing was indeed able to increase her influence by gaining allies among well-known and prestigious actors of the traditional Chinese theatre. One particularly prominent example was Tan Yuanshou, the great-grandson of the famous Beijing Opera actor Tan Xinpei (1847–1917) known as the 'king of the acting world' in the early years of the twentieth century. Tan Yuanshou had been a supporter of the revolutionisation of the Beijing Opera since 1958, but Peng Zhen and others had opposed and thwarted his attempts in that direction. He thus welcomed Jiang Qing's intervention.

The climax of that critical year 1963 came when on 25 December Ke Qingshi opened the East China Drama Festival in Shanghai. He criticised the lack of modern plays in the repertory of certain troupes, and was able to draw attention to the model of the Festival, which was billed to give twenty revolutionary items.

As the struggle developed and the modernists appeared to gain the victory over the traditionalists, the first Festival of Beijing Operas on Contemporary Themes was held in Beijing from 5 June to 31 July 1964. In his opening speech Lu Dingyi, who was the Director of the CCP Central Committee's Propaganda Department, stressed the all-important political connection between the development of the performing arts and the growth of modern revisionism in China. He believed that the revolutionisation of the opera would be a powerful tool to prevent modern revisionism from taking a foothold in China. At the same time, the Festival was not entirely a victory for Jiang Qing. At a symposium held on 23 June and attended by artists and others taking part in the Festival, she made a speech 'On the Revolution of the Beijing Opera', which was not even reported; its full text was published only in May 1967 at the height of the Cultural Revolution.

The results of the struggle were of course felt in the film industry. New films increasingly reflected revolutionary struggle, and public criticism raged in the media against those which did not measure up to the standard of ideological purity demanded. Perhaps the main one was *Zaochun eryue (February in Early Spring)*. Set in the mid-1920s it was based on the tragic and romantic love novel *Eryue (February)*, written by the Communist author Zhao Pingfu (pen-name Rou-Shi), who was arrested and executed by Guomindang authorities early in 1931. As a foreign resident in China from 1964 to 1966 I was among the many thousands of people to whom the film was shown as a 'negative example', and found it perhaps the tenderest Chinese film I had seen. However, by that time tenderness had come to be a vice, not a virtue. A Chinese living in Beijing at the time has since written of *February in Early Spring*:

> Now in 'glorious color', it appeared to be hopelessly treacly and sentimental. It nauseated the virile young people of the postliberation era and even me, of the 1908 generation. . . . When we saw the two star-crossed lovers on the inevitably broken bridge, we groaned and tittered.

One could legitimately ask why public money had been wasted on such films.[11]

Perhaps by way of additional reprimand to 'revisionist' creations like this film, a number of revolutionary works later to become extremely famous as 'models' were given their premiere in 1964. Among the works performed at the first Festival of Beijing Operas on Contemporary Themes, for instance, was *Hongdeng ji (The Story of the Red Lantern)*, in which Jiang Qing had taken a particularly close interest. On 3 October, as part of the celebrations for the fifteenth National Day, the ballet *Hongse niangzi jun (The Red Detachment of Women)* was premiered in Beijing. On the other hand, revolutionary works later condemned as revisionist and consequently suppressed until after the 'smashing of the gang of four' in October 1976 were also among those first publicly performed in 1964. The most prominent case in point is *Dongfang hong (The East is Red)*, a music and dance pageant dealing with the history of the Chinese revolution right from its beginnings to the time of the Korean War; its premiere took place in Beijing on 2 October 1964 as part of the National Day festivities, and it was filmed the same year.

The Cultural Revolution and after

Ideological fervour and struggle had been building up throughout 1964 and 1965; the struggle over the direction of the performing arts was thus in no sense accidental. At the end of 1965 the Cultural Revolution began over issues raised by dramas popular in the period of ideological relaxation which had followed the Great Leap Forward; the main one was *Hai Rui baguan (The Dismissal of Hai Rui)*, by the Deputy Mayor of Beijing Wu Han, which was published in November 1961. As a matter of fact the debate about the drama was one aspect only of a whole series of struggles over the direction of China. They included the model of economic development, and how China was to be governed, among many other matters. One of the critical questions revolved around incentives; should people work for material incentives, that is primarily for their own interests, or for moral, in order to serve the people? In particular, should administrators be allowed to secure privileges for themselves, or should they be encouraged to work wholeheartedly for the masses of the people? Mao saw this question as asking whether the revolution should result in the replacement of one elite by another, or in a genuine difference in the nature of power and influence in society. If the former were the case, then real power would remain with a small group, if the latter then the masses would secure the right to a real input into decisions affecting their own future.

Mao had decided that the CCP was corrupt and revisionist, that is to say, was itself this new elite the growth of which he had feared so much. His answer to the problem was a full-scale frontal attack on the Party bureaucracy and denunciations of those he perceived as its major revisionist leaders, Liu Shaoqi and Deng Xiaoping, by a vanguard which he himself chose: the youth of China and Red Guard organisations which it had built under his instructions. As a result of his policy almost every senior CCP member, other than Mao himself and his chosen deputy Lin Biao, was criticised or even physically attacked during the Cultural Revolution. Among the first to fall were several whose opposition to Jiang Qing in the performing arts field had been most vocal: Peng Zhen, Mayor of Beijing, and other leaders of the Party Propaganda Department, including Zhou Yang and Lu Dingyi. The masses were enthused with the thought of Mao Zedong, which was condensed into the *Quotations from Chairman Mao Zedong*, usually referred to as the *Little Red Book*. First published in Shanghai in September 1966, this work was distributed on a gigantic scale: the New China News Agency reported on 25 December 1967 that, during that year, 350,000,000 copies had been issued.

The problem was that the old guard, that is the Party hierarchy, was not prepared to yield power. It fought back against the young, and because it held more money and arms than they, it could not easily be dislodged. As the struggle grew more intense violence erupted, sometimes resulting in fairly large-scale bloodshed. A particularly serious incident took place in July and August 1967 in Wuhan, the capital city of Hubei province and an important city from a strategic point of view.

A major factional flare-up there resulted in the intervention of the central government, representatives of which flew to the city to arbitrate. The right-wing faction immediately had them arrested. Zhou Enlai succeeded in obtaining their release, but only at the cost of a fortnight's civil war in the region. Although the central government forces won this local conflict, it certainly frightened the leadership in Beijing because the incident crystallised the threat of a revival of warlordism. This the central government could not tolerate.

In terms of power Mao's forces seemed to gain more victories than Liu Shaoqi's. In October 1968 a plenary session of the CCP Central Committee dismissed Liu from all posts and expelled him from the Party. A new form of Maoist administration called the revolutionary committee, a tripartite sharing of power between the army, the old cadres, and the masses, was instituted in all provinces and counties, as well as in local units such as communes, factories, the army, universities and schools. On the whole there was a change of leadership as a result of the Cultural Revolution: yet a fairly long time was to elapse before the disunity which resulted from it could be solved. The Ninth National Congress of the CCP in April 1969 established a new Central Committee which included most of those who had emerged as radicals and supporters of Mao during the Cultural Revolution. It reappointed Mao Zedong as Party Chairman and Lin Biao as Deputy Chairman; moreover it adopted a new CCP Constitution, under which Lin became Mao's formal successor as Chairman. It seemed that Lin Biao, who had in effect been largely responsible for directing the Cultural Revolution, was to reap the rewards of his loyalty to Mao in terms of present and future power. The Ninth Congress forms a convenient milepost ushering in a period of greater stability after the Cultural Revolution. However, the Congress itself certainly did not declare the Cultural Revolution ended despite references to its 'great victory' and in his report Lin Biao approvingly quoted Mao as specifying that 'it is wrong to speak lightly of the final victory of the revolution in our country'.[12]

Meanwhile in the performing arts the Cultural Revolution down to the Ninth CCP Congress followed logically from the earlier period and reflected developments in other areas of society. The struggle became more intense and the radical side appeared to gain the upper hand with ever increasing strength. A drama had formed a starting point for the Cultural Revolution as a whole but Jiang Qing had no intention of leaving it at that. In February 1966, on Lin Biao's instructions, she convened a forum on the work in literature and art in the armed forces; and the ideas which emerged conformed very closely to Mao's thought. In particular the performing arts and art in general were required to reflect the class struggle with total directness. The hero must belong to the proletarian class and embody all its virtues. Correspondingly, the villain must be a class enemy and reflect all his evil. The images of good and bad, of the proletariat and of the enemy classes, should come over to the audience with the utmost clarity.

One of the first results of the implementation of these ideas was the denunciation of performing arts up to this point. Famous actors such as Zhou Xinfang, film producers like Xia Yan, and dramatists, including Tian Han, came under serious attack. Jiang Qing proceeded with the revolutionisation of the performing arts by adapting particularly appropriate dramas of the pre-Cultural Revolution period to suit the theories which she and Mao were espousing. The changes aimed to bring out the class character of each particular person in the dramas more clearly. For example, Western musical instruments were added to emphasise the heroic nature of certain sections, especially those related to the proletarian heroes. The problem was that because there was a limited number of dramas that could be rearranged in this way, the theatre and film diet of the Chinese people at this period became extremely narrow. As in other sectors of society the drama and film organisations more or less suspended operations while they thrashed out how they were to conduct themselves in future and what ideological line they would follow. The professional performing arts all but came to a standstill during the Cultural Revolution.

On the other hand this was a period when the amateur came very much to his own. One of the points of the Cultural Revolution was to give prominence to the non-specialist in all areas of society. The ideologically motivated person was held to be more useful than the professional, even if his actual skill was somewhat slighter, because of his willingness to serve the masses of the peasants, workers and soldiers and not to seek privilege or physical comfort. The radical phases of PRC history have been the high points in the social status of the non-professional. In particular amateur arts flourished during the Cultural Revolution and increasing numbers of people, especially among the young, were encouraged to take part in them and to exercise their creativity.

The years after the Ninth Party Congress, down to the end of 1976, saw a seesaw struggle between those who wished to maintain the ideas and direction of the Cultural Revolution, and those who hoped to undermine them and replace them with rapid modernisation of the Chinese economy and society. The CCP attempted to reunite itself, after the Cultural Revolution, to present an appearance of unity to the people, and thus to re-establish its authority. The major political event of the period did not help its efforts. This was the Lin Biao conspiracy. According to the claims made by the Chinese media, Lin Biao attempted to assassinate Mao Zedong and seize the Party chairmanship himself. The details of the event are shrouded in mystery and controversy. Two points are clear, however. One is that the 'Lin Biao affair' resulted in his death in September 1971 and fall from the CCP's grace. The other is that it caused a major upset within the CCP because of the extreme prestige which the people had been encouraged to accord Lin Biao up to that time and because he was constitutionally Mao's successor.

The radical faction did not give up despite this clear setback. There was a succession of campaigns designed to enhance mass participation in the nation's activities and to maintain the purity of the revolution. Possibly the most significant one was the Campaign to Criticise Lin Biao and Confucius which began in August 1973, and ran through 1974 as a mass movement. It aimed to link the Cultural Revolution and its ideals with an attack on the ideas of the ancient philosopher Confucius (551–479 BC) and his followers throughout the ages. The man held traditionally as a sage was accused of trying to prevent the onflow of history and to bring back the power of former ruling classes. In the same way the CCP's media suggested that Lin

26

Biao had attempted to bring back the power of the bourgeoisie in China; his role in the forefront of the Cultural Revolution was in reality a hypocritical attempt to destroy the dictatorship of the proletariat. A slightly later campaign attempted to denounce the traditional Chinese novel *Shuihu zhuan (The Water Margin)* as revisionist and capitulationist because its hero ends up surrendering to the emperor.

The seesaw struggle over the preservation of the Cultural Revolution was related to and accompanied by the beginnings of a drastic foreign policy realignment. The Cultural Revolution's opposition to revisionism helped produce an ever more intense antagonism towards the Soviet Union culminating in clashes on the Sino-Soviet border in March 1969, but hostility towards the United States was still just as strong as to the Soviet Union, largely because the Americans were still at war in Vietnam on China's southern border and still its close ally. However, the 1969 border clashes appeared to have been the final episode in convincing the Chinese that the Soviet Union was actually a more dangerous enemy than the United States. The time was consequently ripe for the beginning of a Chinese rapprochement with the Americans.

Already in 1970 several important Western countries, including Canada and Italy, set up diplomatic relations with the PRC. From 9 to 11 July 1971 Dr Henry Kissinger, American President Richard Nixon's Assistant for National Security Affairs, visited Beijing and there secretly negotiated with Zhou Enlai for Nixon himself to make a tour to China. On 15 July Nixon announced to an astonished world that Zhou Enlai had invited him to go to China at an appropriate date before May 1972 and that he had accepted the invitation. The visit actually took place in February 1972; it set the seal on each side's determination to relax tension, even though no formal diplomatic relations were yet opened.

Meanwhile the rapprochement had achieved a concrete result in the long postponed invitation in October 1971 for the PRC to join the United Nations. Just as significant as the visit of the American leader was that of the Japanese Prime Minister Tanaka Kakuei in September 1972. Unlike Nixon's, this one did end in formal diplomatic relations between China and a country which had formerly been so antagonistic to it, in this case Japan. The general trend was that China was establishing very direct contacts with the Western and the capitalist world.

As the CCP began to find its feet in the wake of the Cultural Revolution and as China began to realign itself towards the major capitalist nations, the professional performing arts came back to life, but under the heavy influence of Jiang Qing and her Maoist ideology. The revised versions of the model operas were published in succession. The first one was of a drama based on the CCP-Guomindang civil war after 1945, *Zhiqu Weihu shan (Taking Tiger Mountain by Strategy)*, the revised script of which appeared on 29 October 1969. New versions of the Beijing opera *The Story of the Red Lantern* and the ballet *The Red Detachment of Women* followed respectively in May and July 1970.[13] Film producers followed the lead. The major films of the period were colour cinema versions of the models; and January 1971 saw the premiere showings of *Red Lantern* and *Red Detachment*. Yet the range of available dramas and films was still minute and Jiang Qing was able to prevent the return of traditional opera and other works and films of the pre-Cultural Revolution period. Ideological debate in the newspapers revolved around the class struggle and Mao's ideas on the arts.

These points are well exemplified in a press campaign which flowed from the North China Theatrical Festival held in Beijing early in 1974 during the Campaign to Criticise Lin Biao and Confucius. The Festival featured operas on modern revolutionary themes. One of them, *Sanshang Taofeng (Going Up Peach Peak Three Times)*, was later severely attacked in the press, at the instigation of Jiang Qing and her followers, for trying to negate the class struggle and for opposing the line on the arts laid down by Mao Zedong. Yet the drama was set in a post-liberation commune and on the surface very much brought out the ideals and images of contemporary times. To Jiang Qing only the most select, rigidly propagandistic items were acceptable.

The line of the Cultural Revolution was followed also in the realm of the non-professional arts. Amateurs remained very much in favour, so long as they reflected the class struggle properly. Although they too were thus somewhat hamstrung by ideological rigidity, they were certainly able to achieve considerably greater variety than the professionals. Moreover, the fact that the masses were so heavily encouraged to take part in artistic productions must have developed their sense of creativity.

The opening to the West which was an important feature of the political life of the early 1970s seemed to be about to show results in the performing arts when the Vienna Philharmonic Orchestra visited China in April 1973 during a period of relative relaxation. Attitudes to foreign art changed abruptly, however, with the onset of the Campaign to Criticise Lin Biao and Confucius. To appreciate European music again became a capitulation to the bourgeoisie and hence bad. Franz Schubert was among the many composers to come under attack.

Take for instance the representative work *Symphony in B Minor* (the *Unfinished Symphony*) by Schubert (1797–1828), an Austrian bourgeois composer of the romantic school. The class feelings and social content it expresses are quite clear, although it has no descriptive title. This symphony was composed in 1822 when Austria was a reactionary feudal bastion within the German Confederation and the reactionary Austrian authorities not only ruthlessly exploited and oppressed the workers and peasants, but also persecuted and put under surveillance intellectuals with any bourgeois democratic ideas. Petty-bourgeois intellectuals like Schubert saw no way out of the political and economic impasse, and lacking the courage to resist they gave way to melancholy, vacillation, pessimism and despair, evading reality and dreaming of freedom. This work of Schubert's expressed these class feelings and social content. The opening phrase is sombre and gloomy. The whole symphony continues and expands on this emotion, filling it with petty-bourgeois despair, pessimism and solitary distress. At times the dreaming of freedom does come through but this, too, is escapist and negative.[14]

It appears that the trend towards greater contact with the West was being held back, at least for a time and in the cultural sphere.

The year 1976 to the death of Mao

The morning of 8 January 1976 brought to an end the life of the principal architect of the emerging, if temporarily postponed, friendship with the West: Zhou Enlai. His death was the first of a series of major events which make 1976 the major turning-point year in the history of the PRC. Zhou Enlai's passing was not unexpected; he had been suffering from cancer since 1972. Yet there is little doubt that his death provided the cue for a noticeable sharpening in political conflict in China. Zhou Enlai was an immensely popular figure and that meant that he exercised a stabilising political function.

As happens so often in China, and indeed elsewhere, political struggles revolve around individual personalities. It was mentioned earlier that the most notable leaders to suffer degradation and dismissal during the Cultural Revolution included Deng Xiaoping. In 1973 he returned to office and by April had become a Vice-Premier of the State Council, clearly with the warm support of Zhou Enlai. The latter's death removed an obstacle to renewed attacks and criticism against Deng and in February 1976 a wall poster campaign began at Beijing University against a 'capitalist roader' who was clearly Deng Xiaoping, although his name was not specifically mentioned. Over the next few months the campaign against Deng reached an ever greater crescendo.

Deng's enemies were able to make temporary use of vitally important events which occurred early in April in Beijing. In order to mourn Zhou Enlai, hundreds of thousands of people gathered and placed wreaths in Tiananmen Square in the centre of the city on 4 April. The honour paid to him apparently also suggested support of his political heritage, including the personality of his protégé Deng Xiaoping. The following day, continuing demonstrations in honour of Zhou Enlai in Tiananmen Square erupted into violence in which a nearby building was ransacked and set on fire. Many people were arrested. Similar events occurred in other parts of China in the following days. The radical group which opposed Deng Xiaoping stepped in to take advantage of the situation. They were assisted by Hua Guofeng who had been Acting Premier of the State Council

in succession to Zhou Enlai since 3 February. This alliance succeeded in convening immediately a meeting of the Central Committee of the CCP which on 7 April appointed Hua Guofeng as
the permanent Premier of the State Council and as the first
Vice-Chairman of the CCP's Central Committee. This made him
Mao's deputy and automatic provisional successor.

The same meeting of the Central Committee cast the following judgment on Deng Xiaoping and on the events of the preceding days.

> Having discussed the counter-revolutionary incident which
> took place at Tien An Men [Tiananmen] Square and Teng
> Hsiao-ping's [Deng Xiaoping's] latest behaviour, the
> Political Bureau of the Central Committee of the
> Communist Party of China holds that the nature of the
> Teng Hsiao-ping problem has turned into one of
> antagonistic contradiction. On the proposal of our great
> leader Chairman Mao, the Political Bureau unanimously
> agrees to dismiss Teng Hsiao-ping from all posts both
> inside and outside the Party while allowing him to keep his
> Party membership so as to see how he will behave in the
> future.[15]

Hua Guofeng had no intention whatever of remaining merely
the puppet of the radical faction led by Mao Zedong's wife Jiang
Qing. He naturally wished to increase his own personal power
and influence so that, if need be, he could exercise political
power in his own right. He went along with the anti-Deng
campaign and bided his time.

One of his tactics was to dominate the limelight of China's
foreign relations. During the first half of 1976 a succession of
foreign dignitaries visited Beijing and met the ailing Mao Zedong. They included the New Zealand, Singapore and Pakistani
Prime Ministers, respectively Robert Muldoon, Lee Kuan Yew
and Z. A. Bhutto. On each occasion we are ritually informed
that Hua Guofeng was present. In the middle of June the Central Committee decided that Mao should meet no further foreign
visitors. The reason given was that he was too busy, but the
whole world knew that Mao was not long for this life. Mean-

while nature stepped in to give Hua Guofeng a much better political opportunity, even though at the expense of considerable suffering on the part of the ordinary Chinese.

On 28 July the city of Tangshan in Hebei Province was struck by a series of devastating earthquakes. A later reliable report, issued at a seismic conference of November 1979, indicated that the earthquakes had killed some 242,000 people, seriously injuring 164,000 others. If these figures are accurate then, in terms of human casualties, the Tangshan earthquakes rank third in all recorded history only to the Central Chinese earthquake of January 1556, which the Ming dynasty standard history claims 'crushed to death' 830,000 people,[16] and that of Calcutta in 1737 which took some 300,000 lives.

A natural disaster on this scale cannot fail to carry political implications. Jiang Qing and her radical faction continued to fulminate against Deng Xiaoping and in effect blamed his revisionism for the earthquakes. Hua Guofeng, on the other hand, jumped in to offer condolences, visited the devastated area and arranged for what relief he could. Here was the voice of reason, economic stability and good sense in opposition to the ranting and ravings of the radical faction. Indeed, the earthquakes heightened the need for economic stability. In addition to being a populous city, Tangshan was the centre of China's coal producing industry. The importance of this fact is underlined when we remember that China's is still a predominantly coal-based economy. The economic implications of the sudden destruction of Tangshan are therefore not hard to understand.

In traditional Chinese thought major earthquakes were taken as portents. A great emperor or dynasty was about to fall and be replaced by another. It is true that China was now a revolutionary society; its people ought not to believe in such feudal superstitions as portents derived from earthquakes. Yet it is difficult to avoid the suspicion that many people in China saw the great Tangshan earthquake as a portent of the death of Mao and his replacement by an alternative political figure.

Just over a month later Mao Zedong in fact died on 9 September. Massive mourning ceremonies took place throughout China reaching a climax at a mass memorial meeting on 18 September at which Hua Guofeng delivered the memorial speech. Hua now became automatically the Acting Chairman of the Party. Yet the death of Mao created a vacuum which increased the political tension noticeably as the people waited nervously to see what would happen.

The ouster of Deng Xiaoping made these months look like an ideological victory for the continuation of the Cultural Revolution. The evidence in the field of the performing arts is absolutely consistent in pointing to the continuing dominance of Jiang Qing and the Cultural Revolutionary line.

A series of national festivals took place in Beijing, each one giving play to a different branch of the performing arts. The first one was a dance festival beginning on 18 January. The troupes which took part included both professional and amateur and came from all over the country. There were 262 items presented and the themes were strongly in line with the radical nature of the period. 'The whole repertoire accorded warm praise to the Cultural Revolution and new socialist things.' [17]

In the middle of June there was a national festival of *quyi*, that is, ballad-singing, story-telling and cross-talk. Again the troupes came from all over the country and again the themes reflected the period.

> One merit of this short, lively art form is that it is well
> suited to reflecting current struggles. All the items
> presented depicted our new era, new people and new
> deeds and, in addition, quite a few had as their themes the
> struggle to hit back at the Right deviationist wind and the
> struggle of the proletariat against the capitalist-roaders in
> the Party.[18]

Clearly the performing arts were as usual being used for a particular purpose, this time to denounce Deng Xiaoping, the most important capitalist-roader in the Party.

Among the main ideological statements on the arts made during this period was one on the familiar topic of the evils of Deng Xiaoping. He it was who held power in the period before the start of the Cultural Revolution in 1966 and did his best to promote the revisionist line. He tried to restore capitalism, according to the claim, not only in the arena of literature and art, but in the political as well.

The group of people who issued this statement saw as one of Deng's most heinous crimes the fact that he had opposed the model revolutionary theatrical works sponsored by Jiang Qing and her supporters. The following extract illustrates the strength of their feeling on this issue.

> It is crystal clear that the model revolutionary theatrical works have helped bring about the blossoming of a hundred flowers in revolutionary literature and art, but why did Teng Hsiao-ping [Deng Xiaoping] regard this as 'a single flower blossoming'? Did he really want to have a hundred flowers blossom in proletarian literature and art? Not at all. Facts in the past and at present have proved that he, representing the bourgeoisie both inside and outside the Party, always harboured a bitter hatred for the fragrant flowers of socialist literature and art and prostrated himself in admiration before feudal, capitalist and revisionist literature and art. What he tried to do was to smother the fragrant flowers of proletarian literature and art and let feudal, capitalist and revisionist poisonous weeds grow instead, thereby turning literature and art into his tool for restoring capitalism.[19]

The content here resembles so much commentary in China in that it casts judgments on purely political grounds. The group makes an accusation against Deng and assumes him to be guilty because he stands on a different side of the political fence. To judge from his more recent activities, Deng Xiaoping might well have responded simply by agreeing with the charges but by counter-charging that his actions were correct and his value judgments, not those of the group, were sound and rational.

Of course, the model revolutionary operas continued in vogue in those months. Indeed, another was added to their list: *Panshi wan (Boulder Bay)*. It is a Beijing opera set in the early 1960s. Its theme is perfectly typical; a hidden spy and class enemy from the Chiang Kaishek gang is trying to help the enemy launch a raid into Boulder Bay. The Party exposes both the plan and the hidden enemy agent.

A new model theatrical drama may be worthy of note because of the very small number of such pieces produced up to that time. But a more important development was the commencement of publication (late in March) of a number of journals dealing with artistic matters, including *Renmin xiju (People's Theatre)* and *Renmin dianying (People's Cinema)*. These, although but two of several, assume considerable importance because much of the information on which this book is based is derived from them. Both are reasonably comprehensive in the field which they cover, as indicated by their titles, including literary, social and other material applied to the theatre and cinema.

It is only fair to point out that the beginnings of these journals coincide with the end of the Maoist era and not with the new period after Hua Guofeng smashed the 'gang of four'. Conversely, the festivals discussed earlier excited much interest at the time, and the Chinese news media attempted to give the impression that they represented a kind of high tide in the development of the Chinese performing arts in the period after the Cultural Revolution. Some statements such as the following even suggested an acme of success since liberation.

> These festivals, participated by 29 provinces, municipalities and autonomous regions (with the exception of Taiwan Province), are the biggest of their kind since the founding of New China, with the greatest number of performances and new programmes. Workers, peasants and soldiers in the capital saw the performances with great interest and spoke highly of them, many of which reflected the spirit and essence of our times. They have vividly demonstrated that the revolution in literature and art exemplified by the model revolutionary theatrical works has achieved fruitful results.[20]

Clearly the quantity suggested here reflects also the growth in the number of drama forms in China. A particularly interesting genre is the spoken play. As noted earlier, playwrights had been active before the Cultural Revolution and many new plays written. However, the model theatrical works did not include a single spoken play and it was not until the mid-1970s that they were again seen on the stage performed by professionals. However, perhaps the most striking point is that it was while Jiang Qing was still in control of the cultural scene in China that spoken plays again began performance. It is not correct to give all the credit for that trend to the post-Mao leadership.

One must give her some due also in the cinema industry. The question of quality may be more difficult to judge, but in terms of quantity 1976 appears to have been the richest for Chinese films since the Cultural Revolution. On National Day, 1 October, screening began of a series of forty-seven new films of various kinds, including coloured features, documentaries, educational and science items and of course those based on Beijing and regional operas of various styles. A particularly noteworthy film was called *Lu Xun zhandou de yisheng (The Militant Life of Lu Xun)*, a full-length colour documentary which was premiered on 1 October to commemorate the ninety-fifth anniversary of Lu Xun's birth and the fortieth of his death. Although only a few days away from the arrest of the 'gang of four', this film festival undoubtedly belongs to the Jiang Qing era. Lu Xun was famous as almost the only writer of the pre-Liberation period to enjoy full favour with the cultural authorities whom Jiang Qing headed. Certainly the theme of this particular film resembled all other forty-six in being tightly welded into the revolutionary, even dogmatic, line of the left.

Two general points stand out from this treatment of the performing arts in the few months before Jiang Qing's overthrow. One is that the policy line was still in accord with the radical view of the Cultural Revolution and consequently fitted in very well with the campaign against Deng Xiaoping. The other point is that these were in no way months of stagnation. On the contrary, a revolutionary culture was beginning to develop which might easily have been an embarrassment to Hua Guofeng and his followers. In the event it was nipped in the bud and replaced by something new as a result of the smashing of the 'gang of four'.

Conclusion

Virtually all information in the present background chapter supports the broad conclusion that in the PRC, down to the autumn of 1976, overall government policy tended to go hand in hand with that towards the performing arts. So when policy in general emphasised ideas similar to, or along the lines of the Cultural Revolution, then so did that towards the performing arts. When government policy in general took a relatively liberal line, then so did that towards the theatre and other aspects of the performing arts. Trends in one sector of society inevitably brought implications in other areas. The foregoing account shows very few exceptions indeed to these observations. It brings home again how strongly integrated Chinese society has been under the PRC.

In the same way, the various periods of the PRC's history show a continuum and a logical sequence. Thus in the period which is of central concern to this book, namely that from October 1976 onwards, we find a number of phenomena and outcomes which flow logically from the preceding years. All countries rely, at least in part, on their history. China is no exception, and may be even more conscious of its own past than are most other countries. Thus from 1976 on, we find constant references in the literature to the years before, and incessant judgments on whether the trends of particular periods were good or bad. It is partly for this reason that the necessity arises to recapitulate the history both of the PRC in general, and of its performing arts in particular, as a means to understanding how China, its theatre, music and film have developed from 1976 onwards. The relevance of this history will become abundantly clear in later chapters.

2

Performing arts policy in the history of China since Mao Zedong

On 6 October 1976 the year's traumatic events reached their climax in the 'smashing of the gang of four'. The present chapter will discuss the political and general history of China since that time and correlate it with developments in policy towards the performing arts. This procedure, similar to that followed in the previous chapter, will enable the fulfilment of two objectives. First, it will provide a background against which to describe and analyse the various types and categories of performing arts found in China today. Second, it will test whether the hypothesis put forward in the first chapter holds true in the changing conditions in China since the autumn of 1976; that is to say, has China remained a society integrated enough that developments in the general political and social arena are virtually always reflected in that of the performing arts?

From the fall of the 'gang of four' to the Eleventh Party Congress

In concrete terms 'the smashing of the gang of four' meant the arrest, on the orders of Hua Guofeng, of four of China's most prominent radical leaders; Jiang Qing, who was the widow of Mao Zedong, Yao Wenyuan, Zhang Chunqiao and Wang Hongwen. All of these had played leading roles in the Cultural Revolution. The next day, 7 October, the Central Committee of the

CCP appointed Hua Guofeng as its Chairman in succession to Mao Zedong.

At the time that Hua Guofeng overthrew the 'gang of four' there were no reports of his action in the Chinese press. In theory, therefore, the Chinese people knew nothing about what had happened, although in fact news was percolating quite widely among the population. It was not until a fortnight later that official reports of the incident were released. Instantly enormous demonstrations took place all over China to show the people's support for Hua Guofeng's appointment as Chairman of the CCP and his victory over the 'gang of four'.

Thus began the campaign against the four, and it persisted with great enthusiasm and intensity until the end of 1978. The four were collectively accused of every conceivable crime, and individuals among them of particular types. In the initial months the Hua Guofeng leadership laid primary emphasis on the attempt by the gang to seize power by splitting the CCP. His media released reports of factional violence and political instability in the period up to October 1976, and declared them to be deliberate preparations for a takeover. Had the gang not been smashed, so the new regime claimed, China would have been thrown into civil war and the way opened for aggression by foreign powers once again. Clearly Hua Guofeng's principal aim was to establish his own legitimacy, to persuade the people to accept his government.

Meanwhile the new Chairman attempted to work out his policies on particular issues and to that end convened a series of conferences. The first was the National Conference on Learning from Dazhai in Agriculture, held in Beijing from 10 to 27 December. At it Hua Guofeng himself made a major speech on 25 December. He made it clear that from now on China's priorities would be economic, and that consequently revolutionary ideology would take a back seat. Apart from a detailed justification for his own accession to power and attacks on the 'gang of four' for their crimes, he outlined a policy of 'comprehensive modernization of agriculture, industry, national defence and science and technology' (the four modernisations) to raise China's economy 'to the front ranks in the world before the end of the century'.[1] Hua acknowledged that this plan had in fact been first outlined by Zhou Enlai in January 1975. With the removal of the gang it would now be able to proceed without obstruction.

Hua Guofeng's appeal to Zhou Enlai became a characteristic feature of his regime. The first anniversary of Zhou's death saw such extravagant mourning that it appeared to be he, and not Mao Zedong, whom the new government wished to hold first place in the affections of the people. As a matter of fact, my own observations in China in January 1977 and since lead me to believe that it was genuine, and in no way contrived, for the people to show and feel a greater devotion for Zhou than for Mao.

It is most important to note that to reduce emphasis on revolutionary ideology was in no sense tantamount to ignoring it. As a matter of fact, the first months of the Hua Guofeng regime witnessed a number of important initiatives in the ideological sphere which gave the impression of continued, indeed firmer, adherence to Mao Zedong's thought, but at the same time subtly, albeit considerably, changed the direction of China's official ideology. The overall thrust was against the social idealism, the voluntarism and the anti-bureaucratism of the Cultural Revolution, and in favour of economic development, modernisation, expertise and pragmatism.

A principal early symbol of this new direction was the New China News Agency's release, on 25 December, of a speech by Mao Zedong entitled 'Lun shida guanxi' ('On the Ten Major Relationships'). Mao had first made the speech on 25 April 1956 but publication had been delayed for just over twenty years. Clearly China's new policies were to be closer to those of the mid-1950s than those of the Cultural Revolution and early 1970s. The first four of the ten major relationships refer to economic matters, such as those between heavy industry on the one hand and light industry and agriculture on the other, and between industry in the coastal regions and that in the interior.

Another step taking China's ideology in a similar direction was the publication, on 15 April 1977, of the fifth volume of *Mao Zedong xuanji* (*Selected Works of Mao Zedong*). All five volumes present Mao's articles in exactly chronological order. The first four volumes had included what Mao had written down to the time of liberation; the last one took the story to the end of 1957. This date is striking, for it was the eve of the Great Leap Forward, which, as noted in Chapter 1, was the first of Mao's major attempts to introduce radical economic policies. The implication was clear: in so far as Mao Zedong remained a teacher, it was as economic planner and pragmatist, not as cultural revolutionary.

It is natural that as China's economic attitudes and its ideology were changing with the establishment of the new regime, so would some of its social policies. Among the first major areas to show vital alteration was education. When I visited China at the beginning of 1977 I was consistently told in the schools and universities that teachers were now demanding greater discipline and academic skills from their students. They complained that when the gang was 'on the loose' they had been unable to teach because their students criticised them all the time. Zhang Chunqiao, the chief ideologue of the four, was denounced for giving higher priority to the class background of students than to their academic standards. No wonder students knew nothing!

Clearly the revolutionary hysteria of the anti-Deng Xiaoping campaign in 1976 was well and truly over. Predictability and stability were now the order of the day, in fact, the very directions in which Deng himself had striven so hard to drive China. It was only a matter of time before Deng himself would return to power. From 16 to 21 July 1977 the CCP held another plenum, the Third Plenary Session of the Tenth Central Committee of the CCP. Its principal act was to adopt the 'resolution on restoring Comrade Deng Xiaoping to his posts'. These included Vice-Chairman of the CCP Central Committee, Vice-Premier of the State Council and Chief of the General Staff of the Chinese PLA. In addition the Plenum expelled the 'gang of four' from the CCP.

From 12 to 18 August the new leadership, the new economic and other policies were formalised and consolidated at the Eleventh National Congress of the CCP, held in Beijing. The speed with which the Hua–Deng duumvirate had been established was made clear when Hua Guofeng delivered the political report to the Congress and Deng Xiaoping the closing address.

In 1976 it had, as mentioned in Chapter 1, been Deng Xiao-ping who was attacked for revisionist views on politics and the performing arts. As he rode high, Jiang Qing and the other three suffered attacks. She had earlier exercised great influence in the ideology of the performing arts and been possibly the most important single force behind their revolutionisation. So it is not surprising to find that the new policy directions in China under Hua Guofeng brought about substantial changes in the performing arts.

Up to this point discussion of these arts has been general, in that it has included both policy and practice or reality. In this chapter, however, the material on the performing arts will con-centrate entirely on policy, except when reality is the best de-monstration of policy. This is because other chapters deal with the reflection of policy in practice, but only for the period since the autumn of 1976 which is the central focus of this book.

The first major statement on the performing arts came in a major front-page article in the *People's Daily* on 5 November. It centred round a directive which Mao had written on 25 July 1975 about a film called *Chuangye (Pioneers)* concerning the workers of the pace-setting Daqing oilfield. The gang had found serious fault with the film and had it banned. Mao's directive, on the other hand, said that there was no major error in the film and suggested it be approved for distribution. Mao argued that the suppression of the film was based on nitpicking, and hampered the adjustment of the Party's current policy on lit-erature and art. The editorial continues:

Even after Chairman Mao wrote this important directive,
they continued to use the tactics of complying in public
while opposing in private, put up a stubborn resistance,
did everything possible to prevent Chairman Mao's
directive from being known, wantonly distorted it and even
quoted it out of context, claiming that if there were no big
errors, there were medium and small ones. All this was a
wild counterattack against Chairman Mao's directive. Going
from bad to worse, they resorted to persecution, retaliation
and vengeful counterattacks against revolutionary literature
and art and the revolutionary literary and art workers, and

they did not in the least heed what Chairman Mao had said. Such despicable actions thoroughly revealed their true colours as counter-revolutionaries who betrayed Marxism-Leninism-Mao Tsetung [Zedong] Thought, practised revisionism and splittism and engaged in conspiracies.[2]

It is quite clear from this extract that the new leaders consider themselves the true Marxists in the field of the arts and the gang as sham Marxists. In other words, the Marxist revolutionary ideological basis of the arts in theory remains unchanged. Art should still serve the masses, the workers, peasants and soldiers and the images which come over in artistic works should still be those of the workers, peasants and soldiers.

The other major theme to come across from the discussion of the directive is the slogan 'let a hundred flowers blossom, let a hundred schools of thought contend', which is quoted in the editorial. This means not that there should be total freedom in the arts but that a far greater degree of variety and of breadth is not only desirable but essential. As a matter of fact, the slogan had been official policy even in 1976, as the passage quoted in Chapter 1 on Deng Xiaoping's crimes makes clear. The aim of the new leaders was to give the saying more teeth and meaning, greater reality for the Chinese people.

The delicate balance which requires a degree of freedom and yet strong government concern with what happens in the performing arts is amplified further and more clearly in the Central Committee's introduction to the fifth volume of the *Selected Works of Mao Zedong*.

Proceeding from the viewpoint of the unity of opposites, Chairman Mao elaborated on the correctness of the policy of letting a hundred flowers blossom and a hundred schools of thought contend, and criticized Stalin's metaphysics and the erroneous view that only fragrant flowers, but no poisonous weeds, should be allowed to grow, a view that denies the existence of poisonous weeds in a socialist country. He pointed out: 'Fragrant flowers stand in contrast to poisonous weeds and develop in struggle with them. It is a dangerous policy to prohibit people from coming into contact with the false, the ugly and the hostile. . . . It will lead to mental deterioration and one-sided thinking and render people unprepared to face the world and meet challenges.' Poisonous weeds should be weeded out. Harmful statements should be refuted in good time. Evil trends in society must be wiped out and the way to do it is through reasoning.[3]

An early question which faced the leadership in this scenario without Jiang Qing, was what attitude to adopt to the model revolutionary theatrical works which had been fashionable so recently. The solution adopted was twofold.

In the first place credit for the creation of the models was reallocated – instead of to Jiang Qing it went to Mao Zedong and Zhou Enlai; the two leaders are said to have 'nurtured' the models which were created by the literary and art workers 'through painstaking labour'. After that the 'gang of four', and in particular Jiang Qing, 'grabbed the fruits of the revolution in literature and art' and took for themselves the title of standard-bearers in the revolution in literature and art.[4]

Second, the value judgment on the models was changed. Since Mao Zedong and Zhou Enlai nurtured them, one cannot easily condemn them. On the other hand, in the period after October 1976 they were very rarely performed. Attempts which I made during a trip to China in January 1977 to locate performances of the models invariably ended in failure. Three years later, in January 1980, cadres of the literature and arts section of the *People's Daily* told me that the models were still never performed, except for radio broadcasts, and even then the pre-Cultural Revolution versions were used. When Hua Guofeng made his report to the Eleventh Congress of the CCP on 12 August 1977 he made a reference to the problem of the model operas and their place in the theatrical repertoire. He quoted Mao as saying, 'Model operas alone are not enough. What is worse, one comes under fire for the slightest fault. No longer are a hundred flowers blossoming. Others are not allowed to offer any opinion, that's no good.'[5] Hua concluded from this statement that Mao was denouncing the 'gang of four' for cultural autocracy, and pushing for greater variety.

One aspect of the model operas which did early come under very direct attack was its stereotyped method of characterisation (see Chapter 1). One early reference to the 'revolutionary heroes' of the models described them as 'extremely stilted as if there was no one beside them; they regard themselves as holy things and regard the masses as inferior rustics.' [6] Detailed commentary on this question followed in later months, with extremely strong language used to condemn the models' style of characterisation.

All commentators drew attention to the exclusiveness of the models; this leads to the question of what attitude the new leadership might adopt towards foreign and traditional performing arts. The first of the two problems is answered by Mao in the article 'On the Ten Major Relationships', the last or tenth of which is that 'between China and other countries'. He wrote:

Neither the indiscriminate rejection of everything foreign, whether scientific, technological or cultural, nor the indiscriminate imitation of everything foreign as mentioned above, has anything in common with the Marxist attitude, and they in no way benefit our cause. [7]

As we shall see in greater detail later this has meant, in effect, a spectacular reversal of the 1974 policy, mentioned in Chapter 1, which denounced foreign art altogether.

The question of traditional art is actually more important because of the extraordinarily significant place which the traditional performing arts once occupied in the affections of the people. Moreover, Deng Xiaoping had been denounced in 1976 because he wished to restore them in preference to the model revolutionary operas. If Deng Xiaoping came back to power how could the traditional Chinese opera fail to return to the stage? In the event it did not have to wait for Deng's formal return. To commemorate the thirty-fifth anniversary of Mao's most important utterance on the arts, the 'Talks at the Yan'an Forum on Literature and Art' which he gave in May 1942, a revival took place in Beijing of several scenes of a traditional opera called *Bishang Liangshan (Forced Up Mt Liang)* which was adapted as a revolutionary piece in Yan'an not long after the

forum. *People's Daily* described the item as 'a revolutionary historical Beijing Opera', and claimed that it had been 'nurtured
by the glorious thought of the "Talks" ',[8] thus justifying the
resurrection of traditional Beijing opera through an appeal to
Mao's doctrine. In August complete performances of the work
recommenced.

One other area is worth mentioning to illustrate the general
theme of the need for greater variety which characterises this
period; and that is the resurgence of children's theatre. This
had flourished extensively in the period before the Cultural
Revolution; however, with Jiang Qing's accession to power in
cultural matters, performing arts designed specifically for children substantially disappeared. Just as the post-Mao policy of
Hua Guofeng allowed for the return of foreign and traditional
theatre, so it gave active encouragement to children's performing arts as a specific genre. An editorial comment in China's
main theatre journal concluded with this ringing call:

> On the basis of writing good themes on realistic struggle,
> we should also have a few fairy tales and myth dramas, the
> content of which is healthy and has educational
> significance. We should be energetic in ensuring that the
> creation and performance of children's dramas should be
> such as to appeal both visually and aurally to the broad
> masses of youth and children, and even better should give
> play to their educational function and struggle function.
> We must write even more dramas for youth and children.
> We must make a contribution to the growth of the
> revolutionary successors.[9]

As far as both traditional opera and children's theatre are
concerned, it is thus quite clear that the propaganda function
remains intact. The reference to educational significance is a
very clear indication that there must be a moral in any children's
drama performed. The delineation of good and bad, the images
of virtue and evil are to be left in no doubt. On the other hand,
it is a remarkable and dramatic departure from the policy of the
gang's decade 1966–76 to allow the revival of fairy tales and
myths. Anything even slightly bordering on the magic, other

than the almost supernatural powers endowed to Mao Zedong's thought, had been absolutely anathema during those years.

The first few months after the smashing of the 'gang of four' saw a fairly general and important change in direction in policy towards the performing arts. The direction was towards greater variety of form and content, and giving real meaning to the 'hundred flowers' slogan. The directness of the ideological commitment and propaganda was becoming slightly diluted, but there could be no question that these remained in essence unchanged. Attitudes towards the performing arts were developing in a way which conformed with the direction of policy in society at large under the regime of Hua Guofeng.

From the Eleventh Congress to the Third Plenum
(December 1978)

If there is one general feature which characterises the period following that just discussed, it is an acceleration of change; the direction remains the same, the pace gathers momentum. Almost certainly the basic reason underlying the greater speed is the ever increasing confidence and authority of the rehabilitated Deng Xiaoping.

Possibly no field better exemplifies the growing speed of change than foreign relations. After the fall of the 'gang of four' widespread speculation arose, especially in the West, that China might begin to heal its rift with the Soviet Union. After all, the new regime opened the way for a decline in Mao's revolutionary ideas and a consequent moving in the direction of the domestic policies characteristic of the Soviet Union. This trend eventuated as expected, but it gradually became clear that the implied détente with the USSR would not follow, at least in the short term. During 1977 China moved further away from the Soviet Union and closer to the Western powers. But it was in 1978 that the rift became virtually total not only with the Soviet Union itself but with its allies, and it was in the same year that China cemented alliances with the major capitalist countries.

By far the most spectacular case illustrating China's break with formerly friendly Soviet allies was that with Vietnam. For years China and Vietnam had seemed to be on the closest of terms. It is true that there had been signs that not all was well, but only the most perceptive of observers had seen through the implications. To analyse the reasons why relations deteriorated is well beyond the scope of this book. What is important is that in May 1978 China and Vietnam startled the world by making serious and hostile accusations against each other. The Chinese charged that the Vietnamese were ostracising and persecuting Chinese residents in Vietnam and expelling many of them back to China. Vietnam accused China of deliberately stirring up trouble in Vietnam to cause an exodus of Chinese residents back to China. The problem escalated, and by August both sides were publicly declaring that border clashes had begun to take place.

Meanwhile in July the Chinese government had informed the Vietnamese that it would no longer be offering economic or technical aid to Vietnam and was planning to recall its experts and engineers in that country. It is ironic that within a few days of this announcement the Chinese made a similar statement concerning its aid to Albania, formerly among its very closest allies. Clearly China had given up seeking friends among socialist countries, even those hostile to the Soviet Union.

At the same time, the China of Deng Xiaoping moved ever closer to the Western countries and Japan and, in effect, moved to lock its economy into that of the capitalist world. Several stages of this process are visible in 1978. In February China signed a long-term trade agreement with Japan under which it guaranteed to export coal and petroleum in return for Japanese technology, including complete plants. In August 1978 China and Japan formally signed their long awaited Treaty of Peace and Friendship. Japan agreed to China's demands that it should oppose 'efforts by any other country or group of countries to establish . . . hegemony' (Article II). On the other hand it was able to introduce a clause stipulating that the treaty would not affect the relations of either country with any third power (Article IV). The clause denouncing hegemony was clearly aimed specifically against the Soviet Union; Article IV was a Japanese attempt to soften the blow.

The important features of the developing Sino-Japanese relationship extended beyond the strategic implications – a developing alliance aimed against the Soviet Union – to serious economic consequences. China was prepared to export raw materials and to import highly developed industrial goods. No doubt the Chinese were mindful of their past relationship with Japan, and had no intention of repeating imposed unequal treaties so characteristic of the past. On the other hand, it cannot escape attention that the sale of raw materials in return for highly sophisticated technology usually implies an unequal relationship.

As China allowed its economy to move closer to the capitalist world the obvious end result was to seal a friendship with the United States. After a series of diplomatic moves the natural climax was reached when, in the middle of December 1978, the United States and China simultaneously released a joint communiqué announcing their decision to establish diplomatic relations as from 1 January 1979. The United States acknowledged the claim of the People's Republic to Taiwan, but declared that people-to-people unofficial relations would continue between the United States and Taiwan.

A certain logic dictated the moves which the Chinese were making. On the one hand, fear of the Soviet Union remained as strong, if not stronger, than ever, with an added concern that the Russians were using or were about to use Vietnam to threaten China's southern areas. On the other, obsession with the four modernisations required that economic assistance should be sought from any possible source, no matter how counter-revolutionary or non-revolutionary it may be.

The four modernisations also dominate domestic developments in China in the latter half of 1977 and throughout 1978. One result of the emphasis placed on them was that administrative efficiency gained greatly in importance even at the expense of revolutionary ideals. A particularly interesting example of this trend came during the first session of the Fifth National People's Congress held from 26 February to 5 March 1978. On the latter day the Congress adopted a new PRC Constitution under which revolutionary committees were in effect abolished, except as organs of government. It will be recalled that, at the end of the Cultural Revolution, tripartite organs of power called revolutionary committees had been established with the aim of giving greater mass participation in decision-making. Their abolition, except as government organs, meant their total disappearance in factories, institutes and other such organisations, although they remained intact at government levels such as provinces and rural people's communes. The move against the revolutionary committees was justified on the grounds that the Party committees remained unaffected and could cater for any necessary mass participation in decision-making. My specific enquiries in 1973 and 1977 supported the official view that the Party and revolutionary committees tended to consist of the same people and that the overlap was simply inefficient. On the other hand, the abolition of the revolutionary committees was an excellent symbol of the disappearance of the system which the Cultural Revolution had brought into being.

A few other important signs occurred during 1978 suggesting ever more exclusive emphasis on economic modernisation, and pointing to the regrowth of the social and political system which had prevailed before the Cultural Revolution. They include several major conferences.

One was a National Science Conference, which took place in Beijing in March, aimed at harnessing the use of science and technology in the interests of the four modernisations. Deng Xiaoping made a point of specifying at the conference that heads and deputy heads of research institutes were to enjoy a freer hand than in the past in science and technology. This was but a further step in the direction of handing power back to those with specific skills and expertise, in fact making way for the regrowth of the technocratic elite.

In September a National Women's Congress, and the following month the National Congress of the Chinese Trade Unions and National Congress of the Communist Youth League of China were held successively in Beijing. The bodies which these three congresses represented had enjoyed considerable prestige and influence before the Cultural Revolution. They had come under severe attack as revisionist during that movement and their regrowth in the early 1970s was extremely gradual. The more or less simultaneous convention of these three congresses was undoubtedly symbolic of a trend in China's development back to the pre-1966 society, and was certainly due largely to the influence of Deng Xiaoping.

As Deng became more influential and the Chairman and Premier Hua Guofeng correspondingly less so, it was only a matter of time before the Tiananmen Incident of 1976 should be reinterpreted. The incident assumed considerable importance in China's recent history because of its spontaneity. The fact that Deng Xiaoping's opponents had managed to use it to bring about his downfall and that Hua Guofeng had been able, through it, to seize the premiership on a permanent basis made a reinterpretation of the event much more desirable for Deng Xiaoping than for Hua Guofeng. Deng now moved to clear its reputation and thus use it as a stick wherewith to beat further the 'gang of four'. In November 1978 the Beijing Municipal CCP Committee eventually declared that the Tiananmen Incident was not counter-revolutionary at all, as declared by the Central Committee on 7 April 1976, but a 'completely revolutionary action'.

This reinterpretation of an important recent historical event was accompanied by a wall poster campaign similar to that of 1957. On 19 November 1978 a very long poster appeared on the 'Democracy Wall' in Beijing, accusing Mao Zedong himself of having been a supporter of the 'gang of four' and of being responsible for ousting Deng Xiaoping in 1976. This poster undoubtedly expressed the thoughts of many people in China, but actually to state in public that Mao was in league with the 'gang of four' was completely unprecedented. Posters of this kind illustrated dramatically how greatly the atmosphere had changed in China.

A new climax came in Deng Xiaoping's China with the Third Plenary Session of the Eleventh CCP Central Committee held from 18 to 22 December 1978. This plenum reached a number of very important decisions. One was to rehabilitate several very important figures who had been disgraced by Mao Zedong before or during the Cultural Revolution. A second was formally to confirm the reinterpretation of the Tiananmen Incident of 1976. Possibly more important, however, was the decision to end the 'large-scale nationwide mass movement' against the 'gang of four', and 'to shift the emphasis of our Party's work

51

and the attention of the people of the whole country to socialist modernization'.[10] This move formalised and greatly strengthened the trend of the preceding period.

The increased emphasis on economic modernisation had clear implications for the concept of class struggle which in 1976 Deng Xiaoping had been accused of trying to overthrow. The Third Plenum, indeed, made direct reference to the doctrine:

> We must not relax our class struggle against them [counter-revolutionary elements and criminals], nor can we weaken the dictatorship of the proletariat. But as Comrade Mao Tsetung [Zedong] pointed out, the large-scale turbulent class struggles of a mass character have in the main come to an end.[11]

Although the Plenum thus actually quoted Mao in support of its own idea, its statement tended to downplay the class struggle and hence to counter concepts which Mao had valued so highly in the last years of his life.

A concomitant of this re-evaluation of the importance of class struggle was the downgrading of the Cultural Revolution. The Plenum also addressed this problem:

> The session holds that the Great Cultural Revolution should also be viewed historically, scientifically and in a down-to-earth way. Comrade Mao Tsetung [Zedong] initiated this great revolution primarily in the light of the fact that the Soviet Union had turned revisionist and for the purpose of opposing revisionism and preventing its occurrence. As for the shortcomings and mistakes in the actual course of the revolution, they should be summed up at the appropriate time as experience and lessons so as to unify the views of the whole Party and the people of the whole country. However, there should be no haste about this. Shelving this problem will not prevent us from solving all other problems left over from past history in a down-to-earth manner, nor will it affect our concentration of efforts to speed up the four modernizations, the greatest historic task of the time.[12]

Although the Plenum thus appears to leave open the problem of how to assess the Cultural Revolution, this was in fact the first time that an official Party gathering had failed to commend the Cultural Revolution. As a matter of fact, popular opinion appears to have been somewhat quicker even than the Party itself in moving against the Cultural Revolution. When I visited China in September and October 1978 I rarely heard it given any positive evaluation. Virtually all references to it were to suggest how much damage it had caused.

This trend towards negation of the Cultural Revolution lies behind a great deal of what happened in China during this period. Certainly it is at the heart of the major theoretical contribution in the performing arts in the sixteen months that separated the Eleventh Party Congress from the Third Plenum: namely the violent attack on the theory of 'the dictatorship of the sinister line in literature and art' (*wenyi heixian zhuanzheng*). This phrase, couched in the characteristic Marxist jargon so popular in China, requires some explanation and takes us from general policy to that in the performing arts.

In a nutshell the theory of 'the dictatorship of the sinister line' meant simply a harsh verdict on the literature and arts of the first seventeen years after liberation. Since so much depends upon personalities in Chinese affairs, as indeed in others, the concept implied giving all the credit for anything worthwhile to Jiang Qing and her followers, and attacking anything associated with their opponents.

Immediately after the fall of the 'gang of four', films, plays and operas popular before the Cultural Revolution began to return. As time went on, China's post-1976 culture began to resemble more and more that of the period from 1949 to 1966. The theoretical concept which would justify this, however, was not formally devised until late in 1977. On 28 November the editorial department of the magazine *People's Theatre* convened a forum to discuss 'the dictatorship of the sinister line'. A number of very distinguished dramatists of the old school took part in the forum including twentieth-century China's most famous playwright Cao Yu, who had disappeared during the Cultural Revolution and been heavily denounced at that time. Not surprisingly he and the others attacked fiercely the doctrine which had called them reactionary and which had sought to negate all the work which they had created as nothing more than a revisionist line in literature and art. In other words, they were angry at the suggestion implied in the policy of the gang's decade that nothing worthwhile had come forward in the Chinese performing arts until Jiang Qing rose to prominence just before the Cultural Revolution. Cao Yu said:

> I am a literature and art worker of nearly seventy years old and I am willing to write for the people under the guidance of Chairman Mao's revolutionary line in literature and art. But the 'gang of four' branded the group of writers like me as 'representatives of the black line in literature and art' and 'reactionary power holders'. They made us, though having mouths, unable to speak and unable to use our hands to write.[13]

Not long after the forum, the *People's Daily* came out with a major front page article by the 'Commentator Group of the Cultural Department of the General Political Department of the Chinese People's Liberation Army' (PLA) explaining the origin of this theory of 'the dictatorship of the sinister line'. The PLA group related it back to the Forum on Literature and Art in the Armed Forces which, on Lin Biao's instructions, Jiang Qing had held in February 1966 at the very beginning of the Cultural Revolution (see Chapter 1). The Forum had exercised an enormous influence on the Cultural Revolution in the arts and considerably increased the importance of Jiang Qing's role. The PLA group was certainly not about to deny this latter point, but placed an entirely different perspective on it simply by reversing the army's previously favourable value judgment. Referring to the forum the PLA's representatives now stated:

> It was said that since the founding of the country [i.e. the PRC] there had existed a 'black anti-Party, anti-socialist line' in literature and art circles. She [Jiang Qing] declared 'This black line has exercised dictatorship over us for seventeen years, this cannot be allowed to continue. It is high time we exercised dictatorship over them!' This then

was the beginning of the theory of the 'dictatorship of the sinister line in literature and the arts'.[14]

It appears that Jiang Qing and her followers went on after the forum to extend their condemnations of the literary and art productions of the period before the Cultural Revolution even to pre-1949 revolutionary productions.

With the smashing of the 'gang of four' the value judgments which gave credit to Jiang Qing clearly needed revision. She and her followers were now worthless, as was everything they had produced. It was the people they attacked, such as Cao Yu, who became the heroes. Good examples of revolutionary art could now be found in abundance in the years before the Cultural Revolution but the decade 1966 to 1976 was a more or less dead one.

As usual the people began to show support for the new line. The *People's Daily* began to receive letters to that effect from citizens. An ordinary soldier in Kunming called Huang Yanjun had written a particularly interesting example several years earlier but the newspaper had not published it. Dated 9 February 1974, it expressed strong disagreement with the way in which unnecessarily violent attacks on the works produced in the first seventeen years after liberation had distorted the revolutionary movement in literature and the arts.[15] Since that was not the 'correct' line in 1974 one cannot be surprised that *People's Daily* failed to print the letter in that year.

It is very characteristic of China to bring out examples of courageous people who dared to express opposition to a previous policy at the time but whose views were then forbidden publications and hence suppressed. This manner of working has the strength of proving that at least some citizens are not simply wise after the event.

It was earlier noted that 1978 saw the reactivation of a number of bodies which had been important before the Cultural Revolution but disbanded as 'revisionist' during that time. To set the ball rolling for the pre-1966 cultural organisations the All-China Federation of Literature and Art Circles held a national meeting in Beijing from 27 May to 5 June 1978, its first since before the Cultural Revolution.

Not only were organisations revived, but virtually all the old guard of artists were again praised as heroes, many of them persecuted and suppressed by the 'gang of four'. Among them were the two famous actors of the traditional Beijing opera, Mei Lanfang and Zhou Xinfang. The difference between these two and Cao Yu was that they were by now both dead, so that it was not they themselves but their reputations which were rehabilitated. Mei Lanfang had died in 1961 but his family had suffered severely as a result of the Cultural Revolution and the policies of Jiang Qing. On 8 August 1978, that is the seventeenth anniversary of Mei Lanfang's death, his widow Fu Zhifang wrote an article in his praise in *People's Daily* (p. 3) stressing the concern which Mao and Zhou Enlai had shown for his welfare, and his loyalty to the Party, of which he had actually been a member. She dwelt at some length on the particular traditional items which Mei Lanfang had performed after liberation, and on the strenuous efforts which he had made to tour around the countryside so that large numbers of the masses could enjoy and be educated by his art.

Zhou Xinfang's case was slightly different to that of Mei Lanfang, in that Zhou could accurately be described as having been directly persecuted by the 'gang of four'. Although he had been much in favour in the early years after liberation as a revolutionary actor who had contributed directly to the revolutionisation of the traditional opera, Jiang Qing and her followers considered him to be reactionary and would not let him perform. Even in 1966 stories circulated that Red Guards had physically molested him. It was even reported that he had been killed. However, when a memorial service was eventually held in his honour on 16 August 1978 it was officially confirmed that he had not died until 8 March 1975. The importance of his rehabilitation is underlined by the fact that Deng Xiaoping attended the memorial service.

To bring Mei Lanfang and Zhou Xinfang back to favour was one aspect of an ever increasing emphasis on the traditional performing arts. Early in 1978 Deng had visited Burma and Nepal, and on his way back to Beijing spent the Spring Festival (Chinese New Year) in his home province of Sichuan. He saw quite a few operas there at three private performances given him by the Sichuan Provincial Opera Troupe. Actors and actresses of the company told me on 29 January 1980 that Deng had come backstage and 'given us great encouragement'. The pieces played were all traditional, including love stories and comedies. 'We asked him if he thought these were good and healthy items, and he replied they certainly were. Not long after that, we performed the same operas publicly.' Sichuan became a precedent and other provinces followed suit.

In his speech to the Fifth National People's Congress on 26 February 1978 Hua Guofeng had given his official blessing to traditional theatre. The basis on which to choose the particular items to be performed was explained in a later official commentary entitled 'Actively but Cautiously Perform Superior Traditional Theatre Items'. Included among those which should be brought back to the stage were dramas with a patriotic spirit, those which 'sing the praises of the Chinese people's struggle against class oppression, express the industrious, courageous, intelligent and other superior qualities of the Chinese people; or reflect a democratic and revolutionary essence, such as sacrificing one's own interests for others or active optimism'.[16]

These were doubtless laudable sentiments but they were rather broad and unspecific; they allowed considerable room to manoeuvre. Probably Deng Xiaoping's guidance to the Sichuan actors was just as important for those many troupes which came to know about it.

Clearly the major thrust of policy in the sixteen months under discussion here was against the Cultural Revolution. One area, however, which was preserved from that period was an adherence to the mass line. In his speech to the National People's Congress Hua Guofeng stated that the arts 'must keep to the orientation of serving the workers, peasants and soldiers', and he exhorted all those involved in the performing arts 'to go to factories, rural areas and army units to experience life at its source and create more'.[17] Hua's speech came three days after the close of a major amateur theatre festival held in Shanxi province.

Another 'massline' phenomenon to which the press has devoted particular attention has been that of the caravan troupes. These were first founded in 1957 in Inner Mongolia and were designed to be active more or less all the year round in travelling from place to place to perform for the masses, to suit the convenience not of the actors themselves, but of ordinary people. The Cultural Revolution had been particularly enthusiastic about the caravan troupes because of the mass line which they represented, but in 1978 the 'gang of four' was accused of having tried to sabotage them. We are told that most of them, despite the gang, 'persisted in the revolutionary tradition of going up mountains and down to the countryside to bring drama to the doors of the people'. On the other hand, the confession comes forward that 'in truth there were also quite a few theatre troupes which were poisoned'.[18] The four can do nothing right even in cases where the new regime persists in the Cultural Revolution's policies!

Among all the performing arts the one most easily able to reach the masses is film, simply because it does not require the transportation of groups of actors from place to place. Hua Guofeng said about it at the National People's Congress: 'We should give special attention to the film with its huge audience, because its impact is immense. We should redouble our efforts to produce more fine films.' [19]

Naturally enough, official Chinese reports claimed that the gang of four' had suppressed good films and that a revival had taken place since their fall. It is ironic to recall in passing that the very week the four fell had seen the issuing of a particularly large number of new films. Hua's call, however, was not so much for the revival of earlier films as for the production of a great many new ones; this was not so easy to accomplish. A newspaper commentary written specifically to support his call conceded that 'the number of our films, especially features, is not very great and a few problems exist with regard to their quality'.[20]

One final aspect of policy on the performing arts in this period deserves attention because of its particularly close relationship with the political scene. As the Tiananmen Incident was being reassessed, new dramas appeared giving literary and emotional support to the favourable verdict on the event. The best known example was *Yu wusheng chu (Where Silence Reigns)* which was first performed in Beijing on 16 November 1978, the very day

after the Beijing Municipal CCP Committee's declaration in favour of the Tiananmen Incident had been announced. As a
matter of fact, the play had been premiered earlier in Shanghai
but the capital did not see it until the changed verdict on the
Incident became official.

Such plays were important mainly as a symptom of something much more significant: namely the predilection of modern
plays and other works to centre their themes around the evil
actions of the 'gang of four' in suppressing the masses of the
people and upright cadres. By extension, this came to mean
that the evils and injustices of the Cultural Revolution figured
largely in modern plays. The 'smashing of the gang of four' and
its aftermath are typically the climax which rights the wrongs
and eliminates the injustices.

From the Third to the Fifth Plenums (December 1978 to February 1980)

The importance of that event – 'the smashing of the gang of
four' – remained just as significant throughout 1979 and into
1980 as it had been in the earlier period, despite the decision of
the Third Plenum to 'end the large-scale nationwide mass
movement' against the gang. In both foreign and domestic developments the period was one of intensification, even climax,
of the previous line but in both areas there were at least temporary signs of the seeds of a new direction.

This comment applies particularly to China's foreign relations. The policy of accommodation with the United States,
which had begun just after the Cultural Revolution, reached its
logical conclusion with the formal establishment of diplomatic
relations on 1 January 1979, and the visit by Deng Xiaoping to
the United States later the same month and early in February.
This laid the basis for a substantial increase in American social
and cultural influence, as well as economic investment, in
China. Self-reliance in economic production and the intense
desire to find their own way in social development quite irre-
spective of imperialist countries such as the United States now
belonged firmly to the past. The idea of courting the United

States may have been anathema to the 1950s and 1960s. It was now seen virtually as the highest good.

Meanwhile serious trouble was brewing on China's southern borders. On 7 January Vietnamese troops marched into Phnom Penh and overthrew the pro-Chinese Kampuchean government of Pol Pot. The Chinese saw in this action clear evidence of a Vietnamese hegemonism which they had feared for some time. Their anxiety was magnified infinitely through the conviction that this was simply a proxy of the Soviet Union in Southeast Asia, especially since Vietnam and the Soviet Union had signed their Treaty of Friendship and Co-operation on 3 November 1978. While in the United States Deng Xiaoping made several ominous statements hinting at the need to 'punish' the Vietnamese, and on 17 February Chinese troops attacked Vietnam, starting a month-long war which turned out to be extremely costly for both sides, especially the Vietnamese. On 16 March Chinese troops completed their withdrawal from Vietnam but the legacy of bitterness and hatred could not but be long-lasting. Peace talks began not long after the end of the war but neither side was prepared to compromise in any way and the talks produced no results.

At the same time, however, the Chinese showed signs of willingness to tilt towards Vietnam's closest ally and its own strongest foe: the Soviet Union. On 3 April, the Chinese Foreign Ministry sent a note to the Soviet Union with two important messages. One was that China would not extend its 1950 Treaty of Friendship, Alliance and Mutual Assistance with the Soviet Union beyond the date of expiry on 11 April 1980. But, at the same time, the Chinese note proposed 'that negotiations be held between China and the Soviet Union for the solution of outstanding issues and the improvement of relations between the two countries'.[21] The Chinese delegation arrived in Moscow late in September to begin the formal talks. Nobody expected quick results. On the other hand, the past few years had shown how spectacularly the international balance of forces could change in a reasonably short period. The close Sino-American relationship had begun on the basis of just such talks and the Sino-Soviet negotiations could be taken as the seed of a changing line on the part of the Chinese leadership.

By the early months of 1980, however, the situation had changed back to renewed hostility. The reason was the Soviet invasion of Afghanistan at the end of 1979. Just as US intervention in Vietnam had caused the suspension of Sino-American talks, so the Chinese took a similar cue from the Soviet action. A spokesman of the Chinese Ministry of Foreign Affairs said on 20 January 1980:

> The Soviet invasion of Afghanistan menaces world peace and the security of China as well. It has also created new obstacles for the normalization of relations between China and the Soviet Union. It is apparently inappropriate to hold the Sino-Soviet negotiations under the present circumstances.[22]

All this amounted to an apparently temporary feeler towards improving relations with the Soviet Union. In domestic policy, the months between the Third and Fifth Plenums witnessed a major moving forward from the preceding period, coupled with a minor drawing back in some areas. In administration the Second Session of the Fifth National People's Congress, held in June, completed the work of the First Session by altering the Constitution to abolish revolutionary committees completely and at all levels.

Examples of caution include the 'readjustment' of the national economy announced at the Second Session. This meant reducing certain economic targets and scaling down projects of capital construction because they were 'beyond the State's financial means and its available material resources';[23] but that the four modernisations would continue remained in no doubt whatever. Another example of drawing back was the rather deliberate dampener put on the liberalisation movement. The widespread 'democracy walls' which had flourished towards the end of 1978 largely disappeared until only one remained in Beijing.

On the other hand, the atmosphere in the educational and intellectual field did continue to slacken noticeably during 1979. An officially sponsored movement 'to emancipate the mind' reached its high point. Zhou Yang, who had reappeared in

September 1977 after his disgrace in the Cultural Revolution, gave a public address explaining that the movement was in fact rooted in the Tiananmen Incident of 5 April 1976. He went on:

> Over the last two years and more, the Party Central Committee has time and again called on the whole Party and the whole people to understand Mao Zedong Thought as a scientific system in a comprehensive and accurate way, to do away with blind faith and emancipate the mind, to break down all the taboos placed by Lin Biao and the 'gang of four', and to get rid of the pernicious ideological influence they had spread over the years. It also has urged comrades whose thinking is ossified or semi-ossified to correct their stand, keep abreast with the situation, abandon all outdated and obsolete ideas and habits, such as bureaucracy and the force of habit of small producers, and to study new situations and solve new issues and problems which have appeared in the new historical conditions.[24]

Two points stand out from this statement. First, it is in fact a call to break away from Mao Zedong's ideas or at least to allow such departure. The taboos which Zhou mentions amount to vetoes on departing in any way from Mao Zedong thought. The ossification or semi-ossification on which Zhou comments are the bonds which tie the Chinese people to the thought of Mao Zedong. Zhou Yang had himself suffered through the demands of Mao Zedong's ideas (see p. 23). It is perhaps not surprising that he should wish to see their influence disappear.

The second point is that Zhou Yang's declaration can be interpreted as meaning that one type of idea should be banned and another should become fashionable, not that freedom of ideas should flourish. This interpretation would be partly valid. The Hua–Deng regime had no intention of allowing the spread of ideas hostile to its interests or to the four modernisations. On the other hand, the flowering of the social sciences, the praise given to large numbers of specific intellectuals, and the emphasis on the Tiananmen Incident, with its spontaniety, all suggest that 1979 saw greater intellectual breadth in China than any year since 1957.

The changing intellectual climate was accompanied by an admission in 1979 of problems affecting the youth. Delinquency, of which China had earlier claimed to be free, was now publicly declared not only to exist but to be quite serious. Of course the blame was laid on the Cultural Revolution which had removed all discipline from the young and given them the idea that the world should fall down at their feet.

This meant ever more thorough reversal of the policies of the Cultural Revolution. During 1979 there was no aspect of society in which this trend was more obvious than in the legal system. The Third Plenum of December 1978 had called for far more systematic and formal laws which should be strictly enforced and guaranteed, in order to protect the ordinary person and punish lawbreakers. The major rationale lay in the injustices which Lin Biao and the 'gang of four' had wreaked on a horrendous scale on the Chinese people. The media issued disclosures showing how power-holders could trump up charges against innocent people and subject them to lengthy prison sentences, or even have them executed.

A cult began around the figure of Zhang Zhixin, a female cadre and CCP member who was arrested, tortured, then had her throat slit on 4 April 1975 for disagreeing with Lin Biao and speaking out against the crimes of the 'gang of four'. Zhang Zhixin symbolises the need for legal reform. Hers is a powerful case because she was the first Communist martyr to the socialist system by the members of the CCP itself. To torture and kill an innocent CCP member was a crime of which even the cultural revolutionaries had never accused Liu Shaoqi or Deng Xiaoping.

To supervise the reconstruction of a socialist legal system which would prevent the recurrence of such a crime or martyrdom the government established the Commission for Legal Affairs under the National People's Congress Standing Committee, and appointed to direct it Jiang Qing's old adversary Peng Zhen, who had just been rehabilitated after being in disfavour since the beginning of the Cultural Revolution in 1966 (see p. 23). He arranged for the drafting of a number of laws, seven of which were adopted by the Second Session of the Fifth

National People's Congress in June. Perhaps the most important of these was the Criminal Law, the first of its kind to have been adopted in the PRC. Introducing it to the Second Session Peng Zhen said:

> The draft Criminal Law explicitly provides that 'the right of person, democratic rights and other rights of citizens shall be protected against unlawful infringement by any person or institution'. It also provides that extortion of confessions through torture is strictly prohibited; that assembling crowds for 'beating, smashing and looting' is strictly prohibited; that unlawful incarceration is strictly prohibited; and that frame-ups on false charges are strictly prohibited. Whoever fabricates facts to frame up another person (even a convict) shall be held criminally accountable in the light of the nature, seriousness and consequences of the false charges as well as with the criteria for imposing penalties.[25]

He went on to contrast these aims with the actual situation during the Cultural Revolution, when, for instance, the 'practice of extortion of confessions through torture' was 'widespread'. Apparently Zhang Zhixin was very much more than an isolated case. Another of the laws passed was that on Joint Ventures with Chinese and Foreign Investment which paved the way for a rather large influx of foreign capital into China and laid down guidelines for joint enterprises.

Deng Xiaoping and Peng Zhen were undoubtedly well intentioned in their attempts to reform the legal system. It would be quite pointless to deny that there was a problem in China between 1966 and 1976. Deng and Peng had themselves had more than their fair share of experience of the way in which the cultural revolutionary legal system had worked, but clearly there were political motivations as well. A new legal system is possibly the strongest of all bulwarks of a new political and social order. Moreover, it would be too much to expect that the newly devised and codified procedures would not be used against those arch-enemies of the Chinese people, the 'gang of four'. Just as the People's Republic was celebrating its thirtieth anniversary of existence Premier Hua Guofeng announced that the four would be put on trial to answer for their deeds in as fair and formal a fashion as the just established law system allowed.

Some doubt was cast on the legal procedure when on 16 October Wei Jingsheng, who had been believed one of the leaders of the 'democracy movement', was sentenced to fifteen years for 'passing on military intelligence to a foreigner and carrying out counter-revolutionary agitation'.[26] The Western press reacted with some shock to the fact and severity of the sentence, but the Chinese authorities insisted that the judgment was fair and merely an enforcement of the law against those who aimed to overthrow the government under the pretext of democracy and human rights.

The establishment of the new legal system was the forerunner of yet another climax in the dismantlement of the Cultural Revolution, namely the Fifth Plenum of the Eleventh CCP Central Committee, held from 23 to 29 February 1980. Among the Plenum's major decisions were two directly relevant to the Cultural Revolution. One was the formal rehabilitation of Liu Shaoqi, Mao's foremost enemy during that movement, and an explicit condemnation of the October 1968 Plenum which had dismissed Liu from all posts and expelled him from the Party. At the same time as the Plenum it was announced, for the first time, that Liu had died in November 1969 in prison, so that the rehabilitation was posthumous.

The other of the Fifth Plenum's decisions was to alter the PRC Constitution to eliminate the rights of citizens to 'speak out freely, air their views fully, hold great debates and write big-character posters' (Article 45). The rationale for the decision was that these rights had caused great trouble in the past, especially during the Cultural Revolution. They were unnecessary anyway, since there were other mechanisms by which citizens could express views on state affairs.

The Fifth Plenum exemplifies the continuation and intensification of policies found in the period leading up to the end of 1978. The new legal system is a prime illustration of the specifically new social characteristic within this general framework of policies found in the preceding period. If we move attention to attitudes towards the performing arts in 1979 and early 1980 we find, in the same way, certain new trends which exemplify change within the continuity of the previous months. They include the promotion of Zhou Enlai to the status of a major thinker on the arts, and a completely unprecedented emphasis given to foreign theatre.

The unchanged general framework is one of obsession with promoting variety. Ever larger numbers of dramas, especially traditional, must be performed, or restaged; the number of forms of the performing arts must expand. Blame for the previous lack of variety still attaches to the 'gang of four'. It is interesting and significant to find the martyr Zhang Zhixin with strong feelings and views about the performing arts and art in general. Her sayings include the following:

> Many movies and operas are banned. Only a few model theatrical works are left. There are only a few 'quotation' songs to sing. To go on like this can only impoverish the country's art and culture and make them dull. I have my doubts about Jiang Qing. Jiang Qing is not a 'standard-bearer', but a destroyer of China's culture, art and literature.[27]

Zhang gave exact expression to Hua Guofeng's views on variety and Jiang Qing even before the fall of the 'gang of four'.

The other major aspect of policy framework continued from 1978 is the downgrading of the Cultural Revolution. The best illustration of this is the change in attitude towards the drama by Wu Han which, as noted in Chapter 1, was savagely denounced at the very beginning of the Cultural Revolution. Indeed it was an article criticising the drama published in Shanghai in November 1965 by Yao Wenyuan, one of the 'gang of four', which had sparked off the campaign.

It is true that the move to rehabilitate the drama and its author Wu Han had begun in the middle of November 1978[28] and that early in December the editorial department of the journal *People's Theatre* had held a forum to discuss *The Dismissal of Hai Rui*. But it was not until 1979 that its re-establishment as a revolutionary item reached a climax. During that year not only was the play restaged but its author was praised in numerous press articles both as dramatist and as a historian. Of course the sixteenth-century upright magistrate Hai Rui was also reassessed. In 1965 he had been damned as a 'pure official' whose real purpose was not to protect but to exploit the masses because, by his very purity, he helped to uphold a ruthless and exploitative feudal system. In 1978–9 he was judged a proper model who succeeded in overturning corrupt legal verdicts and thus saving innocent people from destruction. So the line was that to dignify Yao Wenyuan's article on Wu Han's work as a prologue to the Cultural Revolution was entirely unwarranted. It was much more reasonable to dub it as 'entirely a big political plot, a trumped-up case concocted by the gang of four' [29] or 'a plot by Jiang Qing to destroy the Great Cultural Revolution'.[30]

This latter description tries to suggest that the reputation of the Cultural Revolution is still intact, and that it was only interference by the 'gang of four' which distorted it. But in fact there could be few developments aimed more strongly at discrediting the Cultural Revolution than to reverse the verdict on Wu Han and his drama. Yao Wenyuan's initial article attacking *The Dismissal of Hai Rui* had been Mao's chosen vehicle for opening the Cultural Revolution. If the drama was to be rehabilitated there could be virtually no way to prevent the Chinese people from drawing the conclusion that the Cultural Revolution itself was under attack. Certainly the rehabilitation of Liu Shaoqi, to which reference has already been made, suggests that the Party gave up any pretence of defending the movement during the period under discussion.

The one figure constantly in favour both in the years of the Cultural Revolution and since the death of Mao has been Zhou Enlai. The extreme affection accorded him, much warmer than that given to Mao, has already been noted in earlier sections. Early in 1979 the inevitable happened when the text of a speech which he had made on 19 June 1961 at a forum on literary and art work was eventually published in the press. The first to print was *People's Daily* on 4 February, but others soon followed. In the same month the People's Press brought out a book entitled *Zhou Enlai lun wenyi (Zhou Enlai Discusses Literature and Art)*. These developments elevated Zhou to a status alongside or above Mao as a thinker in matters related to the arts. The date of the speech is worthy of comment. The middle of 1961 was the height of the relaxation period in artistic matters following the Great Leap Forward. Indeed it was within a few months of the publication of Wu Han's controversial drama *The Dismissal of Hai Rui*.

Zhou Enlai's speech says nothing that actually conflicts with the 'Talks at the Yan'an Forum on Literature and Art' by Mao Zedong. However, it does take a somewhat different emphasis. The major thrust of the speech is to attack commandism, to encourage cadres to allow more discussion in artistic matters. 'We must', says Zhou Enlai, 'create a democratic atmosphere',[31] and again, 'we must allow others to have their own opinions. This is socialist freedom and ease of mind.'

Zhou Enlai elaborates on this theme by advocating less political interference in the arts. He distinguishes clearly between the political and the artistic aspects of works of art of all kinds.

> The leadership have the right to state their views on political questions. Politics must be in command. This means chiefly to determine whether the work is a fragrant flower or a poisonous weed, whether it is anti-Party and anti-socialist. Political acuity should be focussed on these aspects. As far as artistic aspects are concerned, we know very little.
> Since we know very little, we have little right to speak. Therefore we should not interfere unnecessarily. All comrades present are leaders. I hope you will interfere less.[32]

Zhou had quite a bit to say about the force of habit. Writers and artists must overcome it, he says, but should be allowed time to do so. To expect them to break out of old customs and ways of thinking quickly is totally unreasonable. Yet the stress on the breaking down of old ideas suggests a rather deliberate correlation between the publication of this speech and the 'emancipation of the mind' mentioned earlier in this section as a characteristic of 1979.

The former Premier also addresses two political problems which had been much discussed during the Cultural Revolution. One is the question of whom art should serve. Like Mao Zedong, he answers that it is the workers, peasants and soldiers. In this respect his verdict is the same as that which emerged from the Cultural Revolution. On the other question, however, he takes exactly the opposite stand. It relates to which takes precedence, the educational role of literature and art or the recreational. In the days just after the Cultural Revolution the *People's Daily* had seen fit to denounce the idea, attributed to Zhou Yang, that people go to the theatre or cinema not for education but for entertainment as 'a vile slander against our broad masses of workers, peasants and soldiers'.[33] But Zhou Enlai puts forward a completely different perspective. He says: 'The masses who go to see plays or films want to be entertained and to relax and you can educate them through the typified images presented. Education is conducted through entertainment.'[34]

The last point to make about Zhou Enlai's speech is his treatment of subject matter, which he says should suit the particular form of art being used, should be balanced and varied, entertaining, and enriching to the lives of the people. Subjects both from the past and from the present are desirable; those which 'praise the glory of labour' or 'tell young people about the hardships of making revolution' should all be encouraged. 'The Ministry of Culture', said Zhou Enlai, 'should do more work to bring about a general balance as far as subject matter is concerned.' But he added that it 'should not do so by compulsion or commandism and should not interfere too much'.[35]

In an important commentary published some time later the *People's Daily* strongly endorsed Zhou Enlai's view. It listed a whole range of desirable themes and then exhorted writers and dramatists 'to choose topics according to the needs of implementing the four modernisations and of the broad masses of the people, which they themselves understand best and which affect them most'. In the China opening up, 'they may write things which they are able and willing to write', it declared.[36] The phraseology in both Zhou's and *People's Daily*'s statements suggests that the authorities still enjoy some power and responsibility in what happens in the theatres or cinemas. Yet the balance between great and slight concern appears to be moving in favour of the latter.

Several months after the publication of Zhou Enlai's speech yet another ideological contribution was issued for the first time numerous years after its delivery. This time the author was that other leader Mao Zedong. It was a talk which he had given when he met with some of the leading personnel of the National Association of Musicians on 24 August 1956. The talk takes up some of the same themes as Zhou Enlai's speech, such as opposition to dogmatism, but its greatest interest lies in its overwhelming focus on problems related to foreign arts. It is true that Mao repeats his consistent theme of the necessity for a national Chinese culture. But his major thrust is that China should appreciate and make use of foreign cultures as well. 'It's wrong not to translate foreign works', he says, and again he exhorts his hearers, 'don't be afraid to perform a little foreign music'.[37]

If Mao's attitude to foreign productions appears here a little more positive than usual, so is his view on the bourgeoisie. He says:

We can't say the peasants have no culture – intensive
farming, the singing of folksongs and dancing are also
culture. But the majority of them are illiterate and have no
modern culture or technical skills. They can wield hoes and
plows but can't use tractors. In terms of modern culture
and technology, the bourgeoisie is ahead of the other
classes and hence we must unite with them and transform
them. Some bourgeois culture is outdated and can't be
used, but much of it can. Among musicians, there are
many who, in ideology, belong to the bourgeoisie. It was
the same with us in the past. But we've changed over.
Why can't they do so too? [38]

This is a far cry from the kind of interpretations that were being placed upon Mao's declarations during the Cultural Revolution.

The appreciation for foreign cultures which comes so strongly through Mao's 'Talk to Music Workers' was translated into reality in 1979 which saw an unprecedented number of foreign plays and films. Late in March, a Chinese company, for the first time, performed in Chinese translation a play by the famous German socialist playwright Bertolt Brecht (1898–1956): *Leben des Galilei (The Life of Galileo)* or, in Chinese, *Qielilüe zhuan*. The theme has all the makings of popularity in today's China. It deals with Galileo's insistence that the sun and not the earth is the centre of the solar system. Galileo was interested in science not superstition, but he is forced to recant by the medieval inquisition under the threat of torture. Clearly Galileo corresponds to the numerous righteous cadres who succumbed to the pressures of the Cultural Revolution, the inquisition by the 'gang of four'. Production of the play was accompanied by a great deal of favourable discussion in the press of Brecht and his work. At about the same time interest in drama of a different, indeed less revolutionary, kind was displayed when Shanghai's Youth Spoken Play Company put on, in Chinese translation, a production of Shakespeare's comedy *Much Ado About Nothing* under the Chinese title *Wushi shengfei*.

Developments in 1979 set the scene for the convening of the Fourth National Congress of Chinese Writers and Artists, which lasted eighteen days and concluded on 16 November 1979. It elected Zhou Yang, that arch-enemy and victim of the Cultural Revolution, as Chairman of the Chinese Federation of Literary and Art Circles. Zhou made a report to the congress in which he emphasised breadth, both in content and the portrayal of characters. 'Our literature and art', said Zhou Yang, 'should depict heroic people, and also all other kinds of people, including middle characters, backward ones and villains.' [39] Sticking to his earlier theme of the 'emancipation of the mind', he declared that it had still not gone far enough and that 'there are still large numbers of people whose thinking is still ossified or semi-ossified'.[40] Following on Mao's demands for greater appreciation for foreign cultures he concluded with a call for China to 'strengthen and expand cultural exchanges with other countries, and develop friendly contacts with writers and artists in other parts of the world'.[41]

Conclusion

So translated versions of Western works were thus being shown in China and calls for cultural exchanges with foreign countries made at more or less the same time that connections with the West reached a climax through the establishment of diplomatic relations with the United States of America, and just after the rapid growth of economic ties with the Western world and Japan. This suggests an affirmative answer to the question with which this chapter began, namely that political and social developments in China have indeed remained integrated with those in the performing arts.

If one considers the three subperiods discussed one finds very few details indeed which would point against accepting this suggestion. The political turnabout of October 1976 brought a corresponding changeover in the performing arts. The activities of the 'gang of four' were denounced in all their manifestations across Chinese society, but in no field of endeavour were the attacks more savage than in the performing arts. As the line changed towards greater breadth in the field of education, so it did towards far more variety in the performing arts. The explicit use of ideology declined in the economic sector as emphasis on pure production factors rose in the interests of the four modernisations. Correspondingly, the importance of ideology, in its most direct forms of usage, tended to dwindle in the performing arts. On the other hand, an ideological line still remained in all spheres of society, even if of a kind different from that of the period before October 1976.

With the return of Deng Xiaoping in mid-1977 the weight given to profit and all its ramifications, such as material incentives and a downplaying of class struggle, gathered momentum greatly. Links with the capitalist world grew while those with the socialist declined to vanishing point. The Cultural Revolution went from scrutiny to scepticism and then to rejection. All these trends were highly relevant to the performing arts. Tradition came back, gingerly at first, and then like a flood. Not much survived of the Cultural Revolution. Only the seventeen years from liberation to 1966 came in for any praise. Those who had been prominent in those years but then came under criticism or attack during the Cultural Revolution were back in the saddle; apart from the dead, there were virtually no exceptions to this pattern.

Our last subperiod, down to the Fifth Plenum in February 1980, shows a minor exception but a major agreement with the general thesis of social integration. The temporary drawing back or readjustment in the political and economic sphere has no obvious parallel in that of the performing arts. On the other hand, new specific features within the general overall continuation of former policies are clearly visible both in the general and the performing arts spheres. In the former we can single out developments in the legal system; in the latter the promotion of Zhou Enlai as a cultural ideologue and the emphasis on foreign drama.

Despite the massive changes, then, which have taken place in China since October 1976 at least one factor remains constant: it is that China continues to be an integrated society in which the various social features tend to move in harmony with each other and not in different directions. Considering that Western influence is now more than negligible in China and Western societies tend to be anything but integrated, the conclusion reached is not obvious. That it will continue to hold true indefinitely is even less clear.

3

The traditional forms of the performing arts since 1976

China's array of traditional drama forms is rich and varied. To be sure, there are some genres which have long been taken for granted in the West but which did not exist at all in traditional China, such as the spoken play. On the other hand, the range of different styles of opera was very wide, ballad or story-telling forms, nowadays known collectively as *quyi*, flourished all over the country, while acrobats and puppets were also popular.

There was a strong tendency for these theatrical forms to be regional. Each particular district had its own form of musical expression, and the instruments which accompanied the singers differed from region to region. The dialect which the singers enunciated on the stage was chosen to be understandable to the audience; and it is important to note that dialects differ sharply in China so that people who live even quite a short distance apart might not necessarily be comprehensible to each other.

The different styles of regional opera and story-telling, eventually some 300 of them, arose principally in the Ming (1368–1644) and Qing (1644–1911) dynasties. Some were very small in scale, a single person telling a story accompanying himself with a clapper, or a cast of only two or three singing an opera with one or two percussion instruments keeping the beat. According to one contemporary scholar the main artistic features of these small-scale folk styles are: (i) 'the structure is simple, and the plot concentrated', (ii) 'the characters are simple and sharply depicted', and (iii) the styles 'are humorous and witty, and rich in the feeling of authenticity'.[1]

These features have been carried over also to the larger popular regional forms of the big cities. As a general rule, however, the more highly developed the style has become, the more it has tended to lose the simplicity and grass-roots humour of the small-scale folk theatre. The most sophisticated of all is the Beijing Opera. Arising in the capital, as a result of the combination of several different regional forms, towards the end of the eighteenth century, it matured considerably during the nineteenth and produced a series of extremely great actors, of whom the most important and famous was Cheng Zhanggeng (1812–80). It was also influenced by the Qing dynasty court, mainly through the patronage of the famous Empress Dowager Cixi who held effective political power from 1875 till her death in 1908.

Before her time the main drama form, both of the court and the educated classes as a whole, was *Kunqu*. Arising in the sixteenth century near present-day Shanghai, it spread all over China till its virtual demise in the nineteenth century. It has now revived as mass, not elite, drama, but its former appeal to the scholars involved certain characteristics. It is slow-moving, with a regular 4/4 beat, highly elegant and dominated by the sound of the *dizi* (Chinese flute). The words use classical style.

Chinese traditional theatre of all forms is based upon highly stylised and beautifully integrated gestures of the head, face, hands, sleeves and body generally. The actors are classified according to the nature of the part they play, the *xiaosheng* often being a scholar-lover or other positive role, the *laosheng* an old general or minister, and the *hualian* ('painted face') a warrior or heroic official. Makeup is particularly important for 'painted face' characters, as the term implies, but is symbolic for roles of all categories and tells the audience the nature of the person portrayed.

An important characteristic of the Chinese traditional regional theatre, apart from *Kunqu*, was its enormously wide appeal. It was genuinely loved and understood by the people at large in all districts, however lowly and poor, and could truly claim to be mass culture. Indeed, it was for this reason that when the

CCP came to power in 1949 it encouraged and laid great emphasis upon the local drama. Troupes and forms which had fallen into oblivion as a result of the War against Japan and the numerous upheavals and conflicts which had characterised China's modern history were revived and subsidised. The themes underwent some adaptation to suit the demands of the new regime, but the traditional forms were not basically changed. However, Jiang Qing's attempt to revolutionise the theatre from 1963 onwards included the virtual suppression and disappearance of most of the regional styles from 1966. The 'models' were mainly Beijing operas; a few belonged to non-traditional forms such as ballet, but none was a regional drama, other than Beijing opera, or *quyi*. The professional troupes of the regional styles stopped performing, and disbanded. Where the local opera survived at all it was through amateur small-scale productions, and the themes in such cases were of course revolutionary and contemporary.

By the early 1970s Jiang Qing and her supporters saw fit to allow a rather half-hearted revival of the regional opera, provided the modern and revolutionary content was preserved to the total exclusion of the classical. Towards the beginning of 1972, a conference of some 1,000 people took place in Changsha, the capital of Hunan province, with the specific aim of reviving the regional theatre. Shortly afterwards we find reports of model operas being performed in the traditional local styles. *The Story of the Red Lantern* became a Cantonese opera and revolutionary stories were adapted to such minor regional forms as the *huagu xi* ('flower and drum theatre') of Hunan province.

This revival illustrates one interesting point. One has to distinguish clearly between form and content. It is quite possible for a traditional form to be centred on modern content, and the converse is equally true. On the other hand, apart from the period 1963–77, there has been a fairly strong tendency for form and content to go hand in hand with one another. In other words, traditional opera forms normally, although not always, deal with classical content, and non-traditional forms such as the spoken plays have revolved largely around modern themes. In order to reflect reality, therefore, the present chapter on the traditional forms will deal mainly with works on pre-modern themes.

The revival of the regional theatre styles in the early 1970s was a hesitant affair. Jiang Qing and her supporters simply do not appear to have been very keen on any traditional form beside the Beijing opera. The smashing of the 'gang of four' in October 1976, which effectively removed Jiang Qing's influence, opened the way for a vast acceleration in the revitalisation of the traditional regional styles. Figures applying to Zhejiang province to illustrate this point were given me in September 1978 in its capital, Hangzhou, by a group of the province's cultural leaders. They said that before the Cultural Revolution there had been 147 troupes in Zhejiang. Many of these had gone out of business during the years of the four's dominance. In the early 1970s the number had risen again to 80. After the gang was smashed, revival quickened and by September 1978 there were 117 troupes, still lower than before 1966 but expanding. The 117 represented all local opera styles of Zhejiang and most of the story-telling or *quyi* forms, although not all. The 117 companies accounted altogether for more than 6,000 actors and actresses. During a revisit to Hangzhou early in January 1980, I learned that the number of troupes in Zhejiang had risen to 142, almost exactly the same as before the Cultural Revolution.

Comparable figures illustrating several periods for the whole country are unavailable. However, an official figure applying to 1959 showed 3,513 professional companies throughout China at the end of that year.[2] According to a figure given to a reporter by the Minister of Culture on 27 September 1979, and transmitted to me through the Union of Chinese Dramatists, there were at that time a total of over 3,100 professional troupes in the entire country, including those of theatre, such as local opera, *quyi*, plays, acrobatics, *geju*, dance, etc. So the 1979 figure is lower than that of 1959.

Local opera troupes thus remain very important in China and the various regional styles appear again to be strengthening their position. Yet the whole process of revolution and change over the past century, and especially the impact of the CCP, Jiang Qing and the Cultural Revolution, have tended to make the boundaries between the areas of popularity of individual local styles much less clear, especially in the cities. Some cultural leaders in Wuhan, the capital of Hubei province, told me in October 1978 that in the big cities few people were particularly concerned at the type of regional opera they saw or heard. Every provincial capital city now has its own Beijing opera troupe. In Wuhan there is, in addition, a *Yuju* troupe, *Yuju* being the main local style of Henan province, as well as a company specifically designated to perform *Yueju*, the Shaoxing opera of Zhejiang. My informants claimed that it was mainly in the smaller cities and the countryside that attachments and affiliations to regional opera styles survive strongly. In January 1980, Miao Junjie, the cadre responsible for the literature and art section of the *People's Daily*, gave a slightly different, although not contradictory perspective. He claimed that the people retain their affection for the local opera of their own region, but that people with more education, in effect the urban populace, also favour other forms as well.

There is one aspect of this haziness among various local forms that is anything but new, namely the transfer of the stories. The traditional custom, as old as the regional opera itself, was to adapt a particular plot from one style of local theatre to another. A few stories, it is true, were peculiar to one area only, but on the whole each regional style used the major popular stories based on novels, famous dramas and so on. This custom persists today; if a traditional story is performed as a Beijing opera, it is likely to be adapted, almost instantly, to other forms as well such as Cantonese or Hunanese opera. For instance, the reader will recall from Chapter 2 that the first traditional Beijing opera after 1976 was *Forced Up Mt Liang*, revived in the middle of 1977. The *People's Daily* reported on 8 February 1978 (p. 3) that this work was being shown as a Sichuanese opera with all the 'varied musical and performance patterns and rich tunes' of that style, including its characteristic 'drums and gongs' and 'helping chorus'. The very next day the same newspaper noted (p. 2) that the Guangdong Provincial Guangdong Opera Company had 'recently' performed it as a Cantonese opera.

Just as the stories themselves tend to be consistent from one local style to another, so the general themes upon which the stories are based follow certain patterns. Particularly dominant

examples include famous past rebellions against the feudal authorities, the righting of an injustice through the agency of an
upright magistrate of the past, wars of patriotic resistance to
aggression from a foreign power, love stories, and equality for
women, both in political and family matters. Specific items on
these themes will be treated later.

Considering the total prohibition during the decade 1966–76
against traditional themes, even in old theatre forms such as
the Beijing opera, the cultural authorities after 1976 felt called
upon to justify why stories of the dynastic past were returning
so quickly. Vague references to Mao's thought were clearly
insufficient. What had happened to the arguments for aban-
doning traditional themes in the first place? In opening the
famous festival of Beijing operas on contemporary themes in
1964, Lu Dingyi had recorded his belief that there was a connection between the revolutionisation of the opera and the
suppression of modern revisionism (see Chapter 1). Did the
return to historical themes mean the regrowth of revisionism?
The literature does not phrase the question in quite such specific
terms, but it does ask 'can historical dramas become socialist
culture?' and it does raise problems about the function and
status of historical dramas in socialist culture. One specialist
confronts these problems as follows:

> In the past there were comrades who made divisions by
> themes. For instance, content which reflected the New
> Democratic revolution was New Democratic culture, and
> that which reflected the socialist revolution and
> construction was socialist culture. This sort of view on the
> attachment of culture and society is not a rounded one. I
> think that all works created with the viewpoint and stand
> of Marxism-Leninism-Mao Zedong thought and able to
> serve socialism should be counted as socialist culture. Of
> course, the themes are not the same and the degrees of
> embodiment of Marxism-Leninism-Mao Zedong thought
> are not the same. The directness or indirectness of the
> function in socialism is not the same. But although in the
> manner of treatment there should be a distinction between

primary and secondary and greater or lesser emphasis, qualitatively they should all be counted as socialist culture.[3]

Another commentator had just seen and thoroughly enjoyed a play about a righted injustice of ancient times and noted that, although the story took place in the distant past and its heroes had lived a long time ago, 'it most certainly cannot be lost as very good teaching material for the masses of today. It is perfectly normal that the masses should welcome this kind of drama.'[4]

Both writers are saying in effect that historical themes can reflect socialist society, can favourably influence it and can be a suitable method of propaganda within it. This is because some issues remain essentially fairly constant from period to period, even if the way they express themselves in society changes. It follows that themes from the distant past cannot automatically be regarded as 'revisionist'.

It is interesting to note that cultural leaders in contemporary China not only approve historical themes in drama, but also see the study of history through the theatre as a good in itself. The masses 'definitely need historical knowledge, the history of our country is long, so the historical knowledge is really extremely rich.'[5] On the other hand, dramas do not need to reflect exact historical accuracy. After all, as one specialist puts it:

I think that in history there were the ruling classes and the ruled classes, so most of what is recorded in old historical books is the deeds of the rulers. Although it is possible to read between the lines of the historical books and learn about exploitation, making us realise the existence of the ruled, generally speaking, the historical deeds of the ruled are conspicuous by their absence. So in writing a historical drama it is quite correct to give play to the imagination, quite correct to fill in the lacunae from actual fact.[6]

What the writer means by 'to fill in . . . from actual fact' is to imagine what might have been actually so from a socialist viewpoint. This means that the traditional stories must be presented from the viewpoint not of the ruling classes which wrote the records of the past, but of the masses who are now the heroes of history.

Dramas about past rebellions

Let us now turn to an illustration of this point through discussion of a few specific traditional operas on rebellions of the past. These can realistically be described as 'singing the praises of the Chinese people's struggle against class oppression' or expressing the 'courageous, intelligent and other superior qualities of the Chinese people', as mentioned in Chapter 2.

One representative drama in this category is *Forced Up Mt Liang*, which has been mentioned several times and is particularly noteworthy as being the first traditional drama to be performed in China after the smashing of the 'gang of four'.

Having commented on it elsewhere I take up instead another, in many ways similar, drama called *Sanda Zhujiazhuang (Three Attacks on the Zhu Family Village)*, a Beijing opera of which I saw an excellent performance in Wuhan on 11 October 1978 given by the Wuhan Municipal Beijing Opera Troupe with the famous Guan Zhengming in the lead role of Chao Gai.

Like *Forced Up Mt Liang*, this opera is based on the famous novel *Shuihu zhuan (The Water Margin)* and concerns the rebels of Mt Liang during the Song dynasty (960–1279). Near Mt Liang is a village dominated by a big landlord surnamed Zhu, which is being used as a strongpoint to attack the rebels and which the latter, led by Chao Gai, consequently wish to seize. The first attack is aborted. The second is by direct onslaught with some attempt to find out the situation in the village beforehand. It culminates in a typical and spectacular battle scene with plenty of acrobatics and juggling of swords, a generally brilliant display which clearly thrills the audience but does not lead to the successful seizure of the village.

The third and final attack is by far the most important and occupies the most time in the drama. The rebels, to quote the programme's typically Maoist version of the story, 'earnestly sum up the lessons of their experiences and begin by investigating the situation'. This leads them to think that they can

81

undermine the society within the village. They succeed in persuading one of the officials in the village to change sides. Through this means rebel representatives actually infiltrate the village. They find out and play upon a personal squabble between the squad leader of the enemy forces and his deputy, who is desperately jealous of him. Making use of this contradiction, the rebels within the village invite the squad leader for a drink and get him dead drunk, a crime which results in his dismissal. One of the representatives is then able to find out an exactly appropriate time for Chao Gai to lead an attack and sends a message advising him how to proceed. When the attack actually comes the dismissed squad leader is killed in action, and the rebels are able to seize the village without much resistance.

An interesting and unusual feature which this drama shares with *Forced Up Mt Liang* is that Mao Zedong explicitly praised it in writing during the days when Yan'an in northern Shaanxi was still the CCP's headquarters. As early as August 1937 Mao had pointed to the *Water Margin* story of the three attacks on the Zhu family village as one which revolutionaries might use as a positive example. He wrote of the rebel leader:

Twice he was defeated because he was ignorant of the local conditions and used the wrong method. Later he changed his method; first he investigated the situation, and he familiarized himself with the maze of roads, then he broke up the alliance between the . . . [enemy] Villages and sent his men in disguise into the enemy camp to lie in wait, using a stratagem similar to that of the Trojan Horse in the foreign story. And on the third occasion he won.[7]

Because of Mao's enthusiasm for the story, the Yan'an Beiping Opera Company adapted it into a Beijing opera and premiered it on 22 February 1945. According to the programme of the performance I attended in Wuhan, Mao saw the work in March the same year and commented: 'I have seen your drama and think it very good, it has educational significance. Following on *Forced Up Mt Liang* this drama is a successful creation and has consolidated the revolutionary path of the Beiping [Beijing] Opera.'

It is striking that Mao should endorse the revolutionary value of these two dramas, both based on *The Water Margin*. In 1975, Mao had himself begun a campaign to denounce the novel as a capitulationist work (see Chapter 1). As an old man Mao evidently developed more extreme views concerning the continuation of the revolution. Certain it is that the vast majority of his followers adopted the opinions which he had expressed much earlier in life. The drama continued to be performed after liberation and indeed was one of the few which persisted on the stage, during National Day celebrations, even after the 1964 festival of Beijing operas on contemporary themes. One of the reasons for this may have been the special interest in this drama of Peng Zhen, one of the chief opponents of Jiang Qing's attempts to revolutionise the theatre. Three members of the team which arranged the opera from the novel have reported that, when they were actually doing their work and had fallen into difficulties owing to their lack of direct experience in the kind of warfare depicted in the drama, 'Comrade Peng Zhen especially wrote a letter educating us and made us, in the first place, master the correct direction ideologically'.[8]

In fact, *Three Attacks on the Zhu Family Village* is an arranged traditional opera. On the basis of an old story it was composed by Communist writers to serve a particular ideological objective and to portray a specific type of warfare, the kind which the CCP used with such success against the Nationalist Party of Chiang Kaishek. Thus, although it follows the traditional gestures, costumes, music and categorisation of performers which are so characteristic of the classical Beijing opera, in the strictest sense it is not really a traditional opera at all.

Apart from the date of composition there are several features which reflect the modernity of the opera. One is the fact that the producers have used fairly elaborate scenery in specific conflict with traditional practice. Another is that female roles are played by women, not men as in the past. A third is the acting methods of the main negative character. For instance, in the scene where the squad leader gets drunk, he behaves on the stage with mannerisms so similar to those which Nationalist

83

Party agents adopt in Communist plays that the parallel is almost certainly deliberate. In the performance I saw, this section was very amusing and clearly delighted the audience.

Although many of the dramas about rebellions performed in China today follow the example of *Three Attacks on the Zhu Family Village* in taking their plots from *The Water Margin*, this is certainly not the case with all of them. One short piece which I saw in Beijing at the end of September 1978 is set in the year 613, and called *Yandang shan (Mt Yandang)*. Its action is taken up with battle scenes between the rebel and official armies. Naturally the rebels gain the final victory. The good side, that is the rebels, wear purple; the bad, yellow. In this little piece, there is a great deal of spectacular acrobatics, fighting, dancing, musical accompaniment, but no singing at all; the story is simple and easily told through pantomine. This scene was one of four I saw one evening in September 1978. All were performed by students of the China Drama School (*Zhongguo xiqu xuexiao*), which is in Beijing, and each dealt with a completely different theme.

Dramas about patriotic resistance to aggression

Another of the items presented on the same evening was *Yuemu cizi (Yue's Mother Tattoos Characters)*. It deals with Yue Fei, the famous patriot of the Southern Song Dynasty (1125–1279). As a general he had courageously assisted in a war of resistance against the Jin to the north, who have been attacking China. When his commander is killed, an incompetent is sent in replacement. Disgusted, Yue Fei refuses to serve any further and returns home. His mother is furious and persuades him to return to the service. To secure his determination, she tattoos four characters on his back: *jinzhong baoguo*, which mean 'serving one's country with unreserved loyalty'.

Yue Fei was an actual historical figure of the twelfth century; he was killed in a political intrigue at court through the machinations of an enemy, Qin Gui, who opposed his policy of resistance to the Jin. His reputation was later rehabilitated and he became a kind of national hero. He is tailor-made to appeal to post-1976 China where the reputations of so many dead, as well as living, people have been posthumously honoured after suffering denunciations in the Cultural Revolution. Yue Fei himself was honoured by the CCP's government when in 1961 the State Council proclaimed his tomb and the temple built on its site as a national monument. According to the inscription at the temple's entrance, dated July 1979, 'it was destroyed in the autumn of 1966', when the Red Guards of the Cultural Revolution attacked monuments in praise of past heroes, among many others things, 'and in 1979 renewed and restored. This took one year; it cost the energies of 56,000 workers and RMB (people's currency) 400,000 *yuan*'. The rehabilitation of this hero of ancient times was thus worth a great deal of effort and money. In the temple grounds the four characters *jinzhong bao-guo* are inscribed in a prominent place; the slogan is clearly important, not only for the twelfth century, but in the here and now.

The drama which revolves around the four characters is a short one with a small cast, and consists mainly of the exchange between Yue Fei and his mother. Yet the final section where Yue Fei's mother actually tattoos the characters on his back is among the most brilliant pieces of theatre I have ever seen in China because of the masterly manner in which the actor was able to express pain. This he did through staring straight ahead, without blinking for a very long time, and quivering slightly throughout his body. It is part of the skill of a Chinese actor of traditional opera to be able to persist extremely long periods without blinking.

This brief item is distinguished from many other classical operas in China today in not being a Communist composition. Yet it was revised in 1955, and the 1978 production has undergone even further slight changes. Indeed, this last version was specifically praised for 'omitting a whole series of formulae at the entrance of Yue Fei's mother'.[9] Wang Jinghua, who arranged the piece for this particular production, explains that in making the changes he specifically 'strove to express the noble characteristic of her [the mother's] strong love for her country and nation and her qualities of militancy'.[10]

It is striking that the emphasis here is on the woman's patriotism rather than the man's. It is the mother who takes the initiative, Yue Fei who is forced to follow her lead. The idea so popular in the PRC that women should concern themselves with political matters seems here to find vivid expression, especially when one remembers the high status accorded to Yue Fei himself.

Probably the most famous drama to couple the ideals of patriotic resistance to aggression and female participation in politics is *Yangmen nüjiang (Women Generals of the Yang Family)*, a Beijing opera arranged by Lü Ruiming and others in 1960 on the basis of a Yangzhou opera. The original story comes from a classical novel called *Yangmen jiang yanyi (The Romance of the Yang Family Generals)*. The opera is set in the eleventh century. China is being subjected to attack and a faction at court believes it should compromise and seek peace with the enemy. In a fury at this feebleness the dowager of the Yang family, who is 100 years old, whips up the women of the clan to a pitch of enthusiasm in favour of resistance. The emperor is forced to change policy and determines to resist the enemy. He orders the dowager of the Yang family herself to lead the female generals out to battle. In the end, the dowager devises a plan through which the generals are able to attack and annihilate the enemy army, after which they return to court.[11]

Like all other dramas on traditional themes, this one was banned at the time of the Cultural Revolution. Jiang Qing's accusations against it included 'that it attacked Chairman Mao's thought on people's war and opposed all war'. These seem curious charges to make against a work so obviously overflowing with militant patriotism. Certainly one reviewer on seeing the opera again after a long gap during the Cultural Revolution was moved to exclaim: 'These glorious heroic figures of women generals of the Yang family who won the war and won victory; what great inspiration they can give us!'[12]

The audience at the performance which I saw in Hangzhou in September 1978, performed by the local municipal Beijing opera company, would probably have echoed those sentiments, albeit with reservations. They were very clearly on the right side of the debate over whether to resist or not. They laughed enthusiastically at the right places, identified with the heroes

86

and seemed angry with those who wished to compromise with the enemy. Yet it must be added that during the rather long section leading up to the final battle, some members of the audience seemed to lose concentration, and there were even a few who went to sleep. They revived fully for the battle scene. The overall definite sense of enthusiasm may have been due in part to the fact that the theatre was quite full and that all types of people were present, old, young, children, middle-aged.

This varied audience clearly understood what was happening on the stage, not only because of their familiarity with the story but because the script was projected beside the stage. This was particularly important in the present case since the cast, although members of the Hangzhou troupe, sang in standard Chinese, but the audience were presumably mainly people from the city itself and thus most conversant with the local dialect. To project the sung words on the walls beside the stage is a virtually universal practice in contemporary Chinese opera theatre.

Again in accordance with contemporary custom for traditional operas, the orchestra sat behind a screen to the right of the stage. In the past, before liberation, it would normally have been placed right on the stage in full view of the audience. Another contrast with traditional custom was to separate the acts by a curtain.

One advantage of the curtain was that the actors were able to escape the view of the audience. Unlike the performance in Wuhan, this one included an interval, during which the actors changed dress on the stage itself, accompanied and assisted by professional dressers. Dressing-room space is sparse in China and may be totally inadequate if the cast is large. That the stage can substitute for dressing-rooms outside audience view is one function of the curtain.

Through being invited on stage during the interval, I learned that the actors were very young, mostly around twenty years old. Even the centenarian dowager was only twenty-four years old, although her acting was good enough to make her seem like the aged woman she was trying to portray. The players of the instruments in the orchestra were also very young indeed, mostly less than twenty.

Dramas on righted injustices

The theme of female equality comes forward by implication, not only in such patriotic dramas as *Women Generals of the Yang Family* but also in another broad category of works very popular both in the China of the past and of today, namely dramas which deal with righted injustices. Invariably, it is a woman who suffers the injustice at the hands of some local tyrant or her husband. It is she who stands up for herself, will not submit to the injustice and is prepared to take strong action against it. Normally she invokes the aid of a traditional just judge or magistrate who, after some persuasion, successfully helps her and rights the wrongs she has suffered. Such dramas may be said to express 'class oppression' or 'reflect a democratic and revolutionary essence', according to the stipulations mentioned in Chapter 2 as appropriate to traditional operas.

A good example is the Beijing opera *Qin Xianglian*, called after the heroine of the opera. It concerns a scholar called Chen Shimei, married to Qin Xianglian. He goes to the capital to sit for the examinations, does brilliantly well, is asked to marry the daughter of the emperor.and agrees. He then sends someone to murder his previous wife and their two children, but the three escape and go to the capital in search of him. She appeals to the judge Bao Zheng (999–1062), famed for his justice, but two members of the imperial family intervene to persuade him not to help her. Bao turns against Qin Xianglian and tries to induce her to drop the case and go back home. She replies bitterly by declaring her disappointment in this famous upright official who is interested only in protecting rank. The charge stings Bao Zheng into agreeing to help her. He succeeds in bringing Chen Shimei to trial and in the end sentences him to be executed, for, among other crimes, trying to murder his wife and children.

In this opera, the two children play a fairly significant role, even though they do not actually say much. They add greatly to the drama's emotional tension, highlighting it by much weeping, expressed by placing their sleeves over their eyes, and by the dramatic convention, already mentioned in connection with Yue Fei, of holding on for a very long period without blinking.

In the performance which I saw on 4 October 1978 in Nanjing, both were actually performed by children.

Like many other full-length Communist-arranged pieces, this one is extremely lengthy. It lasts over three hours and, in the performance I attended, without interval. Another characteristic it shares with other operas arranged under the auspices of the CCP is its intense moralism. The characters are depicted as evil, heroic or good with very great clarity and firmness. It is certainly Qin Zianglian who is the real heroic figure, not the judge Bao Zheng, for it is she who persuades the wavering official into supporting the side of justice. Just as in the case of Yue Fei and his mother, the woman takes the lead and succeeds in urging the recalcitrant man to abandon the path of weakness and adopt that of righteousness.

The story takes place in the distant past, but nevertheless carries its own significance for the present. The *People's Daily* of 4 June 1980 (p. 3) printed an article about a ' "Chen Shimei" of today', a commune member called Liang Changdong who had married a village girl in 1962 but in 1972 went off to the city to study medicine. His wife did what she could to support his studies; he joined the Party and even became deputy head of a major hospital. He then remarried and when the former wife found out and complained did all he could to interrupt her livelihood. She appealed to higher authorities and, as a consequence, was 'beaten up many times by Liang Changdong'. Punishment for his misdemeanours, which threatened to bring about 'a repeat performance of the tragedy of Qin Xianglian', was Liang's expulsion from the Party. Such a story would most certainly not have found its way into the newspapers before 1976. The article makes no mention of how common the behaviour of Liang Changdong is in China today. However, the reference to Qin Xianglian and Chen Shimei shows the popularity, fame and relevance of this traditional work, and also suggests that the drama is itself a moral warning against flouting the Marriage Law.

Another drama in which Bao Zheng plays a prominent role is *Limao huan taizi* (*Exchange of the Heir-Apparent for a Leopard Cat*), which I saw in Hangzhou on 2 January 1980, performed by the *Shaoju* Troupe of Xiaoshan. *Shaoju* is a local style found in Shaoxing and nearby parts of Zhejiang, while Xiaoshan is a small city, not far to the southeast of Hangzhou. Although this, then, was not a major company from a particularly significant city and did not play one of China's most widespread drama forms, its standard was very high indeed and the work performed both typical and of great interest.

Like *Qin Xianglian*, this opera is set in the eleventh century. It concerns two concubines, surnamed Li and Liu, of the Emperor Zhenzong. Li gains the emperor's favour by announcing she is pregnant and hopes to give birth to the heir-apparent, but Liu, in a jealous fit, conspires with an evil eunuch to exchange the baby for a leopard cat and orders a servant girl to drown the heir. The emperor, believing she has deceived him, places Li under house arrest. Through the agency of a good eunuch, both Li and her baby separately escape; and Li lives in the countryside as a poor woman. Many years later, by which time her son has in fact become emperor without knowing who his mother is, she persuades Bao Zheng to look into the case. As a result of the judge's investigations, the evil machinations of Liu and her eunuch friend are revealed. Liu commits suicide, the eunuch is executed, while Li and all her supporters are reinstated or promoted.

Despite the obvious tragic element in the early stages, the opera follows tradition in its happy ending. It also includes a very important comic element. While she is a poor woman, Li adopts a son called Fan Zhonghua who is the main clown. He does not wear the white painted face of the traditional *chou*, and is a positive character, so the audience laughs with him, never at him. Virtually all the main comic passages are spoken, not sung. Apart from his generally light-hearted and jocular manner in a basically extremely serious situation, what appeared to amuse the audience most was his ambivalent manner and attitude towards the judge. Although Bao Zheng was highly exalted, Fan Zhonghua a mere peasant, Fan behaved without great respect and continued his clownish jocularity in Bao's presence although the latter never smiled once. The biggest laughter of the evening came when Bao, convinced that Concubine Li's story was genuine, knelt down before her and Fan responded by doing a traditional somersault in surprise that so high an official should thus demean himself. It may well be a fantasy of many ordinary Chinese openly to laugh at bureau-crats, even good ones, and their procedures. Certainly this particular audience, and others I have seen in China, derived much fun from the slinging off at relations between high and low.

Humour of this kind is part of the Chinese tradition. The scenery used, however, was very modern indeed. In the first place, it was extremely elaborate with splendid palaces, lakes and mountains depicted. Second, it changed with remarkable speed through a series of curtains at the back of the stage each of which could be raised during a moment of complete darkness to reveal the next magnificent scene.

Although based on an old story this opera has been rear-ranged many times and the production I saw dated only from mid-October 1979. It had an obvious political relevance to that time. Several Chinese friends at the performance agreed with me that it was not too far-fetched to see Concubine Liu as a representation of Jiang Qing and the evil eunuch as the other three members of the 'gang of four'. Perhaps even more striking is the overall theme of rehabilitation which runs through the opera. The many years between the times that Concubine Li suffers her injustice and is brought back to favour as a heroine must surely have reminded the audience of the long years of the Cultural Revolution when so many innocent and good people suffered in the countryside as a result of trumped-up charges. Equally certainly the parallel was intentional, with the final dénouement representing the arrest and fall of the 'gang of four'. Bao Zheng is simply those good political forces which bring about the rehabilitation of the worthy.

This obvious connection between drama and politics raises the suspicion that the plethora of dramas on righted injustices is a political tool designed to encourage the people to support legal reform. It is true that the revival of such dramas belongs initially to 1978 and the year when legal reform began was 1979. On the other hand, preparations were certainly well under way already in 1978 for the changes which were to take place in the legal system. The following comment in an article about Bao

Zheng may be taken as confirmation that the propaganda relationship between drama and law is intentional:

> The fascist dictatorship practised by Lin Biao and the Gang
> of Four over the people enabled us to understand that a
> people's judge must have the revolutionary spirit of self-
> sacrifice in resolute struggle against acts which encroach
> upon the interests of the country and the people. The
> people must be guaranteed equality before their own law
> and no one must be allowed to have privileges above the
> law. . . . Only thus can we give full play to people's
> democracy, maintain socialist rule of law, secure the
> people's trust and united efforts in modernizing our land.[13]

It was not accidental that there was a slogan hanging promi-
nently at the back of the theatre where I saw *Exchange of the
Heir-Apparent for a Leopard Cat*; it read 'give play to socialist
democracy, strengthen socialist legality, all people are equal
before the law'.

Dramas based on love stories

The case of *Qin Xianglian* makes clear that some of the dramas
on righted injustices include a fairly strong component of betrayed love. This is also a branch of the more general classification of dramas based on love stories.

In January 1980 an actively involved theatre worker in Xi'an
told me that dramas on love stories had recommenced performance in Shaanxi and Sichuan provinces in April or May 1978.
This followed on the permission which Deng Xiaoping had
given the members of the Sichuan Provincial Sichuan Opera
Troupe earlier in the year (see Chapter 2), and signalled the
formal and large-scale resurgence of love dramas in the whole
country. Because these two provinces were first and because I
have seen a number of particularly interesting love operas there,
I propose to focus mainly on Shaanxi and Sichuan in drawing
examples for this section.

There appear to be three main types. The first is comedies

where love forms a central interest, second are those where an evil force, principally a religious one, attempts unsuccessfully to destroy the happiness of a pair of lovers, and finally there are the stories of love ending in tragedy, either through the force of circumstances or betrayal by the man. In virtually all cases a central point emerges that one ought to choose a marriage partner freely and not submit unwillingly to the dictates of parents. In other words love operas contain a clear message in favour of the Marriage Law of 1950, mentioned in Chapter 1, which laid down equality of the sexes and outlawed the old system of arranged marriages.

Two full-length examples of the comic love story are the *Wanwanqiang Nangzai* and the Sichuan opera *Qiao laoye qiyu (Lord Qiao's Adventure)*. Both feature absurd situations and disguise. In the former the main character Nangzai succeeds, through a great deal of manoeuvring which includes his disguising himself as a doctor and transporting the hero hidden in a box, in bringing about the marriage of two sisters to men they really love and not to those of their father's choice. He also finds a bride himself. In the second, the central character Lord Qiao, spends the night in a sedan chair because he can find no room in inns. He is abducted by a local bully who believes the occupant to be a beautiful girl as whom Lord Qiao disguises himself to prevent the marriage. The bully arranges a wedding between himself and the girl but it turns out to be between his own sister and Lord Qiao.

From the point of view of content a common point in the two operas is to laugh at the feudal notions which saw great scandal in a man's entering a woman's boudoir or a doctor's touching a female patient. In their technique both are similar and typical. Both give prominence to the traditional stage convention by which the lights do not dim at all even when the scene is supposed to take place in pitch dark. In both it is a source of great amusement for the audience to watch the groping about in full light or to hear the bully addressing fond words to the sedan chair's occupant, in the belief that it is a girl, while Lord Qiao wears a surprised expression.

Nangzai holds an unusual place in the history of Chinese regional theatre, because of its origins. *Wanwanqiang*, the style to which it belongs, is called after a small bell-like instrument named the *wan* which plays an active role in the percussion section of the orchestra. One of the three main forms of the Xi'an region, along with *Qinqiang* (Shaanxi Opera) and *Meihu xi* (Meihu Opera), it originated in the eighteenth century as a form of shadow play in Weinan, a town not far from Xi'an. Unlike most popular theatre styles, which were despised by the educated classes, it attracted the attention of an eighteenth-century Weinan literary figure called Li Shisan. I learned in Xi'an that a stele in Weinan records Li's patronage of the *Wanwanqiang* and his contribution to its development, including composition of ten shadow plays, one of them *Nangzai*.

Written versions of the ten items have not survived from that time. However, they have been transmitted by word of mouth through the training of generations of actors. Not till after liberation were Li Shisan's ten plays written down. They were rearranged and adapted for performance on a full-size stage. The stories were left essentially unchanged, though in the case of *Nangzai* the original included only the marriage of the two sisters and not of Nangzai herself.

Shadow plays are still performed in the villages of Shaanxi Province, though not in Xi'an since the Cultural Revolution. Yet despite the adaptations which it has suffered, *Nangzai* may certainly count as an illustration of the kind of humour and love story which is so basic to real local theatre.

To increase its dramatic importance and intensity true love must be opposed by some force other than the couple concerned. A feudal father is a popular choice, as in *Nangzai*. Another is an abbot, abbess or other religious power. *Baishe zhuan* *(The Story of the White Snake)* is a particularly famous example. A White Snake becomes a beautiful girl and gets married to a young scholar in Hangzhou. The wicked abbot Fahai abducts the husband to destroy the marriage, but the girl summons the magic forces and defeats him. A very similar story is *Hongzhu nü (The Red Pearl Girl)* about a mother-of-pearl fairy who becomes a beautiful girl and marries a mortal. Again a wicked Daoist abbot, a crane turned into a man, kidnaps the husband to destroy the couple's happiness but is defeated by the girl and her supporters.

One of the early surviving love dramas is *Yuzan ji (The Tale of the Jade Hairpin)* by Gao Lian of the Ming dynasty (1368–1644). I saw two scenes from it in the form of Sichuan opera in Chengdu: *Bizhi (Compelling a Nephew)* and the succeeding, and famous, *Qiujiang (Autumn River)*. A nun, Chen Miaochang, falls in love with a scholar, the nephew of her abbess, who refuses them permission to marry and instead forces the young man to sit for the examinations. When he does so the nun flees the convent and, with the aid of a sympathetic old boatman, crosses the river and catches up with him.

Except for the last, magic and fantasy play a significant role in these dramas. The revival of such elements, so strongly denounced in the Cultural Revolution, is a significant characteristic of children's theatre, but it has not taken long for the more general dramas to catch up. Fantasy and magic are, after all, appropriate vehicles to point a moral about equality between the two sexes and free marriage.

The notions are strengthened by the fact that in all three dramas it is the woman who takes the initiative. The same point has emerged in discussions on other types of drama and is even more prominent here. It does not need Jiang Qing to give women the central positive roles in the Chinese theatre. In *The Red Pearl Girl* there is a long and amusing section where the heroine proposes to her young man the first time she has met him. She feigns sore feet to attract his attention and weeps aloud for his benefit while showing a satisfied face to the audience as the plot appears to work. When he refuses her offer of marriage she threatens suicide, which has the desired effect of a speedy change of mind on his part. In all three operas the heroes are but shadowy figures by comparison with the heroines and in the two with battle scenes, *The White Snake* and *The Red Pearl Girl*, it is the women who fight on behalf of the men, not the other way around; and the victories are secured by women against powerful male opponents.

The performances I attended of these operas in January 1980 all illustrated some theatrical practices which are worth recording. *The White Snake* is best known as a Beijing opera, but I saw scenes from it both as *Kunqu* and Sichuan opera. In the latter the heroine's associate, the Green Snake, is a male, not female as in other forms. The battle scene where Fahai is defeated shows several stage techniques peculiar to Sichuan opera. One is a skill originated by the famous actor Kang Zhilin (1870–1931) which enables the actor to kick up his foot and touch the area just above the nose with it, placing the image of a third eye there. The technique requires absolutely accurate placing and perfect control over the foot. Another is the ability of one actor to change facial makeup suddenly and repeatedly with the face hidden only momentarily from the audience's view.

In the case of *Autumn River* the technique to note is actually a more beautiful one, though it may not require the same split-second control as the two just described. It is the way the old boatman and Chen Miaochang evoke the motion of the boat. They sway to and fro, keeping the same distance from one another. The boatman holds an oar which he waves gently to imitate the extraordinarily graceful motion of a real boatman. These actions, which are justly famous, can be varied to show particular sections of the trip such as the boat's being pushed off from the shore or striking a rough patch. All the time the audience imagines both the boat and the water. There are no scenery and no props but an oar.

The Red Pearl Girl illustrates quite another type of practice. I saw this work as a Shaoxing opera (*Yueju*) performed in Suzhou by a touring Xi'an company. In Shaoxing opera the pre-liberation tradition was that the troupes were exclusively female. Since 1949, however, the general policy adopted for all forms of theatre has been that 'men should play men, women portray women'. In *The Red Pearl Girl*, however, all performers were women, except for the wicked Daoist abbot and his army. All positive males, including the husband, were played by relatively young women. The training of female performers of male roles appears to persist in less prestigious training schools which are thus likely to keep this rather beautiful convention alive indefinitely. On the other hand, it is no longer carried on in the main Shaoxing opera schools, such as the one in Shanghai. When I saw there a scene from the famous *Liang Shanbo and Zhu Yingtai*, the part of Liang was played by a young man.

Liang and Zhu is an example of a love opera which ends with the deaths of the lovers, though there is a happy note to the conclusion when they are reunited as butterflies. My example for the third category of love dramas, those ending in tragedy, is thus more appropriately another opera *Dashen (Beating the God)*, which I saw as a Sichuan opera with the famous Sichuanese actress Jing Hua as Jiao Guiying. The opera is part of a much longer work which concerns a scholar Wang Kui who falls in love with the prostitute Jiao at a time when he is desperately poor. She saves him from disaster and they marry. At the Temple of the Seagod they swear eternal fidelity and he goes off to the capital to sit for the inevitable examinations. He comes top, is given high office and marries the prime minister's daughter. Jiao appeals to the Seagod for help. When this proves ineffective she beats its image and hangs herself.

As theatre *Beating the God* is a gem. It is a concentrated and intense piece lasting less than an hour but expressing deep feeling. It belongs to that very special brand of drama, real tragedy. On the whole the Chinese much prefer a happy ending and, unlike its converse comedy, tragedy is not a strong element in traditional Chinese opera. During the Cultural Revolution tragedy as an art-form was totally unknown, because a revolutionary hero never admits defeat, even in death. Even since 1976, though tragic elements abound in spoken plays and operas, real tragedy remains rare.

The tragedy in *Beating the God* was heightened by several factors. One was the superb acting of Jing Hua. Though she is already somewhat older than Jiao is supposed to be, she succeeded in capturing the distraught mood of the deserted wife to perfection. Another was the dramatic imitation of puppets. In this piece there are, besides Jiao herself, only two characters, the images of the god's attendants. When she strikes them down they come alive briefly. The actors make puppet-like motions to illustrate the futility of her action before departing from the stage. This convention is not found in China outside Sichuan opera.

Beating the God was part of the repertoire which the Chengdu Municipal Opera Company, of which Jing Hua is a member, took to Eastern Europe in 1959, in the days when China enjoyed reasonably friendly relations with most countries there. Jing Hua told me that the opera had been much changed for the

tour and also still further since 1976. The opera had been somewhat shortened to sharpen the character of Jiao Guiying. The
puppets were in the original but were omitted for the 1959 tour.
She said that they had been later restored. This was a wise
move, because they add greatly to the mood of the opera.

In its dramatic force, in its capture of the essence of real
tragedy, and in the superb intensity of Jing Hua's acting, this
item struck me as probably the finest piece of theatre I have
even seen in China.

Dramas about Monkey

A tragic story of betrayed love may appear to stretch the definition of what constitutes a revolutionary and consequently
acceptable traditional drama. In the middle of 1978, however,
performers reached an even further stage when they began to
put on dramas about Monkey (Sun Wukong), the mythical companion of Xuanzang in his journey to India, lasting from 629 to
645, to collect Buddhist scriptures and images. The story of this
famous monk of the Tang dynasty (618–907) has been fiction-
alised in the novel *Xiyou ji (Journey to the West)*, which forms
the basis of many Chinese dramas.

If the standard is set against the official *People's Daily* commentary of 13 July 1978 on what kinds of traditional operas
should be performed (see Chapter 2), it appears that the only
possible justification for reviving dramas about Monkey comes
under the heading of 'active optimism'. Certainly they can claim
to propagate that important revolutionary quality. Good is always victorious over evil. On the other hand, the less revolutionary symbols of magic, fantasy and religion are also vital
components and, in contrast to love story operas like *The Red
Pearl Girl* or *The White Snake*, the religious element is not always
evil. The real reason why Monkey dramas have been revived is
the simplest one: Chinese people love them, no matter of what
age, sex or political colouring. This has been so for centuries
and will quite likely remain so for more.

Monkey dramas exist in numerous regional forms. Their central characteristic from a technical point of view is their empha-

sis on acrobatics. The situation which makes the opera exciting is the need for a battle, and such are the scenes upon which acrobatic skills thrive. Such operas are traditionally termed *wuxi* (military dramas) and stand in contrast to *wenxi* (civil dramas), which deal with such topics as love. It is of course possible to combine both types into a single work, such as in *The White Snake*. By comparison with civil dramas, military have but few sung sections, but much stylised dialogue and a great deal of action, accompanied by the percussion instruments appropriate to the particular regional style.

The actor who portrays Monkey is always a 'painted face'. This enables him both to appear as a magnificent general, suitable for military drama, and to look like a real monkey. To imitate the facial and other mannerisms of a monkey is part of the skill of performers of this role, and some of them achieve it with a perfection which is almost weird.

Nowadays by far the best known of the Monkey dramas is *Nao tiangong (Havoc in Heaven)*. It concerns Monkey's eating the magic peaches of heaven's orchard, and other heavenly commodities. Heavenly troops come out to arrest him but he defeats them all. Another is *Shuiyan Sizhou (Flood in Sizhou)*, about an underwater female goblin who eats people. She forces a young man to marry her, but he obtains her permission to return home to Sizhou to tell his parents the news. When he fails to return, she goes off with an army to seize him, but the goddess Guanyin gets Monkey and others to battle, successfully of course, on his behalf.

Both items are short and each formed the climax of a series when I saw them in January 1980, *Havoc in Heaven* as a *Kunqu* in Beijing, and *Flood in Sizhou* as a Shaanxi opera in Xi'an. In both cases the realism of Monkey's mannerisms was extraordinary, particularly his actual eating of the peaches in the first one. The acrobatics in both included unbelievably rapid twirling of spears, bouncing swords neatly on a spear one after another and thus juggling them from person to person, and the inevitable cartwheels. Brilliant displays of this kind never fail to amaze or thrill a Chinese audience.

Monkey is not the only character who performs acrobatics. In the second item, the goblin does so even more than he. In the performance I saw it was a man who performed this female role because of the superb dexterity in 'military' acting of the particular actor, Li Zhenmin. It is very rare nowadays for a man to perform a woman's role and he was the only one I saw thus trained since liberation. The exception is due to the demands of the role, since acrobatics are actually far more characteristic of male than female parts, because of the military connection. The goblin has hardly any sung or even spoken lines, and Li Zhenmin did not imitate a woman's voice well.

Another notable feature of the action in this opera is the representation of underwater scenes. These are shown in the traditional manner. Numerous people wave long blue cloths quickly up and down, and this action creates an overall undulating impression on the stage reminiscent of waves.

It appears to be mainly the form and action of *Havoc in Heaven* and *Flood in Sizhou* that account for their appeal. Yet content should also be considered. It is possible to seek progressive ideas in either. *Havoc* appears to be hostile to the gods and *Flood* to forced marriages. Yet in *Flood*, Guanyin, as much a positive character as Monkey, is just as divine as the wicked heavenly soldiers of *Havoc*. There are scenes there, in contrast, which outweigh the positive aspects of *Flood* in the realm of ideology on family or women. In one place Monkey is confronted by a female adversary. He makes gestures sneeringly suggesting that it is ridiculous for a woman to take part in a battle. His subsequent easy victory over her appears to confirm his most unprogressive attitude.

One observer of the Chinese scene suggested that Monkey is a representation of Deng Xiaoping who, like Monkey, 'has laid about him with his magic cudgel, radically altering the lives and prospects of China's billion people'.[14] The parallel is a possible one, and would make Monkey dramas political in nature. Given Monkey's sexism, to which I have just referred, the comparison may not be too flattering for Deng. Yet surely the basic lesson of Monkey dramas that difficulties can be overcome, however great, is a political one with a considerable importance in a China bent on modernisation.

Quyi

In terms of the speed of the actors' movements traditional Chinese theatre reaches its pinnacle in military dramas such as those about Monkey. At the other extreme, where in many regional styles the performers simply sit, is the genre known as *quyi*, a general term covering popular forms such as ballad-singing, story-telling, comic dialogues, cross-talk and others.

The *quyi* arts are extremely ancient in China. Primary sources attest to popular story-telling in the ninth century, but it is probably much older. Over the centuries *quyi* has blossomed into many different forms which, like the popular theatre, are largely regional. On 23 January 1980 I was informed that the Central People's Radio had broadcast, since the fall of the 'gang of four' in October 1976, *quyi* items of 294 different styles, and expected more still to emerge in the course of time.

By the very nature of ballad-singing and the other aims of *quyi*, it is a small-scale art. There may be one to three performers, sometimes four or five, but rarely more. They may play a role, or simply recite a story.

In many forms talking predominates, but in the great majority music also plays an important role. Since the art is largely regional, it shows heavy local flavour and the influence of the folk songs of the area. Both the recited and sung sections use the dialect of the region of provenance.

Just as with local opera, the people retain an affection for their own area's particular variety, but regional loyalties are breaking down in the major cities in the sense that a *quyi* troupe of one province or region often performs items belonging to a form of another and the audience will appreciate the music and style. However, this tolerance extends less to the countryside, where the peasantry still tend to be unused to, and hence reject, any forms but their own.

No matter what the style, the content of *quyi* items may concern either a traditional or contemporary story. During the period 1966–76 the former was banned altogether along with the pre-CCP stories in all branches of the Chinese performing arts. However, since the fall of the 'gang of four', ballads, stories and dialogues on themes of dynastic or ancient times have

101

returned strongly, although traditional content has not by any means ousted contemporary which the young people still greatly prefer.

At a performance I saw of a regional Sichuanese form of *quyi* in Chengdu, the provincial capital, in January 1980, all items were traditional. One concerned the meeting between Chen Miaochang and her lover just after the boatman, in *Autumn River*, brings her across the river in his pursuit; another, an ancient Chinese patriot resisting foreign aggression. There were five performers for each item; all wore everyday clothes, and played musical instruments as they sang. In the first item two young women portrayed respectively Chen and her lover, in the second all five actors were men and all old. One of them played the role of the patriot, another that of his lover and future wife, imitating the voice of a woman. A feature strikingly shared by all five old actors was blindness. In the old society, *quyi* performers were often without sight because by its very nature *quyi* artistry was virtually the only profession a blind person could choose without becoming totally dependent on others.

Despite this grim social phenomenon, probably the most important characteristic of *quyi* from a content point of view is its humour. Actually there is no doubt that of all branches of the performing arts the one which provides most laughter to the Chinese people is the *quyi* form *xiangsheng*, meaning literally 'face and voice'. It reaches a particularly wide audience through radio, television and flesh performance and among the Chinese its best known living exponent Hou Baolin is certainly one of the most famous men in the whole country, even though he is now too old to give public performances.

Although up to four performers can take part in *xiangsheng*, the most usual number is two, one of whom cracks the jokes, while the other provides the foil which makes and increases the comedy. A *xiangsheng* item is extremely pointed, fine and witty and lasts generally only about fifteen minutes.

There is a vital implication in the small scale and popularity of this medium, well summed up as follows:

Xiangsheng exceeds other art forms, in fact it may be second only to word of mouth in the speed with which it reflects popular concerns. While contemporary short stories and stage plays are also good at such reflection, and are warmly received, there is at least a half-year's time lag between their conception and their publication or performance. Movies and novels are of necessity even slower. But *xiangsheng* can pop up in a matter of days. After the fall of the 'gang of four' *xiangsheng* was by far the first to the trigger in attacking them.[15]

Social commentary is thus a prime function of *xiangsheng* and also one of the types of its content which the artists use to make people laugh. Hou Baolin and others have said that *xiangsheng* items are 'works of comic nature which use satire and humour as their principal base. Their satirical content strikes home at contemporary malpractices and also often includes political satire.'[16]

In items with traditional content, attacks on bureaucracy and corrupt officials through slinging off at their greed are an element of political satire. This survives strongly in post-1976 *xiangsheng*. When I was in China early in 1980 the special privileges of high-level cadres and their abuse by certain individuals was a topic of great interest among the people and in *xiangsheng* items. It was certainly not out of bounds to laugh at Party members. To make fun of the CCP itself as an entity, however, was quite another matter. I did not hear this done openly, either in *xiangsheng* or anywhere else.

When I asked Hou Baolin to list the elements that made a good *xiangsheng* item funny, he named satire as the first and most important one. Another was the more general playing on weaknesses in character, not only corruption in bureaucrats but any fault in any person. A further general area was coincidence and trivial misunderstanding, a subdivision of the second being the familiar device of the pun. Hou Baolin claimed that the general area of what he termed 'language art' (*yuyan yishu*) had been developed into a new comic technique since liberation. Of course the pun can be regarded as under the heading of 'language art' and is very much older than liberation in the *xiangsheng*. But Hou had in mind such other matters as greater skill and refinement in methods of speaking, and playing on contradictions between the standard *putonghua* and the language of the ordinary people.

It is likely that these elements which make *xiangsheng* funny can be applied more generally to Chinese humour as a whole. The satire of bureaucracy has already been mentioned in another art-form altogether, the *Shaoju Exchange of the Heir-Apparent for a Leopard Cat*. In fact, the revival of the *xiangsheng* and *quyi* since 1976 almost certainly reflects a regrowth of humour in Chinese society as a whole. This is not to say that the Chinese never laughed under the 'gang of four' – they most certainly did so. Nor would it be fair to argue that there was no political comedy at that time. The 'gang of four' permitted satire on its enemies, just as the Hua–Deng duumvirate does on the four themselves. Nevertheless, there is definitely a difference between the two periods 1966–76 and after 1976. A politically narrow leadership, such as the Chinese undoubtedly was in Mao Zedong's last years, fears and constricts comedy. While there are limits to the breadth of the successors, there is much more room to manoeuvre for comedians, far fewer restrictions on their possible areas of satire. As in so many other spheres of society, the closest parallel is the period before the Cultural Revolution.

This chapter has focused on particular types and examples of the traditional performing arts because they are most interesting or representative. It makes no claim, however, to being exhaustive. Acrobatics shows have been mentioned only as part of opera, where they are in my opinion at their greatest significance, but they exist also in their own right and demonstrate the Chinese finesse for split-second timing and control. Of all major traditional forms of the performing arts, acrobatics were virtually the only one to continue without drastic revision during the years of 'gang of four' rule.

On the other hand, a form lost due to the Cultural Revolution is puppetry. It deserves at least passing mention for the attempts made in 1978 to revive it.

In April 1978 the Fujian Provincial Art School organised a training class for the purpose of teaching children the skills of

Quanzhou marionettes, a particularly famous and old form of puppetry in China. The School invited veteran artists who had not worked at their skills since before the Cultural Revolution to teach young people their trade.

Stories of these revived forms of puppetry are similar to those of local and Beijing opera, including modern and traditional themes. On the other hand, it is only fair to add an exception which was when the Puppet Art Company of China specially commissioned a composer to arrange Hans Andersen's story, 'The Wild Swans' for the Chinese puppets. Yet even in this case, the initiative appears less great when we remember that Peter Tchaikovsky's ballet *Swan Lake*, based on 'The Wild Swans', was popular in Beijing before the Cultural Revolution and has been revived since 1976. A commentary on 'The Wild Swans' describes how the heroine, Princess Elisa, saves her eleven brothers, enchanted by the wicked queen into swans, 'through the spirit of strong fortitude and precious self sacrifice'.[17]

In other words, the moralism is as strong as ever. The ideals are somewhat different from the period of the Cultural Revolution. The propaganda may be less nauseating, the moral tone broader, but the doctrinal moralism is still there explicitly and deliberately. This point comes loudly and clearly through the commentaries in the Chinese daily and periodic press on puppetry and most other items of the traditional performing arts.

The propaganda content is at its most obvious in those operas in the traditional forms which deal with contemporary problems. Examples are numerous. In Xi'an the life of the martyr Zhang Zhixin (see Chapter 2) has been dramatised in the form of *Pingju*, a Hebei regional style. Called *Shei zhi zui? (Whose Crime?)*, 'the script concentrates on describing the heroic deeds of Comrade Zhang Zhixin's life-and-death struggle with Lin Biao and the "gang of four", and enthusiastically eulogises her indomitable, magnificent and dauntless heroic spirit'.[18] Another case in point is a *Pingju* called *Chuigushou gaozhuang (The Actress Places an Accusation)* which I saw in Beijing in January 1980. It deals with corruption in the countryside since the smashing of the 'gang of four'. Not only relatively recent forms like *Pingju*, but also very old ones have taken on some up-to-date themes, such as the Sichuan Opera *Jiujiu ta (Save Her)*, which is simply an adaptation of the play of the same name discussed in Chapter 4.

Although these works are reminiscent of Jiang Qing's 'model operas' in their attempt to blend modern content with old forms, they are not necessarily bad theatre and appear to gain some acceptance. Should the current emphasis on return to tradition ever lose its attraction, then dramas of this kind could easily turn out to be highly relevant to the needs of contemporary society.

4

Theatre in its modern forms

Apart from those performing arts forms which have enjoyed popularity in China for many centuries and consequently belong firmly to its tradition, there are a number which are relatively recent introductions. Some are of Western origin, others are a mixture of Chinese and Western culture. The term 'modern' in the title of the chapter implies only that these forms do not have a long history in China. In general, the content of specific items belonging to the modern forms tends to reflect contemporary society more directly than does that of the traditional. Yet there are certainly exceptions to this pattern, some of them quite important.

Possibly the two most important performing arts forms to blend Chinese and Western culture are the *geju* (sung opera) and *wuju* (dance-drama). The two major forms which come originally from the West are the film and *huaju* (spoken play). In addition, ballet has some following in China. The film is important enough to merit a chapter by itself, and will be considered separately.

The geju

The *geju* consists of singers who act out roles on stage to the accompaniment of an orchestra. It is in this sense similar both to the Western opera and to traditional Chinese operatic forms. However, the orchestra comprises mainly Western instruments and an admixture of Chinese. The melodies which the performers sing are based on Chinese folk songs but their form and style show Western influence and they in no way resemble the tunes of the traditional theatre. The *geju* stage includes scenery and props, just like the Western opera's.

The *geju* form dates from the 1920s, when Li Jinhui wrote two small-scale operas on children's problems. Although they were in no way revolutionary in content, the form was soon adopted by progressives and not long before his death in 1935 at the early age of 23 the famous revolutionary composer Nie Er wrote the music and Tian Han the libretto for a short *geju* called *Yangzi jiang de baofengyu* (*Storm on the Yangzi River*). In Yan'an the form became popular, especially after Mao Zedong's 'Talks at the Yan'an Forum on Literature and Art' gave impetus there to a propaganda art aimed at developing a national spirit and defeating Japan. Early in 1944 the first medium-scale *geju*, lasting about ninety minutes, was performed. Called *Zhou Zishan*, it concerned a CCP supporter of the same name involved in the land movement who turns traitor and is finally arrested and executed. It is of collective composition, including He Jingzhi, later the main author of the first full-scale *geju*, *Baimao nü* (*The White-haired Girl*), premiered in April 1945 in Yan'an during the Seventh CCP Congress.

Despite its non-revolutionary beginnings, the *geju* is thus a form very closely associated with Yan'an and the CCP. It remained in vogue after the CCP established power all over China. However, with the onset of the Cultural Revolution it disappeared completely from the stage. When I met him in January 1980, He Jingzhi, who was then Deputy Minister of Culture, told me that Jiang Qing and her followers had absolutely forbidden all *geju* performances, even those at amateur level. After the smashing of the 'gang of four', the form was among the first to reappear.

By far the best known *geju* is the first major work in the form, *The White-haired Girl*. The plot concerns a peasant girl called Xier. Her father commits suicide owing to his inability to pay his debts to the landlord and general exploitation. Xier is raped by the landlord and flees to the mountains where she lives in a cave and eventually bears a child. Her whole ordeal causes her hair to turn white. Later, however, she is saved by the CCP's Eighth Route Army and at the time of Liberation takes the forefront in accusing the landlord of his crimes.

After its first performance in Yan'an in 1945, this opera remained possibly the most popular of all the *geju* from 1949 to 1966 and I saw it in Beijing in 1965. Although Jiang Qing hated the form, she liked the story, or most of it. She had it rearranged into a ballet and changed the story somewhat, to eliminate such unhealthy aspects as the rape of the heroine. According to a contemporary commentator, the survival of *The White-haired Girl* 'was also in fact a serious threat to the "gang of four" and in particular was an even more deadly blow to the topsy-turvy so-called "theory of literature and art" which they fabricated so contrary to Mao Zedong's thought'.[1] The reason for this claim lies in the fact that the opera was originally written specifically to conform to the 'Talks at the Yan'an Forum on Literature and Art' and was approved by Mao Zedong after he saw the piece. Moreover, its popularity belied the theories which the gang had put forward.

Another particularly popular *geju* is *Honghu chiwei dui* (*Red Guards of Honghu Lake*), which concerns the struggle of the CCP in the late 1920s against the Guomindang in the lake district of southern Hubei province. The leading character, Han Ying, is a female party leader who, having mobilised the people of a lakeside village against local tyrants then leads them to join Mao Zedong's Soviet in Jiangxi province.

The opera not only takes place in Hubei province, it was also 'created and performed' by the Hubei Provincial *Geju* Troupe, to music composed by Zhang Jing'an and Ouyang Qianshu. The first public performance was in 1959. The 'gang of four', according to present claims, prevented performances of the opera and 'put it into cold storage'.[2] In November 1976, the very month following the smashing of the 'gang of four', it was back again on the stage in Wuhan. When I visited China in January 1977, the major tunes from the opera were heard everywhere. They were constantly broadcast and the people whistled and hummed them.

According to the script and musical score of *Red Guards of Honghu Lake*, which was republished a few months after the

109

reappearance of the opera on the stage, one of the reasons why the 'gang of four' had been so hostile to the opera was because they wished to get rid of the political influence of He Long, a leading revolutionary hero of the early days who was particularly active in the Hubei region in the late 1920s. It was he who co-ordinated the CCP's military endeavours there and under him many successes were won. During the Cultural Revolution he came under savage attack as a 'conspirator', but his memory was among the first to be rehabilitated after the fall of the gang. He is but one among many examples of heroes in Chinese dramas who dominate through influence without actually appearing on the stage.

Among the heroic figures who are indeed present, the role of Han Ying has become very much associated with the actress Wang Yuzhen, through public performances, gramophone records and a film of the opera. I was able to meet Wang Yuzhen in Wuhan in mid-October 1978. She told me that the suppression of the opera by the then cultural authorities led by Jiang Qing had included serious discrimination and persecution against her as the leading actress in the opera. She stated that the followers of the 'gang of four', that is the left cultural authorities in Wuhan, had forbidden her to perform, threatened her life, had a dunce's hat placed on her head and shut her up in a dark room. She claimed that they had smeared her reputation and called her 'the black flower of Hubei'. They had arranged for slogans to be posted up calling for her to be hanged.

On the other hand, Wang told me, the people at large had protected her from her enemies and she had slept in peasants' houses. Members of the PLA had hid her in their barracks. The masses had responded to the title 'black flower of Hubei' by calling her the 'red flower'. They had secretly invited her to give performances of the *Red Guards of Honghu Lake* in their homes. Wang Yuzhen was naturally very bitter against the 'gang of four' and believed that they had caused her to lose ten years of her life.

The claim that Wang had been invited to give secret performances in private homes is extremely interesting. We can, I believe, extrapolate from it to suggest that private performances of banned dramas may well be reasonably common in China. Certainly they are much more common than the authorities of any period are prepared to admit, or indeed may know about. In view of the extreme narrowness of the people's public theatrical diet during the decade of the 'gang of four', 1966 to 1976, it is perfectly possible that private performances were commoner then than at any other time. Several people knowledgeable on theatre in China with whom I discussed this matter were convinced that underground drama, or anything approaching it, would have been absolutely out of the question in Beijing between 1966 and 1976, because controls were too tight. They agreed, however, that it was possible in the countryside and away from major centres of the 'gang of four's' influence. A Cantonese theatre specialist assured me that traditional operas, to which Party authorities turned a blind eye, had been reasonably frequent in the Guangdong countryside in those years. There is thus no reason to doubt Wang Yuzhen's story. It is even interesting to speculate whether underground theatre of any kind continues to take place in the more relaxed atmosphere of contemporary China, since 1976.

Another point of interest in Wang Yuzhen's story is the association of particular important roles with individual artists. The phenomenon is, of course, found in other countries and, in China, is not peculiar to the post-Mao era. For instance the performers most closely associated with the main roles in the 'model' operas were virtually national heroes during the decade 1966 to 1976 but have now fallen from grace. The point reemphasises that the general rehabilitation of personalities from before the Cultural Revolution applies to the theatre as much as to other spheres of life. Another example is Guo Lanying, the famous Xier in *The White-haired Girl*, who has a story to tell similar to Wang Yuzhen's.

The two *geju* which feature this pair of distinguished actresses have a number of things in common. Both are based upon revolutionary history, although *Honghu* takes place more than a decade earlier than *The White-haired Girl*. In both cases, the leading role is a woman. In *Honghu*, she is a party cadre and a heroine; in *The White-haired Girl*, she is a member of the oppressed masses who eventually gets her revenge and overturns

111

the existing power. From an artistic point of view, also, common points can be observed. The orchestration is similar in each case and the tunes are memorable and catchy, the type of melody which cannot easily be cast from the mind.

Dance-drama and ballet

Melodic inventiveness and charm are features also of another performing arts form which mixes Chinese and Western culture: the dance-drama. Further general characteristics are well described by one Western observer as follows:

> It is difficult to think of Western equivalent, although it is similar to ballet. There are no spoken or sung parts. An off-stage chorus at one or two points adds the only verbal interpretation, other than the programme notes. The dance form, however, is not ballet, but a modern use of traditional Chinese dances. As is common in Chinese dance, acrobatics are used effectively. The music is a beautiful combination of traditional and new.[3]

The work under discussion here is *Xiaodao hui* (*The Small Sword Society*), which I saw in Shanghai in January 1977. The dance-drama form was relatively popular before 1966, but from that year until 1976, no examples at all were shown. Along with the form it represented, *The Small Sword Society* was also totally absent from the stage during the 'gang of four's' decade.

The plot concerns a society which leads a rebellion in Shanghai against the Manchu dynasty in the 1850s, during the time of the Taiping Revolution. The Manchu officials conspire with the British to suppress the rebellion. They succeed in so doing and in the end the rebel leader is killed, along with many of his followers. Although the uprising is totally suppressed, the audience knows that this is but the beginning of the revolutionary movement of the next century.

A few interesting points stand out from this dance-drama. One is that this was the first piece shown in China, since the beginning of the Cultural Revolution, which dealt with the period before the rise of the CCP. Although it does not fall into the category of traditional opera, its reperformance does represent a sharp break in the direction of tradition.

A second point relates to the status of the Taiping Revolution in China. The CCP has always regarded the Taipings as revolutionary precursors and it continued to do so throughout the Cultural Revolution. The Small Sword Society was indeed not the same as the Taipings, but there were apparently links between the two movements and the programme notes give the impression that the society was not unlike a subsidiary of the Taiping Revolutionary movement as a whole. With some justification, the Chinese take the ban on dramas about the Taipings or their allies from 1966 to 1976, despite the Cultural Revolution's overall positive evaluation of the Taipings, as a sign of the extreme narrowness of the 'gang of four'. On the other hand, *The Small Sword Society*'s early revival after October 1976 suggests at least a measure of continuity in attitudes towards historical events before and after 1976. Chinese scholars have commented endlessly on the Taipings since then, and changed their verdict on many features of the movement, but retained their overall positive assessment of it as revolutionary.[4]

One may note that the end of the dance-drama is explicitly tragic in that the revolution is crushed. It is true that the audience knows that in reality this is not the end. Yet on stage, the action proceeds no further than defeat. This fact brings out a sharp contrast to the practice during the period 1966 to 1976. The 'model' revolutionary dramas invariably ended with a victory by the revolutionaries.

The dance-drama contains elements of ballet, but is not ballet itself. That latter form enjoys some popularity in Chinese cities, although it must be added that it cannot compete with several forms which the Chinese have come to regard truly as their own. It will be treated briefly again in Chapter 6, because in China it often constitutes part of primarily musical concerts.

The irony of the situation is that the impact of ballet comes principally through Russian influence, yet at the very time when the Cultural Revolution was intensifying anti-Soviet feeling, the ballet enjoyed two major examples among Jiang Qing's 'models', namely *The White-haired Girl* and *Hongse niangzi jun* (*The*

Red Detachment of Women). In other words, it cannot be claimed that Jiang Qing and the 'gang of four' suppressed the form of the ballet, although it is true that they prohibited particular examples.

Before the Cultural Revolution, China had taken some steps towards establishing a classical European ballet repertoire. Restaging of works like *Giselle* and *Swan Lake* has also taken a fairly high priority in the 'new period' since 1976. Yet the problem of creating a national ballet is clearly greater than this, as explained below:

> At present there are two important themes in the art of ballet. One is to create items on subjects which express the struggle of life of the people of our own country, including also international history and modern life struggle. At the same time as creating new items, those of the past, such as *The White-haired Girl*, can be constantly performed. Simultaneously, we should revive a few superior foreign ballets that we have studied in the past. Even if we have our own new ballets, we should not rule out the performance of superior world items.[5]

That *The White-haired Girl* should continue to receive praise is curious. It was, after all, among Jiang Qing's 'models'. The solution to the problem is that it is an earlier version which is well regarded, in other words, before Jiang Qing interfered in the production. As a matter of fact, Miao Junjie, the cadre responsible for the literature and arts section of the *People's Daily*, told me that *The White-haired Girl* had not been much performed as a ballet since 1976, and nor had *The Red Detachment of Women*. He said that progress towards a national ballet had been very slow and not high in the priorities of artists in China. He knew of only one Chinese ballet written since 1976, a *pas-de-deux* lasting about fifteen minutes about the female martyr Zhang Zhixin.

114

The spoken play

The literature and Miao Junjie both leave the strong impression that few people in China envisage ballet as a form of the performing arts available to the masses. It is likely to remain city-bound and the preserve of a fairly highly educated and possibly even relatively Westernised audience. It is, after all, very difficult to perform.

A genre of the performing arts which is becoming much more widely accepted in China is the spoken play.

Until the twentieth century virtually all drama in China was in one or other operatic form. The idea of a play entirely without music, in which the actors and actresses simply spoke to each other on the stage, was quite contrary to the Chinese tradition, and took its first concrete expression as late as 1907. Since then, the spoken play has enjoyed ups and down, but overall can be said to have gathered momentum. The May Fourth Movement generation contributed greatly to the composition of spoken plays and the 1930s were a particularly rich decade, producing as they did the first works of such great playwrights as Cao Yu.

One particularly important characteristic of the Chinese spoken play, beginning right from 1907, was its tendency towards social commentary. All the major plays, and a fairly high proportion of the minor ones, concerned modern times, the contemporary political and social order; and they did not hesitate to cast judgments, usually unfavourable to the social patterns inherited from the past. One particularly popular topic was to denounce traditional family life and point out the miseries which it created.

An important point which relates to social context, not to content, is that the spoken play remained an almost exclusively urban phenomenon until the late 1930s. It is true that during the War against Japan, real efforts were made to bring spoken plays to the countryside. However, even these attempts proved only temporarily successful; the peasants continued to appreciate the traditional operatic forms much more.

After liberation, the spoken play continued in reasonable strength. It was particularly popular among amateurs because it was easier and cheaper to perform than the traditional opera.

It required no expensive costumes and could be managed successfully without years of arduous training. The Cultural Revolution put a temporary end to professional performances of the spoken play, but, as noted in Chapter 1, the early months of the year 1976 were a high point, at least in terms of quantity. In other words, the revival of the spoken play was a phenomenon which preceded the smashing of the 'gang of four'.

The trend immediately after that event was for a whole range of spoken plays which had been condemned by Jiang Qing and her followers to return to the stage. They still concerned revolutionary history or post-1949 social and political events. One which I saw in Nanjing in January 1977 was called *Bayi fengbao* (*August 1st Storm*) and dealt with the Nanchang Uprising, a political and military event beginning on 1 August 1927 in which Zhou Enlai played a very important role. References were made to the late premier and at one point the glory of his virtue shone onto the stage from a room upstairs where Zhou Enlai was supposedly sitting, but the hero himself did not actually appear on the stage. After a few months, completely new plays began production and performance. One which aroused particularly strong interest was called *Yang Kaihui*.

This was the name of Mao Zedong's wife, who was executed on 14 November 1930 on the orders of the Guomindang Chairman of Hunan, the warlord He Jian. She was only twenty-nine at the time. The first part of the play portrays Mao and Yang together leading revolutionary struggle, both against the Guomindang and against the opponents of Mao in the CCP itself. Later, the action shifts to the year 1927 when the Guomindang turned fiercely against the Communists and began suppressing them with the utmost savagery. Finally, the heroine is arrested. The last act 'ends with the image of glowing flames representing the heroine's death for the cause of the people'.[6] An epilogue shows Mao and his wife walking side by side amidst blossoms.[7]

The play *Yang Kaihui* is significant in three ways. First, it is largely historical, in two senses; one is that it follows a well laid tradition of focusing on the history of the CCP, the other is that it accords basically with historical fact. No doubt the figure of Yang Kaihui is somewhat idealised and even the marriage between Mao and Yang may well be presented to show a much

116

rosier picture than reality might have warranted. Nevertheless, the playwrights have striven consciously to adhere to the portrayal of actual incidents and people.

In the second place, the play is very much part of a cult: the attempt to portray Yang Kaihui as an ideal wife for Mao. While Jiang Qing held great power it was very difficult to suggest perfection for any of her predecessors. On the other hand, to denounce Jiang Qing in the way that has been done since October 1976 implies that Mao chose his wives badly. It was thus necessary to put all the blame on Jiang Qing and to suggest that Mao's earlier wife had been a model of perfection, as well as pointing out that she was a martyr to the revolutionary cause. To dramatise this episode in Mao's life and in the revolution brought much greater weight emotionally than any simple rewriting of history could have done, and served further to play up the negative historical role of Jiang Qing.

The third and most important area of significance about this play is that Mao Zedong himself plays a dominant role on stage in it. The role of Zhou Enlai in *August 1st Storm* offstage was noted earlier. To portray a hero such as Mao on the stage itself, with so large a role, had up to now been considered slightly sacrilegious, just as in imperial China edicts severely forbade actors to portray the emperor on the stage. One commentator of *People's Theatre* wrote:

> To mould artistic images of proletarian revolutionaries of the older generation, is a new topic in artistic creation. Theatrical creation has already achieved some preliminary results but is still in a probing experimental stage; already we have a few experiments but not many. From now on, in concrete creation, whether it is in ideological knowledge or in artistic display, we are bound to strike problems. These problems can only be raised in practice and also it is only through practice that they can be solved.[8]

Since the production of this play there have been numerous others, including several popular and important ones, which have revolved around the careers of the great revolutionaries of the past. Naturally enough, Zhou Enlai, Mao Zedong and Zhu

117

De, have been the best represented on the stage. One play called *Xi'an shibian* (*The Xi'an Incident*) which, as its title implies, deals with the Xi'an Incident at the end of 1936 which forced Chiang Kaishek to resist the Japanese, actually places all three of these leading revolutionaries on the stage in dominant roles.

The dramatisation of general revolutionary history is nothing new in China. One kind of play, however, which is a really radical departure from anything found before, is that which deals with the period of the 'gang of four' and portrays it in the black terms current in the PRC today. Spoken plays on themes of this kind are part of the whole new literature which has developed in China since the smashing of the 'gang of four', but especially since 1978. It is closely related to the whole social movement which attaches to the reinterpretation of the Tiananmen Incident (see Chapter 2). It is officially termed 'new wave literature' (*chaotou wenxue*) but there are several sub-branches including 'the literature of the wound' (*shanghen wenxue*). The latter is based on a story called 'The Wound' by Lu Xinhua published in August 1978 which deals with a female cadre attacked during the Cultural Revolution. Her daughter breaks off relations with her, but after the smashing of the 'gang of four', she is rehabilitated and wishes to see her daughter again. The latter comes back to see her but does not arrive until just after she dies. Clearly, blame for the tragedy attaches to the Cultural Revolution and to the 'gang of four'.[9]

A pioneering play of a similar kind is *Danxin pu* (*Red Hearts*). It is also set in the years 1975 and 1976, that is not long before the 'gang of four' fell from power. It concerns an old doctor called Fang Lingxuan who leads a research group trying to develop a new medicine which can prevent and treat coronary heart disease. Their research comes under attack by followers of the 'gang of four', who accuse it of being divorced from the masses. The research is encouraged by Premier Zhou Enlai, whom the author, Su Shuyang, claims as 'the main and most glorious hero of this play, although he never once appears on the stage'.[10] His is certainly the main 'red heart' to which the title refers. As the play ends, the struggle to bring the research successfully to an end emerges victorious. Fang Lingxuan is

5   A scene from the Clapper Opera of Puzhou *Xu Ce paocheng* (*Xu Ce Runs on the City Wall*). This opera is set in the Tang dynasty (618-907) and describes how Xu Ce helps right an injustice perpetrated by the wicked minister Zhang Tai against a worthy official and his clan. In this scene Zhang Tai sits on the ground, defeated by the heroes. (Photo taken by the author in January 1980)

6   The Shaoxing opera *Hongzhu nü* (*The Red Pearl Girl*) is a fairy story based on the love of peasant Zhao Hai and the Red Pearl Girl, a clam immortal changed into a beautiful girl. It is discussed in Chapter 3. In this scene the wicked crane (*left*), turned into a Daoist monk, plots with one of his forces, a bird, to capture the magic pearl. The performance was given in Suzhou by the Xi'an Shaoxing Opera Company. (Photo taken by Judith Cooney in January 1980)

7   The Red Pearl Girl plots to entice and marry Zhao Hai, who is resting
behind. Note the picture projected at the back as a form of scenery. In this
performance the part of Zhao Hai was played by a woman. (Photo taken by
Judith Cooney in January 1980)

8   The wicked monk (*second from left*) secures an invitation to eat with Zhao
Hai (*left*) and his brother (*second from right*) and sister-in-law (*right*). He had
saved Zhao Hai's brother from wolves, and is plotting to destroy the
happiness of Zhao Hai and the Red Pearl Girl, by now married. (Photo taken
by Judith Cooney in January 1980)

9   The Red Pearl Girl (*left*) summons the aid of the Underwater Mother (*fourth from left*) and her forces to help defeat the wicked crane, turned monk. In the end the crane is defeated. (Photo taken by Judith Cooney in 1980)

10   In the *Kunqu* drama *Nao tiangong* (*Havoc in Heaven*), Monkey has stolen the heavenly peaches. Here various heavenly generals, soldiers and gods gather to seize and punish him. Of course he defeats them all. The drama is discussed in Chapter 3. (Photo taken by the author during an actual performance in January 1980)

11   The famous Sichuanese actor Zhou Qihe playing the part of a comic old woman. Zhou plays mainly male roles; he is not a *nandan* (see Chapter 7), even though he plays this female part. Comedy is an important feature of small-scale regional theatre

12 A *quyi* performance in Chengdu, Sichuan Province. This is larger than most *quyi* groups and the performers are relatively young. The two women are the singers. The one on the right is playing the *sanxian,* a plucked, three-stringed instrument. The picture was given to the author by the performers whom he met in a Chengdu teahouse in January 1980. See Chapter 3

13, 14 Scenes from an acrobatics performance in Beijing. Acrobatics is not only a vital attribute of Chinese opera, but also a significant form of theatre in itself. The extraordinary dexterity and precision of Chinese acrobats has long amazed audiences throughout the world. (Photos taken by Judith Cooney during a performance in January 1980)

15 A scene from the modern *Pingju Chuigushou gaozhuang* (*The Actress Places an Accusation*), briefly noted in Chapter 3. The opera is set in the period since 1976 and deals with a corrupt Party secretary and his followers in the countryside. The drama is based on an actual report in the *People's Daily* about an actress in Anhui province. In the present scene the actress (*third from the left*), berates the Party secretary (*second from the right*), who looks away shamefacedly as various ruffians look on. Note that in this modern opera there is simple scenery at the back and the props are somewhat more complicated than in the pure traditional opera. (Photo taken by the author during a performance in January 1980)

16   The full cast of the modern *Pingju The Actress Places an Accusation* (see also plate 15). The picture here includes He Jingzhi (*tenth from right*), Vice Minister of Culture, from whom the author obtained some of the material in this book, especially Chapter 7. He went backstage with the author, who took the picture, to congratulate the cast after the performance

17   The author (*third from left*), together with various cadres of the Literature
and Arts Section of the *Guangming Daily*

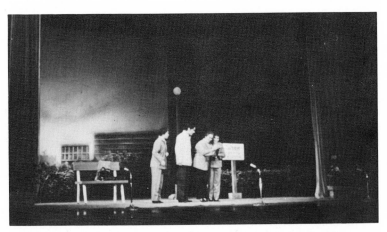

18   The final scene of the spoken play *Jiujiu ta* (*Save Her*), discussed in
Chapter 4. The scene is at the university which it has been the ambition of the
central character Li Xiaoxia to enter. She is shown at the right together with
her fiancé and others. (Photo taken by the author during a performance in
December 1979)

19 The spoken play *Qinggong waishi* (*Unofficial History of the Qing Court*) is
based on true events in the last years of the nineteenth century. It deals with
court machinations of the Empress Dowager Cixi and her attempts to
dominate the Emperor Guangxu. This picture was taken backstage by the
author after a performance in January 1980. It shows the young Emperor
(*right*), the Empress Dowager (*centre*), and her favourite eunuch Li Lianying
(*left*)

20 Part of a Chinese orchestra. The pear-shaped instrument on the right is
the *pipa,* which is plucked. Just to its left is the plucked moon quitar *(yueqin).*
Front left is the bowed Chinese fiddle (*huqin*). (Photo taken by Robert Ross)

21 Children dance at a primary school. Amateur performing is an important part of the curriculum in China (see Chapter 5). (Photo taken by the author)

22 Cartoon films for children have recently come back to prominence in China (see Chapter 5). This picture shows Nezha, the hero of one of them. Nezha is a small boy, born of a magic pregnancy and endowed with magic powers. He succeeds in conquering the evil Dragon King who steals children to eat. (Source: *China's Screen* 1 (1980), p. 15)

23   The film *Erquan yingyue* (*Moon Reflected on the Second Springs*) concerns the life of the famous people's musician Abing (see discussion in Chapter 5). Here he is shown, carrying his musical instruments, together with his wife. Abing is played by Zheng Songmao, his wife by Yuan Mengya. (Source: *China's Screen* 2 (1980), p. 14)

24   The film *Xiaohua (Little Flower)* is among the most popular features of 1979 (see discussion in Chapter 5). Set in the 1940s, it concerns the search of the girl Little Flower for her brother. This picture shows the heroine Little Flower. The actress is Chen Chong, probably China's best known up-and-coming film star. (Source: *China's Screen* 1 (1980), p. 8)

25   Little Flower finally finds her brother. (Source: *Ibid.*, pp. 10-11)

26   The film *Languang shanguo zhi hou* (*After the Blue Light Flashed*) is a
fictionalized account based on the real events of the great Tangshan
earthquake of July 1976. (The earthquake is discussed in Chapter 1, the film
in Chapter 5.) Here the young doctor meets her beloved at a bridge broken
by the earthquake. Each had believed the other dead. (Source: *China's Screen* 2
(1980), p. 18)

27 The famous actor Zhang Junqiu photographed in September 1979 in
full costume. The original of the picture was given by Zhang himself to the
author in January 1980. Zhang Junqiu is the last of the famous male *dan*.
Both Zhang and the male *dan* are discussed in Chapter 7

28 Learning to do cartwheels at a training school in China. Acrobatics are a vital part of the training of Chinese performers and of the practice of Chinese theatre. (Photo taken by the author)

29, 30 Training young actors and actresses. (Photos taken by the author)

about to report this fact to the Premier when the news arrives of the latter's death.

In a sense, *Red Hearts* thus resembles 'The Wound' in its tragic ending. Some people wanted this changed so an epilogue was added set in 1978. This makes for a happier ending because it shows the 'gang of four' smashed and the four modernisations under way. Producers may either include or omit the epilogue as they see fit.[11]

A major feature of this play is the explicit praise it gives to intellectuals and their work. The core of the play is the necessity for medical research; the hero is a prominent intellectual who devotes his entire life to learning and to pushing back the boundaries of knowledge. It was mentioned in Chapter 2 that one of the earliest priorities of the new regime was to remove a perceived stigma against education and research and to accuse the 'gang of four' of having done their best to sabotage these activities. The play highlights this theme. 'When the "gang of four" held sway over literature and art, intellectuals were often reflected on the stage as negative characters, if at all.'[12] *Red Hearts* was, in fact, the first play to be produced for many years which made intellectuals the heroes.

But above all the play is significant for its relationship to the 'literature of the wound' with the latter's emphasis both on tragedy and on joy or relief; tragedy because of the intense suffering, much of it irredeemable, which the Cultural Revolution caused, and relief and joy because the period is now over. The author expresses his feeling on this issue very clearly when he says:

What *Red Hearts* reflects is this special historical period from 1975 to 1976. This was a period of joy and sorrow, bewilderment and puzzlement, of ample hope but great worry. In the face of the social reality of the gathering crisis, people were raising questions, probing and answering. In realistic life, I feel that revolutionary cadres who persisted in the proletarian Party principles, proletarian intellectuals and literature and art workers were the ones most seriously hurt and persecuted by the 'gang of four'. Their individual fates were closely bound up with

119

the fate of the Party and that of their country. Because of this, I chose old Chinese doctors, Party cadres, reporters, national dance performers etc. etc. as the characters in the play, and attempted through expressing their joy and sorrow to reflect the emotions of the broad people.[13]

In every sense then, this play is social commentary and political propaganda, and to that extent carries on the tradition which has prevailed since 1907 in the spoken play movement. Yet, on the other hand, it is the past which it criticises, not the present, and that past still lies in the period since liberation. For the first time in the PRC, a spoken play places earlier years after 1949 under severe attack. This is something entirely new in the history of Chinese spoken plays.

In October 1978, I saw in Shanghai a rather similar play by Qin Peichun called *Tong Xin*, the name of the hero but also meaning 'children's heart'. It was set in the autumn of 1975 and concerned the former school teacher Tong Xin, forced into retirement by 'gang of four' supporters. He is much loved by most of his former students but some have been influenced by the 'gang of four' against him. He comes under attack as a reactionary follower of Confucius and after a fierce struggle is eventually sent off to prison as a counter-revolutionary.

As with *Red Hearts*, the ending is overtly tragic. Evil appears to have won out over good. On the other hand, the audience knows that very soon the 'gang of four' will be smashed and the hero and villain will change places, so that the former will be released as a persecuted model, while the latter who effected Tong's arrest in the first place will himself be put in jail.

Qin Peichun has himself commented on the tragic element not only in this play but in the recent Chinese performing arts in general. Its development, he claims, 'is determined by its existence in society'. The reason for this is 'the appearance and influence of the "gang of four" on China's political stage', which was 'tragedy for the Party, the nation's tragedy and the people's tragedy'.[14]

To blame a political faction is an interesting, and no doubt reasonable, way of reintroducing an important dramatic convention, but it does not really explain how this particular play written after October 1976 can end tragically. Qin goes on:

> The tragic conclusion is not the aim but only a method. It can expose even more keenly the disaster of the mistaken line of the 'gang of four' and provide a foil for the great significance of the Party Central Committee's smashing of the 'gang of four'. . . . If one made Tong Xin and the few people round him win a light and easy success, that could weaken the criticism of the harm [caused by] the 'gang of four', and reduce the tremendous social significance of the smashing of the 'gang of four'.[15]

Qin suggests that there is greater dramatic intensity in allowing the audience to imagine what happens after the play's end. Having seen the play, I believe his judgment is sound.

Despite the serious subject matter there were many scenes of considerable charm and humour. In one place, for instance, a character wants to relax by turning on the wireless. The only programme available is revolutionary model opera, so she turns it off in disgust. The reaction of the audience suggested that this had been a fairly common real-life experience in those years.

The place where I attended a performance of this drama was the Children's Art Theatre. One reviewer described it as a 'children's play' (*ertong huaju*) which had been 'warmly welcomed by audiences of all circles, and especially educational circles and secondary and primary school students'.[16] In fact, there were not many children at the show and the 'all circles' segment appeared to outweigh at least the primary students. On the other hand, the audience was distinctly young, with a majority of late teenagers or people in their early twenties, including many courting couples. They clearly loved the play and concentrated hard throughout, although following normal Chinese practice they did not applaud very much.

Plays dealing with particular social problems rarely run for very long in China. They arouse great interest, if they are good, and then move off to be replaced by others dealing with more topical questions. When I returned to China late in 1979, *Tong*

Xin was a play of the past. By then juvenile delinquency was more pressing and interesting as an overt social problem than respect for teachers, so plays on the new theme came forward. A famous one was *Jiujiu ta* (*Save Her*), which concerns a delinquent young girl called Li Xiaoxia. The major theme of delinquency comes through in Li's past behaviour – among other crimes she lied to get into university for which she was placed in detention for a week – and in the offhand way both she and her negative friends behave. They smoke, are rude to their parents and teachers, and swagger about. Young people of this kind clearly represent a feature of Chinese society. What is important is that 1979 was the first year it could be portrayed on the stage.

Even more striking is the open discussion of delinquent sexual problems. Li Xiaoxia becomes pregnant to one of her friends, a bad influence of course, who has drugged her. She has an abortion, which throws her into a fit of shame. When she tells her main male friend Xu Zhiwei, who is a positive character, he rushes away in a rage at her perfidy and infidelity. In itself the stage portrayal of such an attitude by a good young man towards premarital sexual intercourse (with someone else) and abortion reveals something about Chinese society. The female is ashamed, the male enraged and shocked.

The secondary theme relates to the education system. Li was sent to the countryside at the time of the Campaign to Criticise Lin Biao and Confucius. When she went she was a very good girl, but turned bad after. The moral seems to be that the down-to-the-countryside movement, which the audience well knows to have been mainly a result of the Cultural Revolution, was a wrong move with a harmful impact on youth.

Li's old teacher Fang Ai was denounced as reactionary owing to 'gang of four' influence but comes back to favour after 1976. She plays an important role in the inevitable process of remoulding and 'saving' Li Xiaoxia. The reviewer in the *People's Daily*, Gao Zhanxiang, found 'the image of Teacher Fang to be authentic and moving' and said of her treatment of her student that she 'melts the layers of ice frozen into Li Xiaoxia's heart through motherly warmth'.

Unlike *Tong Xin* the play ends happily. The last scene falls in the autumn of 1977 by which time the 'gang' is well and truly smashed. Xu Zhiwei returns to Li Xiaoxia and they become engaged. The heroine, now reformed, fulfils her long-standing ambition and goes to university. One is reminded of a traditional love drama, where a typical ending shows the hero having passed the exams and married to his beloved, only now the roles are reversed and it is the female who stands in the centre position.

The major political point of the play is clearly the evil influence of the Cultural Revolution and the 'gang of four'. After all it is this pair of now inseparable twins which has led Li Xiaoxia astray. She requires discipline, and this she gets through the 'new period' of Hua Guofeng and Deng Xiaoping, and the good rehabilitated teachers it brings. Blame for the evil seducer and credit for the faithful lover can be similarly distributed to draw a political lesson.

We may say that without the victory of smashing the 'gang of four', without the power of the Party's policies, and without the help of Teacher Fang, Xu Zhiwei and other people, there would have been no new life for Li Xiaoxia.[17]

Save Her is far more interesting as a sociopolitical document than an artistic experience. As a play it is unremarkable. Yet two technical points of different kinds stand out. One is the use of flashback. At one point Fang Ai, the old teacher, talks about how Li Xiaoxia went to the countryside. As she begins her explanation the lights change, Li appears on the stage as her former self and a dialogue ensues which recreates the past scene not only in words but actuality.

The other point goes to the use of Standard Chinese or *putonghua*. The performance I saw of *Save Her* was given by the Guangxi *Huaju* Troupe in Guilin, in other words by a provincial company which might well have spoken more comfortably in dialect and to an audience which almost certainly would have understood local speech more easily. Yet the language used was *putonghua*. This was a play shown throughout China by a range of troupes. Consequently the national language was essential. In the *huaju* form, only a small number of items with local themes and shown in a narrow region use dialect. *Putonghua* is virtually universal.

Tong Xin and *Jiujiu ta* are intended specifically as plays for the young. They deal with educational and other social problems focusing on the reactions of the young. In this respect, they differ from *Red Hearts*. On the other hand, they do give us a bridge to the subject of theatre for younger children which, as mentioned in Chapter 2, has returned to favour once again. It has also enjoyed a considerable revival in reality.

An illustrative item is *Malan hua* (*Indigo Flower*), which I saw as an 'experimental performance' before a full audience in October 1978. The final 'nonexperimental' version was staged by the Children's Art Theatre in Beijing on 1 June 1979 to celebrate International Children's Day.

The play is based on a fairy tale and concerns a wicked old cat who attempts to mislead people and make them unhappy. There is a struggle between two sisters, one lazy, the other diligent. The cat plots to persuade the lazy girl to drown and kill the diligent one. In the end the cat is himself hunted and killed while the diligent girl is saved and the lazy one remoulded.

Animals play an important part in this drama. Though the cat is the symbol of wickedness, most of them are rabbits, deer, squirrels and birds, which represent hard work and goodness. To give animals so important a role is typical of contemporary Chinese children's theatre, as of that before 1966, and a major departure from Cultural Revolutionary drama.

As expected from the criteria laid down for children's theatre already in 1977 and discussed in Chapter 2, there is an important place given to magic and enchantment. Indeed the indigo flower of the title has magic properties to bring about happiness, of which it is the symbol. A parallel aspect is the portrayal of dreams on the stage. In one section, the leading male actor goes to sleep and the scenery changes to show his dream. It takes place under water, so a gauze is lowered at the front of the stage to create the impression of action in the sea. Fishes dart to and fro and nymphs dance around, making for a scene of considerable charm.

The revival of fantasy in the form of magic and dreams in no way lessens the intended moral force of the play. One teacher is reported to have said after seeing the play:

> Before I brought my grandchildren to see this play, they did not like to do any manual labour at home and never washed their hands before they ate. But after they saw the play, they cultivated the habit of cleanliness and loved to help their parents in household chores.[18]

Although this item is specifically designed for children, the performance I attended began at 7.00 p.m. and finished after 10.00, in other words its timing was exactly the same as a play for adults might have been. As a matter of fact, the audience were mostly not children at all, although a substantial proportion was under fifteen. On the other hand, the cast was much older than for most performances I have seen in China. The performers who played the parts of the cat and the two girls were all in their forties. Of course, the latter looked and acted appropriately young and the same could be said of the array of positive animal figures. Whatever the age of the cast, the play itself seemed to give the clear impression that youth is good.

Conclusion

In one sense a children's spoken play is a form most antithetical to the Chinese tradition, because not only is the idea of the spoken play relatively new, but that of children's literature is also so. In form children's plays stand at one extreme of the various types of theatre considered in this chapter. Somewhat closer to tradition is the dance-drama with its Chinese classical dances. Yet although these forms differ in the extent of their modernity, in content and manner of presentation all are recognisably and totally Chinese. A spoken play may not have been initially a Chinese form – it is clearly a foreign and ultimately Western import – but it has now become an indispensable part of the Chinese theatre scene. It is, for instance, perfectly natural that twentieth-century China's most distinguished playwright Cao Yu, disgraced during the Cultural Revolution but back in a leadership role since 1978, should write a play which deals with an ancient Chinese historical theme. *Wang Zhaojun*, Cao's first production after 1976, was published on 20 November 1978[19] and performed in July 1979. Set in the year 33 BC it deals with the famous Chinese woman Wang Zhaojun, who at the age of nineteen goes to marry a ruler of the Xiongnu, a people living to China's north. This episode in China's history, in typically Chinese manner, 'expresses the mutual exchange between Han and non-Han and their long history of peaceful coexistence, and sings the praises of unity among nationalities'.[20] The play has thus become a genuine Chinese form.

Despite its ancient theme, Wang Zhaojun is clearly a new play. To a greater extent than the traditional forms discussed in Chapter 3, the modern have produced works which are in no way revivals from the pre-Cultural Revolutionary period. Some were actually written during the decade 1966–76 but not allowed publication until after the 'gang of four' fell. But the most important group of all the new dramas is those plays which deal specifically with the miseries and injustices of the Cultural Revolution and its aftermath. One can divide these into categories, including plays belonging to the theatrical branch of 'the literature of the wound', such as *Red Hearts* and *Where Silence Reigns*; and the more recent 'items which bring out all kinds of social questions',[21] for example, *Save Her*. Although the form and style of pieces in both classifications retain strong links with those of earlier periods, the content is a radical break with the past.

It is noteworthy that plays on contemporary themes actually deal more with urban than rural life. Two responsible cadres of the *People's Daily* literature and arts section told me that this was because most authors lived in the cities, many having returned from the countryside where the 'gang of four' had sent them. The urban emphasis may well be a temporary phenomenon. City people can easily write of rural problems, especially if they have lived in the countryside. The two cadres in fact noted that several items were coming forward which would alter the urban–rural balance in drama content.

So the scale of change in the Chinese theatre in its modern forms reflects the development of society as a whole. The style retains similarities to the period before 1976, the content shows much that is creative and new, as well as much adherence to the old, especially the harking back to the pre-1966 days and the attempt to revive its good features. Unless the political line changes radically again, creativity and revival may well remain two major watchwords, both in theatre and society at large.

5

The cinema

The reason why the peoples of our country and the world love cinema is because it can, in a meticulous and subtle way, reflect every kind of life picture and complicated emotion accurately, distinctly and vividly. It not only possesses the great artistic ability, the equal of literature and drama, to depict and express characters and their surroundings, but is also rich in the lucid, concrete visible characteristics of sculpture, painting, architecture and other plastic arts, as well as music's particular power to excite and affect the mood.[1]

These words come from the foremost academic treatment of cinema to emerge from China since the death of Mao and amply explain the importance of the motion picture industry there. Films not only enjoy a peculiar combination of power over the emotions, but of all forms of performing arts they are also the most 'modern' in the sense that they demand the highest level of technological expertise. Of course, it is possible to apply advanced technology to operas, plays or puppets, but these can succeed perfectly well without. However, there can be no cinema without such modern commodities as cameras, electricity, and film itself.

The background

The scholar quoted above has claimed that 'in a sense, the forefather who explained and put in practice the principles of cinema was our China',[2] because written records prove the existence of shadow theatre already in the eleventh century, that is to say earlier in China than anywhere else. Be that as it may, it is certainly true that film antedates the spoken play in China. The first films ever shown there were in Shanghai on 11 August 1896, in fact over a decade before the origin of the spoken play and, incidentally, only a few months after Thomas Edison launched motion pictures as a medium of popular entertainment with a public presentation in New York of his projector, the Vitascope. Very little is known about the films seen in Shanghai that August day, but they occupied but a small part of a variety show which included acrobats, juggling and a magician, and were certainly foreign.

By 1916, however, the cinema had advanced to the point where the first Chinese motion picture production company was set up. Yet of course the film industry in China remained a heavily foreign-dominated affair. One visitor to Beijing in May 1919 commented on the popularity of cinema with 'an average daily attendance of 3,000 at the half dozen picture palaces'; these numbers were remarkable because 'the films all depicted Occidental life, or a strange version of it, and had their captions in English'.[3]

At about the same time we find early serious attempts, though not the absolute beginning, of a practice which remains very popular in China today, namely that of adapting operas and plays to the cinema. Mei Lanfang, certainly the most internationally famous Chinese actor ever to have performed, began making films in 1920. He explains that 'although there was no sound in the cinema, one could add a character screen to the film.'[4] However, the lack of sound affects films of opera with particular severity because, although captions may be able to record a dialogue or explain a narrative, they certainly cannot make up for the lack of music.

The first Chinese sound film was *Genü Hong Mudan* (*Singing Girl Red Peony*) which was premiered on 15 March 1931. It included dialogue and songs, but otherwise the sound effects were very meagre indeed. For the dialogues an important decision had to be taken: which dialect to use. The result was the adoption of the national language, *Guoyu*, not Shanghai dialect, even though the film was made in Shanghai. This choice was of great significance because it laid down a precedent which is still followed to this day and because it became one factor helping towards unification of the Chinese language.

During the period of the Guomindang, film-makers and producers operated under fairly fierce censorship. Regulations which came into operation on 1 January 1930 gave the authorities extremely wide-ranging powers, especially as regards the political content of films. Notwithstanding this fact, a fairly high number of good films was produced in the 1930s and 1940s including some with a very definite political message not always sympathetic to the Guomindang.

When the CCP took power in China, it was just as anxious as the Guomindang had been to prevent the production of films that would be hostile to its government. With great enthusiasm it set about building up a socialist film industry which it believed would help propagate its cause. The foreign assistant was at first Soviet, but the split with the Russians in the late 1950s forced the Chinese to rely only on themselves in their cinema industry as in other areas of life. From about 1960, China began to introduce an exclusively Chinese film industry.

However, when the Cultural Revolution began in the mid-1960s the early hopes for the development of really good Chinese films had to be postponed. Apart from a few documentaries, virtually no new films were brought out during those years. By the early 1970s activity had begun again, with increasing numbers as the decade wore on, and reached a peak in 1976, just as the 'new period' was about to begin.

The smashing of the 'gang of four' brought about great and immediate changes in the type and number of films available to Chinese audiences. A Chinese press account claimed in May 1979 that 'in the last three years', presumably meaning since October 1976, over 60 new feature films had been made and that over 200 of those produced before the Cultural Revolution had been rescreened.[5]

That the latter category should outnumber the former is not surprising. It is quicker and easier to bring films back than to make them. Films are the easiest to revive of all the performing arts. They do not need to be rerehearsed before production, but can simply be taken out of the store. Clearly the turmoil of the Cultural Revolution had not resulted in the destruction of all copies of these films.

Including both those made before the Cultural Revolution and since 1976, there are several different types of films seen in the PRC today. They include theatre films, documentaries, reportage, children's films and features.

Theatre films, documentaries, children's cinema

Theatre films are simply adaptations of operas for the cinema. Many of the major productions of operas and plays have been made into films and some have already been mentioned elsewhere, such as *A Dream of Red Mansions* and *Liang Shanbo and Zhu Yingtai*, both traditional Shaoxing operas set in the dynastic period.

A good instance of a filmed opera on a more recent theme is the Shaoxing opera *Xiang Lin sao*. This is based on a short story by Lu Xun and depicts the ageing of a woman in the old society. Because the story covers her life from a young woman to her death as a useless outcast beggar, two actresses perform the title role, one for the young Xiang Lin sao, another for the old. Two films which I saw in China in January 1977, just after the smashing of the 'gang of four', were both adaptations of theatrical works. One was *The Red Guards of Honghu Lake*, discussed in Chapter 4, and the other was *The East is Red*, depicting the history of the Chinese Revolution.

All the theatre films here mentioned were made before the Cultural Revolution, and all were forbidden screening by the cultural authorities under the 'gang of four'. Considering the directness of the propaganda in *The East is Red* and the fact that Lu Xun was one of the few writers who remained in favour throughout the decade 1966–76, two of these films might have been spared had the 'gang' been even slightly broader in its attitudes. In 1975, the novel *A Dream of Red Mansions* was described by firm supporters of the 'gang' as 'an outstanding political-historical novel' which 'reflects the class struggle and the contradictions within the ruling class'[6] in the eighteenth century when it was written. Why the logical step of rescreening the film based on so fine a novel was not taken was never made clear.

Theatre films are not simply screened performances. They make use of cinema techniques such as closeups and the increased flexibility of scenery. However, they do retain the costumes, music and script of the original. Invariably captions show the words being sung.

One reason for this need is that theatre films differ from most others in not necessarily using the Standard Chinese, before liberation called *Guoyu*, but now *putonghua*. Regional operas are sung in the relevant dialect because they are designed to be comprehensible to local audiences. It is not easy to translate sung dialect into *putonghua* and in an opera may not be appropriate to do so. The captions correspond to the projection of the text onto the screens beside the stage during an actual opera performance.

Theatre films (*xiqu pian*) are treated here separately from features (*gushi pian*) because the Chinese place the two types in separate categories. However, theatre films usually do tell a story and in that sense are a kind of feature. By contrast, documentary and reportage films aim to explain and depict an actual happening, institution, custom, achievement, person, etc. Of all categories of the performing arts discussed so far, they are the two most true to life. It may be because they are not fictional that the 'gang of four' encouraged them more than other types of film. By comparison with other forms they have declined in importance since the fall of the four. On the other hand, when newsworthy international or national events take place, one can be reasonably certain that they will be made into short films and displayed widely throughout the country. Thus, considerable praise is given in the literature to a film about Hua Guofeng's trip to the Democratic People's Republic of Korea in May 1978.

Because documentary and reportage films are often very

short, sometimes lasting only a few minutes, they can function as a convenient means of filling up a time slot for a cinema session, which typically lasts about two hours without interval. Newspaper advertisements frequently list 'also screened' items along with feature films. One such reportage segment I saw showed China in 1979 by detailing achievements or features province by province. It reflected China's overall development admirably. The section on Jiangsu was almost an advertisement for a set of particularly comfort-oriented products, suggesting a growth in consumerism, while that on Sichuan showed the return of interest in tradition by focusing on an ancient and beautiful park.

Documentaries can themselves be subdivided into different categories. In all there are seven major studios in China, other than those making feature films. They are two scientific and educational studios, in Beijing and Shanghai, one reportage, one fine arts, one agricultural, one educational, and one translation. Other than the last, all can be loosely described as documentary.

To judge by the numbers, the subdivision of greatest importance to the Chinese is scientific and educational documentaries. As the name implies, these films aim to be educational and highly practical, and to impart to the people information which can be used to promote production. One journalist's claim in 1978 was that 'each year now over one hundred films on different subjects, mostly concerning industrial and particularly agricultural production, are being put out'.[7] He states that these scientific educational films are an effective means of bringing about better and greater production, and cites as example a film on a new kind of rice seedling, particularly resistant to cold, which led to its popularisation in the vital rice-growing province of Hubei.

Another kind of film is that designed specifically for children, the regrowth of which follows logically from the revival of children's literature and plays. Situ Huimin, Deputy Minister of Culture in charge of cinema, told me during our interview in January 1980 that up to then rather few full-length children's films had been produced since 1976, but the Cinema Bureau was aware of greater demand from the people and planned action to satisfy it.

Up to January 1980 greater attention had been given to another branch of children's cinema, namely cartoons, a genre of art not found at all under the 'gang of four'. These 'are not only films reflecting modern children's life, but also films on fairy tales, scientific fairy tales, folk legends and historical stories'.[8] Like documentaries, they are sometimes used as shorts to accompany major films, such as one I saw screened together with *Languang shanguo zhihou* (*After the Blue Light Flashed*), to be discussed below. Absolutely delightful and extremely funny, it was called *Ciwei bei xigua* (*The Hedgehog Carries a Watermelon*) and told of a mother hedgehog which gets herself into trouble by trying to prove to her young that she can transport a watermelon in the traditional manner by carrying it on her back. She is saved by good fortune, help from neighbouring animals and the young hedgehogs' willingness to break with traditional ways of doing things. It was an interesting contrast to *After the Blue Light Flashed*, because the latter is anything but a children's film and features children who have lost their parents under singularly tragic circumstances.

Although there is an identifiable children's cinema in China, it is worth pointing out that, in fact, virtually all films are available to children. There are no censors' gradings declaring that for such-and-such a film no person under eighteen should be allowed into the cinema, or that another is for general exhibition. Kissing is occasionally seen in foreign, although not in Chinese, films but the sex films characteristic of Western countries have not yet found their way to China, and are unlikely to do so in the near future. Another type of 'adults only' motion picture so far conspicuously absent in China is the suspense horror film. While in Beijing I heard stories that it may not be an impossibility even within the foreseeable future.

That children up to now take it for granted that virtually all films should be available to them is obvious from the following letter by two primary school sisters on a commune in Shandong Province:

Uncles and Aunties of the cinema world, How are you? We

two sisters are both little film fans. Whenever we hear
there is a film, we sometimes can't even think about eating.
Whenever we have finished watching a film, we study
according to the heroic figures in the film. Since the
overthrow of the 'gang of four', very many good films have
been liberated and we are both very happy. These good
films as far as we're concerned are new films, but we've
heard grown-ups say that they were shown before the
Cultural Revolution but afterwards put into cold storage by
the 'gang of four'. The 'gang of four' are really too bad.
These good films reflected the heroic deeds of Uncles and
Aunties in every business, every profession, on every
front, but we have never seen films which reflect our
teachers.[9]

The two girls go on to praise the work which their teachers
do and express their admiration for how hard such people
work. The editors comment on the letter that it has 'expressed
the aspirations of millions upon millions of young children in
our country, but it is also not the aspiration only of young
children'. Clearly this letter fulfils a propaganda function and
is related to the revival of respect for teachers which has followed the smashing of the 'gang of four'. Nevertheless, the
way it is phrased and the observation of the editors make clear
that the existence of children's films does not automatically
imply a cinema specially for adults.

Feature films

In their reference to 'films which reflect our teachers', the two
girls appear to have had principally feature films in mind. Nowadays these are the most important category of film in China,
at least in that they occupy by far the most space in journals
devoted specifically to cinema.

There are currently eleven feature film studios in China.
Every year the Ministry of Culture draws up targets for them.
I was told in October 1978, at the Shanghai Film Studio, that
nationally it was fifty-two films for 1979; the aim was to accord

with Chairman Mao's reported wish for one new feature film each week. The number was confirmed by the directors of the eleven feature film studios, who met in February 1979 to draw up their plans for the year. The proposed breakdown by topic of the fifty-two films was two-thirds on revolutionary or contemporary themes, 'while the remainder are adapted from well-known literary works including stories about historical figures, traditional operas, mythological and fairy tales'.[10]

By the time the plan had become reality the content of the two-thirds on revolution and contemporary life broke down as follows:

> Some films reflected the line struggle within the Party and especially wrote of the losses which the rule of the 'left' opportunist line created for the revolutionary cause; some reflected the struggle of the revolutionary people against the 'gang of four'; some reflected the sincere love between men and women; and some expressed the life and struggle of the revolutionary intellectuals. Above all, the film workers, with very great enthusiasm, made useful attempts in moulding the images of the old generation of proletarian revolutionaries, such as Chairman Mao, Premier Zhou, Chen Yi, and He Long, and gained some experience.[11]

In January 1980 Situ Huimin told me that in fact the 1979 target had been exceeded by thirteen, and sixty-five feature films had been issued. The proposed target for 1980 was sixty-five. Content was likely to be broader than in 1979 with more films on topics relating to revolutionary and earlier history and friendship with foreign peoples, about ten opera items, and only about one-third of the total on contemporary life.

To cope with content of this kind a studio includes an editorial board which actively seeks out scripts. The precise choice of which films each makes depends upon the studio itself. In the Shanghai Film Studio, I was told that it was the studio director who made the selection and that he took the proportions of the themes into account to ensure that there were not too many on historical, too few on contemporary, and so on. However, according to the actress Yu Lan, a leader of the Beijing Film

Studio, there are often quite fierce debates over which story to use and 'if there is no agreement on an issue, then the majority wins'.[12] Once the choice of script is made, it is the director of the film who selects the cast. Generally speaking, others will be consulted, including the studio leadership, colleagues and, of course, the actors and actresses themselves. But the final decision rests with the director alone.

The serious development of feature films, as distinct from film versions of plays and operas, has raised discussion in China about how to write a film script and how to create a specifically Chinese style of film acting. The problems are not new, but they have assumed particular importance since October 1976, because the Chinese are anxious to develop their film industry with particular speed as part of their overall demonstration to the world that they are capable of modernising their country.

Clearly there is a great deal in common between writing scripts for plays and for films. It is equally apparent that there are differences, among other reasons because of the greater ability in a film than in a play or especially an opera to change scene quickly and frequently. In an important article on the writing of film scripts, the dramatist Su Shuyang, mentioned in Chapter 4 as the author of the play *Red Hearts,* bemoans that 'the length of the period of our film production is frightening'[13] and not nearly fast enough to keep up with the demands of the people. He lists a number of criteria for good film script-writing, but although he shows awareness of the difference between those for a play and a film, most of them could apply equally to either genre. The first is 'it is not appropriate for plays in cinema literature to be too long.' This is an important point because he believes 'there is nowadays apparently a tendency for plays to become longer and longer every day'.[14] He also calls for the provision of a poetic atmosphere in scripts and for vivid characterisation. Another important point is 'new meaning', because 'the precious value of art is in creating something new'. He regrets the continuing survival of the idea of the 'model' so closely associated with Jiang Qing and the 'gang of four'. 'In fact', he says, 'in art it is quite impossible to have any "model"'.[15] The reason for this is that models imply stereotypes and these must be avoided at all costs.

The other artistic problem the Chinese have raised goes to the development of a Chinese style of acting. It is clearly an important problem in the growth of any nation's cinema industry. To judge from the Chinese films which I have seen, I believe that such a Chinese acting style does exist, in the sense that it is possible to distinguish a Chinese film from that of any other country by the acting alone and without hearing the language spoken or seeing the background scenery. The mannerisms, hand gestures, the walking style and the general way of integrating the movements of the various parts of the body are quite distinctive and identifiable.

One of China's most famous actors of the old school, Zhao Dan, has discussed this problem and reached a somewhat less optimistic verdict than the one just outlined. He believes that this process of 'seeking, groping, trying to find a national style of acting' is only just beginning, and it may thus take a long time before one really develops. When asked if there was a recognisable Chinese style of acting he replied:

> I've been seeking it all my life. For example, in our
> traditional Chinese operas, in all our local operas, we have
> a rich heritage in acting. It is like a Chinese painting. The
> more sophisticated it becomes, the simpler it gets. It is the
> most concentrated form of expression. You never do with
> ten strokes what you can do with one. Films are a modern
> art, so obviously you can't just copy straight from a
> Chinese opera. If anything is offered abroad, we should
> learn from it. We should digest it ourselves until it becomes
> part of our national heritage. Chinese people express their
> feelings in a different manner from people elsewhere in the
> world.[16]

Zhao's statement is a curious blend of a recognition of Chinese inferiority to other countries and its desire to develop its own national way of doing things.

With this background, and other ideas in different chapters, in mind, it will be useful to discuss in greater detail some particular feature films. All are interesting, although from rather

different points of view, and illustrate some general characteristics of contemporary Chinese film.

One is *February in Early Spring*. The reader will recall that it
had been condemned as revisionist just before the Cultural
Revolution. A Chinese living in Beijing at that time, clearly
following the official line, had described it as 'hopelessly treacly
and sentimental' (see Chapter 1). However, at the very end of
1978, the Ministry of Culture formally reversed the verdict on
this film. Reporting the decision, China's main cinema journal
declared *February in Early Spring* 'to be a good and comparatively
good film, to dub it a poisonous weed film was very wrong.
This was nothing more than a grave injustice trumped up by
Jiang Qing and her followers to push "the theory of the dictatorship of the sinister line in literature and art" '[17] as discussed
in Chapter 2. Certainly this film can claim a 'poetic atmosphere',
one of Su Shuyang's criteria for a good script. The strong emotionalism which characterises the film and which had seemed
treacly in 1965, has now become a matter for strong praise from
the critics. One of them wrote:

> It is only because the creators of *February in Early Spring*
> have been able to expose and express the changes in the
> emotions of the characters so realistically and so vividly
> through the characters' actions and language and through
> the background natural scenery. . . and other aspects, that
> they have been able to make the film achieve artistic
> strength that can move people in the way it does.[18]

Clearly the reviewer has no objection whatever to the fact
that this is a love film, the central theme of which is the tragedy
which prevents the two main characters from marrying each
other. Love and tenderness, which during the Cultural Revolution and the early 1970s came close to being forbidden in the
Chinese cinema, have now returned as major topics. This is in
accord with developments in other areas of society. Nowadays
the Chinese press writes much more openly and frequently of
love and marriage than it did before 1976. Whereas at that time,
it placed its thrust on late marriage, rarely mentioning love,
nowadays it has changed its emphasis dramatically away from

self-sacrifice and towards happiness and warmth for the individual man and woman.

The shift is but part of the move away from the Cultural Revolution. Although the period when *February in Early Spring* was criticised was actually just before the Cultural Revolution, the attacks on the film were undoubtedly part of the process which led up to that movement. The political motivation for the reversal of the verdict on the film is thus very obvious. Just as suddenly to start praising the 'pure official' Hai Rui was undoubtedly a political move to condemn the Cultural Revolution, so praise for *February in Early Spring* clearly aims to fulfil a similar objective.

It is obvious from this point that *February in Early Spring* is a rescreened film. A second individual film to discuss belongs to the opposite category and was among the early crop of films to follow the fall of the four. Issued in September 1979, it is called *Erquan yingyue* (*Moon Reflected on the Second Springs*) and is similar to *February in Early Spring* in including a strong love interest.

Second Springs, which I saw in Guilin late in December 1979, is a historical film centring around the career of the people's musician Hua Yanjun, also called Abing (1893–1950), who spent his life roaming round the shores of Lake Tai in Jiangsu province and in the nearby city of Wuxi, playing his *erhu* or *pipa*. His most famous piece is called 'Moon Reflected on the Second Springs' and is the theme of the film. There is a temple there which contains the 'Second Springs under Heaven', and a pagoda on top of a hill, the latter shown several times with the full moon shining behind it. The Second Springs, where Abing is often seen playing his instruments, and full moon give the musical theme, the film and its hero their title and flavour.

As the film begins, Abing loses his mother and with his father goes to a Taoist temple, where he becomes his father's music disciple. He accompanies the singing of a beautiful girl, Qinmei (Little Sister Qin), but after her father dies she is enslaved to a landlord and separated from Abing. He searches for her and they are reunited at the Second Springs, after which they marry and briefly live happily together. Later Abing performs at a banquet given by a high official, but the latter regards his music as subversive and has him beaten up so savagely that he is permanently blinded. The official tries to rape Qinmei who, believing Abing dead, commits suicide. Abing joins the revolution and, through his patriotic and progressive music, contributes to its triumph. After liberation he is appointed a professor and becomes a cultural hero, but his happiness is blighted when he learns for the first time of his wife's suicide.

From a technical point of view this is a good film. In the first place, it follows Su Shuyang's dictum on length; at just under two hours it is long enough to develop a magic atmosphere, but short enough never to become boring. Second, the photography is excellent and captures the magnificent scenery of Wuxi and Lake Tai to perfection, including the bright red colours of the flowers in spring and the exquisite whiteness of the winter snow. I would endorse one Chinese viewer's comment that 'the film fully and appropriately makes use of lyrical scenery for description, thus shaping the film's unique style'.[19] The beautifully played music of the *erhu* and *pipa* combines with the scenic background of the film to create a quiet and unpretentious magic such as I have rarely seen in the Chinese cinema.

The techniques include the alternation, towards the end of the film, of colour with black and white. After the only violent scene where Abing is beaten up and blinded, the colour vanishes from the screen. It returns mildly and again fades several times. This effectively denotes the suffering of the hero. Full and bright colours come suddenly back to announce the arrival of liberation. Only in the flashbacks at the film's end which show Abing's memories of bitterness in the old society does the colour disappear again. The best example is Qinmei's suicide, for it is not only Abing, but also the audience which has till then remained ignorant of this tragedy.

The acting is very fine, especially that of the negative characters: landlords, evil officials and others. The hero, played by Zheng Songmao, himself from a family of folk musicians, captures the persistent selflessness of the character well without the sanctimoniousness which often intrudes into the less aggressive 'goodies' of the Chinese cinema. The heroine, acted by Yuan Mengya, is less convincing. She is a bit too much the model of weak femininity for a progressive film and her overloud weeping and emotionalism sometimes cross the border between strong feeling and sentimentality.

From the point of view of content, the major interest of *Second Springs* lies in the attempt to recreate a historical atmosphere. The relative historical veracity of the play *Yang Kaihui* and the deliberate use of traditional opera to remember the nation's past, discussed in earlier chapters, are here carried over into the cinema. This film is the perfect instrument for reviving the memory of the people's musician and is part of a campaign in favour of old artists in music circles who include Abing. Actually, the picture of the hero is much romanticised, even falsified, for dramatic effect. For instance, Abing's total blindness was 'due to illness when he was thirty-six (1929)',[20] and I understand the sickness was in fact venereal disease; it had nothing to do with any beating at a banquet, which is not portrayed as happening until 1947. Moreover, most of the characters are fictitious. Yet there is unquestionably a portion of essential truth in the film: Abing did exist, he did live in Wuxi and he did sing of its beauty in his music; he did compose the music which gives the film its title. The director of the film, Yan Jizhou, has justified his approach to Abing by saying that this is a feature film based on the life of a historical figure, not a biographical account.[21]

Another point is the centrality of the love theme. The tender relationship between Abing and Qinmei occupies a place more vital to the overall plot than in any spoken play I have seen in China. Yet it is striking how bodily contact between the lovers remains absent. Even in the emotion-charged reunion between the two at the Second Springs, when they rush towards each other, all contact is in the hands, they do not even embrace, let alone kiss. The dictates of traditional, as well as contemporary, Chinese custom forbid public contact between adult members of the opposite sex on the stage or screen.

The importance of the love theme highlights the tragic element in *Second Springs*. Despite the happiness inherent in the liberation which ends the film, the focus is clearly on the death of Qinmei. The final scene does not show an Abing cheered by liberation but his sadness at the loss of his beloved and his bitter feelings towards the oppressors who have caused him and others so much suffering. To judge from their reaction, the audience certainly found the film an immensely sad and moving experience.

A film about the life of a musician invites comparison with Ken Russell's superb *Mahler* of 1974 on the career of the famous composer. The same splendid attention to the background music and scenery is evident in both, the same focus on the love interest. Two major contrasts, however, show a great deal about the differing cinema orientation of China and Great Britain. One is the imagery which shows Mahler's wife Alma in various contorted postures and situations and thus reveals the strange fantasies of Mahler's morbid genius. Such scenes would be impossible in the Chinese cinema which creates its atmospheres in more realistic ways. The other contrast is that the British film places all interest on Mahler as an individual but ignores the political background almost totally as irrelevant to the artist. The Chinese film, on the other hand, gives major attention to the historical period against which it is set. It implies, even stresses, that nothing which happens to Abing can be separated from his function and status in the black society which produced him. Despite its tragedy, love interest and musical focus, *Second Springs* thus conforms to the pattern of other items of the performing arts in contemporary China in being an intensely political document.

Two films which resemble *Second Springs* in the importance of their political setting are *Xiaohua* (*Little Flower*) and *A! Yaolan* (*Ah! Cradle*). Although they do not really fit into the tight categories raised in the quotation at the beginning of this section, they do belong to the very important broad classification of revolutionary history, since both are stories of the War of Liberation (1946–49).

Both films were issued in 1979 and both were well received. On 21 January 1980, when I interviewed several cadres responsible for reviews in the literature and arts section of the *Guangming Daily*, they named *Little Flower* as China's best film for 1979 according to the four broad criteria which they agreed upon as generally appropriate: (i) content and concrete thought, (ii) artistic features, (iii) audience reaction, and (iv) personal reaction.

Little Flower is the name of an eighteen-year-old girl who has been separated from her parents very young and is seeking her elder brother as she takes part in the revolution. In the end a woman with whom she has become coincidentally involved in the war turns out to be her mother. She is not the girl she believes herself to be, and the elder brother not hers at all but that of another Little Flower whom she has befriended as a comrade in the revolutionary war. *Ah! Cradle* is about a young woman who has been grossly ill-treated by her former husband and is consequently determined never to marry again. She is given the task of looking after small children separated from their parents, or orphaned by the war. In the end, having brought about the reunion of the children with any surviving parents, she marries a revolutionary comrade and adopts one of the orphans.

In each film the central character is a young female driven to join the revolution by resentment against aspects of the old society which have hurt her deeply. In both films family relationships are of great importance with emphasis on the separation of parents and children or brothers and sisters as a major aspect of tragedy caused by war and exploitation. So strong is the family theme that it may be asked if the two films are not symptomatic of a strengthening of family ties in Chinese society as a whole. *Ah! Cradle* and *Little Flower* differ in that children play a greater role in the former than the latter. Almost all the actual time of screening is about looking after small children without parents, while they appear only in flashback scenes in *Little Flower*.

Another contrast in content lies in the question of violence. The prevalence of violence in the films of the West, especially the United States of America, has been a major source of controversy in those countries. In China, violence is not a topic often mentioned in reviews. The *Guangming Daily* cadres told me, however, that their attitude, which they believed a general one in China, was that the presentation of violence for its own sake should be regarded as an unhealthy characteristic of cinema. On the other hand, war films should be realistic and not shrink from necessary violence. They believed that Chinese films in general were not especially violent and that *Little Flower*

in particular had not overstepped the boundary between necessary and excessive violence.

Such judgments can never be more than personal. Going by
the Chinese films I have seen I would certainly support the
Guangming Daily cadres' general verdict and apply it to *Ah!
Cradle*. In that film there are shooting scenes and deaths, but
no gory particulars. In *Little Flower*, however, there is fairly
extensive violent detail. Two scenes stand out. In one the heroine, her face burning with hatred, flicks her enormously long
plait around her neck; she flourishes her knife and kicks violently, preparing to slit the throat of a reactionary against whom
she has a childhood score to settle. In the other the enemy
chieftain has two girls violently whipped and orders flames to
be taken towards them in preparation for burning them alive.
In fairness it must be added that in both cases Party representatives intervene to prevent the climax. Little Flower is forcefully
stopped from knifing her enemy; vengeance is not what the
revolution is supposed to be all about. The two girls are saved
from the fire by a bullet in the chieftain's back fired by an
ambushing Communist force. It is arguable, then, that *Little
Flower* is quite mild from the point of view of violence. Certainly
it is not nearly as savage as any number of American or Hong
Kong films I have seen. But I still believe the same points could
have been effectively made in *Little Flower* through different
methods.

Another virtue my *Guangming Daily* informants found in this
film was the acting. Many Chinese viewers have shared their
view. A reader of *Cinema for the Masses* remarked that 'the main
performers, through sincere emotional changes, deeply revealed the inner world of the characters and made the images
of the characters true to life and moving'.[22] Most commentators
have especially noted the performance of the heroine; the
Guangming Daily cadres described it as 'very authentic, vivid,
and attentive to detail'. Chen Chong, the girl on whom they
lavished this praise, was an eighteen-year-old student at the
Shanghai Foreign Languages Institute at the time she made the
film. As such she was an amateur but appeared set for a successful professional career as a film-star. Actually I found her
slightly artificial, even a bit innocent and sentimental at times.

The description 'very authentic' is better applied to the acting in *Ah! Cradle*, not only to that of the lead role but of the numerous children.

In both these two films the sound is excellently produced and the photography superb. Both are coloured, narrow-screen pictures which demonstrate beautifully the magnificent scenery of northwestern China where both are set. From the point of view of technique neither is particularly original, but both make good use of production methods developed elsewhere. Both films employ flashbacks extensively to show bitter memories which have driven the major characters to revolution. In *Little Flower* all the flashbacks are in black-and-white to intensify the dark atmosphere which is supposed to surround them. According to my *Guangming Daily* informants, this alternation of colour with black-and-white, a feature also of *Second Springs*, had never been used in China before 1979. This technique is not found in *Ah! Cradle*, but a striking one there is the sudden transfer from normal to slow-speed projection at a particularly dramatic moment where one of the young girl revolutionaries is shot dead.

The four feature films discussed so far share the common feature of being set entirely or almost entirely in the old society. We now take up an important film about the new China, the story of which takes place entirely in the summer of 1976. It is *Languang shanguo zhihou (After the Blue Light Flashed)*, a colour narrow-screen item produced by the Shanghai Film Studio and released in the middle of 1979. It concerns the impact of a devastating earthquake on a mythical city called Yannan. Obviously it is intended as a dramatisation of the great Tangshan earthquake of 28 July 1976, mentioned in Chapter 2.

The film most certainly produced a great impact on the audience of which I was part in January 1980. If they were typical of the Beijing populace as a whole, a substantial proportion had friends or relations killed in that overwhelming disaster. The film brought out vividly the horrors of the incident and a woman sitting behind me exclaimed several times 'that's exactly what it was like in Tangshan'. Compared with the documentary on the same subject it was less horrific in the fewer shots of dead bodies, but more moving in the explanation of exactly how the Tangshan earthquake affected individual people. The cinema is the perfect medium for such a story because of its unique ability to combine emotion with physical background. No play can show the reality of an earthquake like a motion picture, but the latter can develop characters or reveal emotions as well as a play.

The film begins with an open-air concert which has two functions. First it introduces the main characters, and second it shows an unusually cheerful and happy atmosphere in order to heighten the contrast with the next scene. The central character is Xing Huiming whose daughter is the lead dancer in the concert. After its conclusion all return home and go to bed. In the dead of night, just as in Tangshan, a prolonged blue light flashes in the sky and heralds the violent rocking of the earth which brings all the houses down into rubble. Xing Huiming's wife and daughter are killed. He reacts by leading a group to save and look after the numerous orphans created by the earthquake.

A major characteristic of the film is the important role given to children. Much of the most moving tragedy of the drama revolves around the loss of parents or children to each other, and disappointments of various kinds caused to the latter. In this respect the film has much in common with *Ah! Cradle*. On the other hand, possibly the main point of *After the Blue Light Flashed* is the way everybody unites in the face of distress to help the children. A key moment is when Xing and one of the little girls rush into each other's arms, he imagining she is his dead daughter, she that Xing is her dead father. Film can show what goes on in the mind of the characters through flashbacks to happier moments in a way impossible in any other medium. One of the concluding scenes shows the children departing in brand new buses for a happier life in a different and better city. A later newspaper article responded to an obvious question raised by many people who had seen the film: 'what is the life of the Tangshan orphans like?' It summed up by saying, 'we can tell everybody: their life is very good', and goes on to paint a glowing picture of their progress and happiness under the care of the Party.[23]

So despite the elements of desperate misery in the film, the end gives grounds for hope. The final shot shows a young doctor in the arms of – though not kissing – her beloved, whom she has believed dead. Their reunion takes place where proverbially lovers should meet, a broken bridge, damaged by the earthquake.

Since the film concludes on a note of hope for the future, one can argue a political moral of faith in the Party and persuasion to the people never to give up in the face of adversity. This was certainly the lesson that the *People's Daily* felt its readers should draw from a forum held by the orphans themselves and their teachers. Apart from the realism of the film, the main point to come over from seeing *After the Blue Light Flashed*, as one teacher put it, was 'to add even further to our firm faith in the leadership of the Party, and our firm faith in the superiority of socialism. I feel that the film has really played an active role in educating and encouraging people.'[24]

However, in this film it was the lack of politics, not the converse, that impressed me most forcefully. The happiness of the first scene and the hope of the last one both belonged to the period of the 'gang of four'. There was no reference at all to the currently popular line that the 'gang of four' made no attempt to send relief to Tangshan, and even prevented it by demanding denunciation for Deng Xiaoping and revolution in preference to such bourgeois humanitarianism. Virtually the only political reference was expressions of joy that Premier Hua was planning to visit the devastated city. The reader will recall that Hua Guofeng did in fact go to Tangshan after the earthquake.

It is emotion that strikes the viewer of *After the Blue Light Flashed* rather than politics. There are more tears in it than any other Chinese film I have seen, and that is saying a great deal. One could charge it with sentimentality, but this would be unfair. The event which forms its basis was so overwhelming in scope, and so far-reaching in the effects produced on the lives of people, that to exaggerate the emotional traumas would be difficult indeed.

A final feature which differs from any considered so far in straddling both the old and new societies is *Dahe benliu* (*The Great River Flows On*). It is important, and also different from the other films discussed, in being a two-part item, the first produced in China since the fall of the 'gang of four'.

The first of the two parts concerns the pre-liberation history of the Yellow River, the 'great river' of the title, and the second part, that since 1949. The main character is Li Mai, a peasant woman, who is played in the film by the well-known actress Zhang Ruifang. The picture begins with a spectacular scene set in June 1938, when Chiang Kaishek had the dykes of the Yellow River broken near Zhengzhou in Henan province, ostensibly in order to prevent the southward movement of the Japanese who had just occupied the then capital of Henan, Kaifeng, but according to CCP claims to massacre Communist supporters in the area. Li Mai becomes a refugee but takes an active part in the struggles both against the Japanese and the Guomindang. The second part of the film revolves around an attempt to control the Yellow River. When a serious flood threatens, Zhou Enlai intervenes, inspects the site and decides to evacuate everyone, after which the dykes are strengthened and the river harnessed.

The scriptwriter of this film, Li Zhun, finished his work in 1975, but according to contemporary Chinese claims, political interference from the 'gang of four' and their followers made it impossible to do anything about making the script into a film until after October 1976. Already in 1975, Li Zhun had wanted Zhang Ruifang to play the part of Li Mai. She was enthusiastic, but only after the director of the film, Xie Tieli, and others had agreed on her suitability for the role was work actually able to begin. Part of the job of production necessary for so large-scale a film was for the cast and other relevant people to spend about a year on location in Henan province. As a result of the long process of manufacture, *The Great River Flows On* was not actually released for public screening until early in 1979.

There is an obvious political message in the film. With its two parts before and after liberation it emphasises the contrast between the two periods and leaves the audience with the conclusion that Chiang Kaishek's government actually encouraged the flooding of the Yellow River while the CCP's has done everything it can to prevent it. If there are two contrasting political figures they are Chiang Kaishek and Zhou Enlai.

Chiang Kaishek does not actually appear on the screen, but Zhou Enlai's presence there is quite substantial. As for the other revolutionary whose name is so often linked with Zhou's there is 'a scene where Chairman Mao meets Li Mai on the great dyke and they chat cordially'.[25]

A related point is that although both have been dominant figures in innumerable reportage reels, *The Great River Flows On* is the first feature film ever made in China in which either Mao Zedong or Zhou Enlai appears on the screen. It is the first of the 'useful attempts in moulding the images of the old generation of proletarian revolutionaries', to which reference was made earlier. It will be recalled that it was over a year before that both had begun to be represented on the stage, and the profession of portraying the two great revolutionaries in theatre was now applied also to the cinema. In this film Zhou Enlai is the more important of the two. As a matter of fact, this point even aroused comment among viewers, one of whom remarked that 'the creation of the glorious image of Chairman Mao is still not full enough; it is not depicted as finely or as true to life nor created as vividly or as movingly as the image of Zhou Enlai'.[26] He intended this observation as a justification for his view that there were still some inadequacies in the film.

The reaction exemplifies the extremely mixed reception which has been accorded this film. Although *The Great River Flows On* is clearly a positive work, the public and others have gone out of their way to point out faults. One viewer, while conceding that 'the relevant newspapers and cinema journals had repeatedly done propaganda for it, and given it extremely high evaluation', declared that 'having seen this film, I could not help being a bit disappointed'.[27] Another pointed out that there were still traces of the 'gang of four's' theories on characterisation. 'The film makes the enemy so weak and incompetent just so as to "give prominence" to Li Mai's heroic courage.'[28] There is a feeling about her of being just a little bit too good, not unlike the heroes in the 'model' operas. Even Zhang Ruifang has conceded about the role of Li Mai, which she herself created:

Her starting point, her political consciousness is too high. She knows everything. She can easily distinguish the

150

Communist Party from the Kuomintang [*sic*]. She's just like a Communist Party member from the beginning. She never has room to develop as a character.[29]

Most interesting of all was a survey taken by a research unit in the Ministry of Culture. Over 600 people filled out and returned a questionnaire, part of which related to this film. Sixty per cent of respondents declared that the film was 'not bad' and 'progressive', and 'the first part was comparatively good'. On the other hand, with echoes of Su Shuyang's views, they thought that the film was too long. Some respondents found the second part not concentrated enough, so that they tended to lose interest. Some said 'the scriptwriter, director and cast are all first rate, but the film is not shot at all well; it is too scattered.'[30]

Frank commentary of this sort through surveys had been unknown in China for many years; responsible cadres of the Literature and Arts section of the *Guangming Daily*, which printed the results of the survey, told me that it had been the first of its kind since 1966. The views cover not only political but also technical matters, whereas most public commentary in China in the decade 1966–76 tended to focus on political aspects, and invariably supported the government line. The political comments here do not exactly conflict with official opinion, but it is nevertheless striking that the less popular part of the film is the second, that is to say, the section set in the People's Republic which praises Zhou Enlai and Mao Zedong. Probably Jiang Qing would have seen innuendos of insult to the CCP in this verdict.

This survey appears to be part of the movement, discussed in Chapter 2, 'to emancipate the mind', which to some extent abandoned the social and ideological values which had prevailed in the PRC up to that point, and in particular relinquished the halo which had circled around the head of Mao Zedong's thought. The Ministry of Culture stated in the press article that 'through the investigation, we have heard sounds from the minds of the cinema-going masses: an earnest hope to improve the cause of our country's films'.[31] It follows directly from this comment that it would be legitimate to extrapolate from the example of the single film *The Great River Flows On* to cinema in general; and to conclude that commentary on motion pictures, not only from critics but also from ordinary citizens, is likely to be more sophisticated in the future than it has been in the past.

One area where the Chinese have not yet developed selective capacities is foreign films. This is probably because they saw absolutely none between 1966 and 1976, and only a limited number from a small range of countries before then. Now, however, foreign films dubbed into Chinese occupy a proportion of the total offering high enough to create an impact, if still much smaller than local productions. The overseas motion pictures come from a large variety of countries, especially those of the West, and include such works as *Death on the Nile*, the thriller based on Agatha Christie's novel of the same name, *The Slipper and the Rose*, the story of Cinderella, and *Zorro*.

It is of course a healthy development that China should accept foreign films. No country should cut itself off from foreign cinema to the extent of the 1966–76 decade in China. It would, however, be a great pity if China were to allow itself to be swamped so completely by foreign films as to inhibit the growth of its own cinema. Such a fate has befallen many countries because of the hunger of large film-producing companies for profits and their supreme, and often unjustified, confidence in their own products. Probably China has a large enough demand for its own style of film and enough national confidence and competence to prevent the onslaughts of such cultural imperialism. In the meantime those examples I have seen of Chinese films, and in particular those made since 1976, have convinced me that the Chinese cinema industry is doing well at least in terms of quality. Originality may not be its central hallmark, but the techniques, photography, sound and other features are considerably better than adequate and mesh well with the content. But above all, the stories and acting display a good range of moods, as well as providing the interest and excitement appropriate to the tastes of the Chinese people. Comparisons with other countries are pointless, but judged by its own criteria, Chinese cinema certainly gives evidence of substantial achievement and demonstrates the continuing artistry and skill of its film-makers.

6

Music in the performing arts

China's tradition of music and musical instruments is a most ancient and highly developed one. Early Chinese sources attest the existence, among other instruments, of the seven-string zither, *qin*, from the most ancient times; later the *qin* functioned both as solo instrument – the preserve of the educated classes – and as one instrument of a ritual orchestra which accompanied ceremonial occasions. Apart from instruments originating in China, there are a number which are introductions from foreign countries but have become so much part of Chinese culture over the centuries that they can also be considered Chinese. They include the pear-shaped lute (*pipa*) and the Chinese fiddle (*huqin*).

Traditionally, the Chinese divided their musical instruments into categories reflecting the composition of their major sound-producing component, such as silk, bamboo or gourd. But it is also both easy and appropriate to classify them in the Western manner: stringed, wind or percussion. Among the string instruments, some are plucked, such as the *qin*, the *pipa* and the three-stringed *sanxian*. The latter two are in extremely widespread use in the *quyi* forms, as well as local opera. Others are bowed, including the *huqin* family of fiddles which have two strings. The player places the instrument upright on the thigh, the bow being fitted between the two strings so that he pushes it to play one string, and pulls for the other. Fiddles of one kind or another are vitally important in the orchestras of the regional theatre, in particular the Beijing opera.

The most important of the wind instruments is the Chinese flute (*dizi*). This is also frequently heard in various types of Chinese theatrical music, especially the formerly aristocratic *Kunqu*. Other types of wind instruments include the single-reeded *guanzi* and the *suona*, which has a double reed like the Western oboe, but is smaller and somewhat shriller. The third category, percussion, is well represented with a large variety of instruments, which are used in most types of Chinese music, principally as accompaniment.

These traditional musical instruments have retained their importance in all periods of the PRC, including, naturally, that since the smashing of the 'gang of four'. There is, however, another side to Chinese music, namely that which depends upon instruments introduced relatively recently from European countries. These include the standard members of the symphony orchestra, such as the violin, cello, flute, oboe, trumpet and tympani or kettledrum. To mix traditional Chinese and Western instruments in a single piece is a particularly common phenomenon in contemporary Chinese music.

In a book on the performing arts there are two ways to regard music; one is as a form of the performing arts in itself, and the other is as an accompaniment to others of their branches, especially theatre, film and dance. In several chapters reference has been made to the importance of music in providing interludes or accompaniment for other forms of art; even the spoken play, the essence of which is ordinary speaking not song, actually quite often includes some music as well.

Music as a performing arts branch

The first category – to treat it as an end in itself – shows music in a more important, because independent, role, although in the Chinese context the musical art actually accompanies at least as often, and probably more so, than it dominates.

Interest in playing musical instruments, whether originally Chinese or Western, was retained uninterrupted throughout the decade of the 'gang of four'. It would be quite unfair to charge them with having tried to kill music as an art. I have myself attended well patronised concerts of Chinese music during that period. On the other hand, music by European composers was but rarely performed, and the reader will recall the savage tirades against such foreign items in 1974 (see Chapter 1).

As far as their own national art was concerned, one area that did come under fire as unnecessary, even though it had encountered much success before the Cultural Revolution, was explorations into unusual or obsolescent Chinese instruments and music. One reason for this was that virtually all those people competent to carry out such investigations were under a cloud or labouring in the countryside and thus unavailable.

The removal of the 'gang of four' changed this situation and research activity gradually recommenced. On 23 May 1979, the National Music Committee of the Association of Chinese Musicians held its second expanded conference in Beijing and it discussed the problem 'of the project to collect and arrange the national music legacy'. This involved sending experts out into the field to find out what they could about music still surviving in all the different areas of China, and above all those of the National Minorities. The overall intention was to 'collect, arrange and edit five "compilations" of Chinese folksongs, tunes of Chinese folk instruments, tunes of the Chinese *qin*, the music of Chinese story-telling and the music of the Chinese theatre etc.'[1]

In the same year conferences were taking place locally to stimulate activity in various parts of China. For instance, in June there was a 'work conference for the collection of folk music of Shanxi' in Taiyuan, the capital of Shanxi province, and in March a similar forum in Jiangxi province.

That the possibility remains open for this exploration activity to be translated into performable items is shown through the example of an ancient Mongolian instrument called *huposzu*, a stringed plucked instrument known in the thirteenth century and medieval times, but subsequently lost. One professional performing musician of Inner Mongolia took an interest in this extinct instrument, he 'referred to a large amount of related data, consulted music specialists and conducted an extensive survey among old herdsmen in the grasslands'.[2] By this means he was able to reconstruct the instrument and then gave public performances on it.

Such collected material, apart from opera, tends to consist of reasonably short items and is in this respect like traditional Chinese music as a whole. This means that the concert, which is so familiar a form of entertainment in the West, has not been so in China. There are of course symphony orchestras in China nowadays, and these will be considered shortly, but the most popular type of 'concert' for the Chinese is somewhat more similar to a variety show in which a number of different kinds of musical items are performed. Because such shows include short dance excerpts, it is necessary to include them in this section, even though it is arguable that the music is merely the companion to the dance.

A typical variety show which I attended in Wuhan in October 1978 – in a more comfortable, better appointed, and cleaner theatre than anywhere I saw a traditional opera – consisted of various traditional songs, instrumental pieces and dances. For the first item, a traditional orchestra with gong sets and other instruments accompanied a *suona* solo. Several items featured classical pieces played by an orchestra consisting wholly, or almost entirely, of traditional musical instruments. It needs to be added here that traditional Chinese instruments tend towards the higher rather than the lower extremities of the range. For this reason, cellos and double basses are sometimes added to Chinese orchestras. This was certainly the case at the concert I attended in Wuhan. It is also noteworthy that traditional Chinese music does not make a big feature of harmonic progression. The tendency is for the instruments to play in unison. Such was the case for the traditional items played, even though they were not in their original form but had been arranged. For different items of the programme, a separate set of instrumental players came onto the stage. Orchestral pieces were separated by dances, often of the National Minorities, though accompanied by traditional Chinese instruments. For these items, which were based on folk songs and folk dances, complex and beautiful scenery appeared at the back of the stage.

Another concert I attended was in Shanghai late in 1978. It consisted of three basic sections. The first was a symphony orchestra, which performed some Chinese compositions, but mainly those from the standard classical Western repertory, including for instance, the Blue Danube Waltz and selections from Tchaikovsky's *Swan Lake*. The second was soprano solos, and the third was traditional Chinese dances. This took place in a gigantic stadium which could hold many thousands of people.

These two concerts reflect a differing balance between traditional Chinese and European music. A third one, which I heard in Guangzhou's enormous Sun Yatsen Memorial Hall at the end of December 1979 given by the Ballet Troupe of the Central *Geju* and Dance-Drama Company, represents a further stage in the direction of the Western idiom, while retaining the basic form of the variety show with excerpts of various kinds. While it was at that time possible to find concerts of traditional Chinese music, I suspect strongly that the heavy dominance of Western music at this Guangzhou performance, given before a gigantic and overwhelmingly Chinese capacity audience, can be related to tightening relations with major Western powers during 1979 and the gradual growth in influence of Western social values in that year.

There were two sections, dance and music. Each item was short with dance sometimes following dance, sometimes alternating with music. The programme divided the items neatly into the two parts, but, in accordance with common Chinese custom, the order did not follow the programme strictly.

The dances were mainly ballet, including short extracts from famous European works; the climax to the evening was a scene from *Swan Lake*. Others were Spanish dances performed with such verve, aplomb and obvious enjoyment that one almost felt the Chinese dancers had temporarily become Spaniards. Only one of the dances was Chinese, a snake dance done in the form of a ballet *pas-de-deux*, with the girl imitating, amazingly realistically, the movements of a snake. The music for the dance section came from a tape-recorder in the orchestra pit; there were no players there.

The music section was dominated by a series of short instrumental pieces from European countries, including a Hungarian Dance by Brahms and a Romanian folk song. The orchestra here consisted of three violins, one double bass, clarinet, flute, guitar, side drum, and a piano. Again the performers were very enthusiastic and appeared to be enjoying themselves immensely. All but the pianist were men and wore standard Western lounge suits.

Audience reaction to this orgy of Occidentalia was mixed. As usual there was much talking throughout the performance and very little applause. *Swan Lake*, for instance, drew hardly a patter from all but a few members of this enormous gathering. One particularly virtuoso performance of a very fast Spanish musical item drew real and thunderous applause, but this was exceptional. The constant bodily contact of the dances in the Western ballet was clearly a source of bemusement and wonder, even pleasure. But the expressions on the faces of the watchers betokened some slight surprised shock as well, for in the Chinese tradition men and women do not touch each other in public and certainly not on the stage. What appeared to delight most was the display of great technical skill, such as *prestissimo* and perfectly executed extracts on a musical instrument. This pattern is not unlike the Beijing opera where it is the technical skill of the acrobatics which draws the most applause.

Variety shows or concerts with numerous short items of different kinds are nothing new in China and were common also during the period of the 'gang of four', although at that time they did not include the Western classics. However, one phenomenon not found from 1966 to 1976 was the symphony concert in which a Western-style symphony orchestra, including a full range of violins and other string instruments, oboes, clarinets, brass, percussion, etc., plays both extended and short pieces on the stage, but without dance or other diversion. It is certainly no revelation of the contemporary authorities that symphonic concerts simply did not take place during the decade 1966–76. I can testify from my own experience that it was a matter of pride on the part of the cultural authorities at the time.

With the gang's fall the way became clear for the return of symphonic music and concerts. Shanghai has its own Philharmonic Orchestra which I heard play Beethoven's Symphony No. 7 in October 1978, and Beijing is the seat of the Central Philharmonic Society which in July 1978 resumed weekend symphony concerts after a twelve-year suspension, claimed, of course, to be due to the political interference of the 'gang of four'. The first concert included symphonic music entitled 'Heroic Epic', which is of recent composition, as well as the violin concerto *Liang Shanbo and Zhu Yingtai*. This is a setting, with a full symphony orchestra and a violin solo, of the famous story of the butterfly lovers mentioned several times elsewhere. Written by He Zhanhao and Chen Gang before the Cultural Revolution, this has now come back to popularity and is regularly heard in China. It was first recorded in 1961 and reissued in 1977.

The musical works just mentioned fall into four different categories. One is the standard Western classical repertory which includes work such as the Beethoven symphonies, Tchaikovsky and so on. The more famous of these works are making a return in China, but it is still very tentative and by comparison with a country such as, say, Japan, very preliminary. A music professor whom I met in Shanghai in October 1978 was prepared to express enthusiasm to me for the music of Arnold Schönberg, but I believe it will be a long time before the public at large in China, even the urban people, develop any real interest in such modern Western music.

The second category is Chinese works written in the Western idiom and with entirely Western musical instruments, composed before the Cultural Revolution. There has been a revival of symphonic music from before the Cultural Revolution which parallels that of spoken plays and modern and traditional operas. Third are the minor and small-scale foreign folk songs or pieces.

The last category is symphonic Chinese works written since the smashing of the 'gang of four'. Just as with plays and operas, these have taken a little time to come forward. One cannot write symphonic music overnight. But the resumption of regular concerts in Beijing on a professional level, including modern works, indicates the rebeginnings of symphonic musical creativity among Chinese composers.

In a sense this is the most important of the four categories because it is the one where Chinese inventiveness is most obviously judged. It is of course desirable that people should appreciate each other's cultures and hence that Chinese should hear and enjoy such works as *Swan Lake* or Spanish dances. However, the relevance of such music to the lives of most Chinese is so hard to demonstrate that they may not wish to accelerate appreciation for it indefinitely. A modern musical expression, on the other hand, reflects the growth of a society and is consequently highly relevant. I could not help being struck by the beauty and inventiveness of the Snake Dance at the Guangzhou concert. It demonstrated, both from a dance and musical point of view, how well good artists can adapt a traditional item to a foreign form like ballet and make something new and alive. Yet as far as music in the Western idiom is concerned, the Chinese are not interested in adapting to contemporary European or American style, nor have they so far developed their own stamp. They still appear content to copy from the masters of the past.

Music as accompaniment to other performing arts

The 'concert' has here been treated as a form illustrating music in its own right. Yet it will have become clear that in fact most include items where the music acts as companion to another branch of the performing arts, especially dance. We move now to the general topic of how the Chinese regard the musical side of other performing arts forms.

Because of their closeness to the masses of people the traditional drama styles occupy a particularly important place. Controversy has arisen over how to react to the very substantial changes which Jiang Qing and her followers made during the decade 1966 to 1976 in the orchestra and music of the regional opera forms and the Beijing Opera itself. The essence of the alterations was to expand the size of the orchestra from the traditional ten or so to about thirty, and to include Western musical instruments as well as Chinese traditional, the former frequently in a dominating role. When I visited China in 1973, I learned during an interview with Li Xifan, who was at that time the literature and arts editor of the *People's Daily*, that the addition of Western instruments was supposed to make the music sound much more heroic, and that this was appropriate to the 'model' operas with their strong emphasis on heroism.

After the production of *Forced Up Mt Liang* in May 1977 made old-costume opera acceptable again, some items gradually came back which were purely traditional in the sense that their music was changed but minimally from the Qing or even Ming dynasties. These caused no problem because very little rearrangement was desirable. But they are but a small minority. In most cases of operas in traditional forms on historical or ancient themes, a great deal of musical rearranging or completely new writing by an identifiable composer has taken place. Such people, among others, have raised serious questions over the Cultural Revolutionary approach supported by Li Xifan.

Since October 1976 it has naturally become necessary to ascribe evil intentions to the four's activities. One writer, called Wei Zhou, summed up the influence which he perceived them as having exerted as follows:

> The 'gang of four', riding roughshod over the theatre
> cause, seriously sabotaged the superior traditions of all
> kinds of local theatre, and smothered the style and special
> features of their theatrical music. They only allowed a few
> items adapted and transplanted from Beijing Opera, and
> suppressed and struck down other new creations. No kind
> of opera was allowed to choose the topics it was good at
> expressing or to create melodies according to its intrinsic
> language or libretto rules. The main accompanying
> instruments of the original kind of opera became merely
> ornamental things in the vast band. The music of some
> operas arbitrarily applied the methods of foreign operas
> and sought after 'the symphonic nature' or monotonous
> 'overtures' or 'entr'actes'.[3]

Wei Zhou here raises three problems. They concern, first, the size of the theatrical orchestra, second, the mixture of Chinese and Western instruments there, and third, the retention of the Chinese essence in the face of the conventions of Western music.

On the first problem, Wei Zhou implies that the new size of

about thirty instruments is far too large. He suggests later that small orchestras should revert to ten players or so and that large should consist of about twenty, depending upon the circumstances.

Responses to Wei's suggestion have not been unanimous. One member of a Beijing opera troupe in Henan province took the line that the music of the local operas develops as time goes on, and must therefore be subject to change; so to require a return to smaller orchestras, just because the 'gang of four' had been the cause of their expansion, he believed was quite wrong, 'as if to be small was the superior tradition of opera orchestras and to be large was not to honour tradition'.[4]

Actually, to expand the size of drama orchestra is nothing new to the Cultural Revolution. There is one form of Sichuanese opera which by tradition is accompanied only by percussion and a 'helping chorus' consisting of two or three offstage singers. In the famous item *Autumn River*, four instruments were added in the 1950s, including the Chinese flute and pear-shaped lute, and were still there in the performance I saw in Chengdu in January 1980. Apparently 'discussion is continuing' on the suitability of the additions. Including *Autumn River*, I have seen virtually no traditional opera in Chinese style where the orchestra had much more than ten players, although there may be fifteen or more for items on modern themes.

It is perfectly true that a large orchestra can retain the feeling of the sound of the traditional music. A more important point to flow from Wei Zhou's remarks goes to the mixture of European and Chinese instruments. In some styles the use of Western instruments has become fully absorbed into the music. One case in point is the Cantonese opera (*Yueju*), where the violin and saxophone were normal parts of the orchestra already in the 1930s and are still so now, although only the violin has been consistently in use throughout the whole period. In other styles Western instruments are sometimes found but it is just as common to hear only Chinese. For example, the Shaoxing opera orchestra generally contains only traditional instruments, but the orchestra of a full dress performance of *Liang Shanbo and Zhu Yingtai* which I attended at the Shanghai Shaoxing Opera Training School on 5 January 1980 consisted of thirteen players, one of whom played the Chinese *dizi* at times and the Western flute at others; there were also two violins, one cello and one double bass as well as the traditional *yueqin*, two *pipa*, *huqin*, *yangqin* or dulcimer, and percussion, in fact quite a substantial representation of European instruments in a traditional Chinese opera. In a Shanghai opera I had seen not long before called *Ai yu hen* (*Love and Hate*), which was based on a twentieth-century theme, the clarinet was used several times, but the vast majority of instruments was traditional.

In my observation, the orchestras of most regional styles include Western instrumentation more often than not, especially the strings, and do so more persistently and in greater numbers for items with contemporary themes than for those with traditional. However, the balance of mixed orchestras usually remains strongly in favour of Chinese instruments. As far as *quyi* forms are concerned, the very small groups make the inclusion of Western instruments difficult. Hou Baolin and several other *quyi* experts told me that accompanying instruments were almost always exclusively Chinese and my own experience corroborates this. The rare exceptions, they said, laughing, were due to 'gang of four' influence.

General discussion in the press on the mixing of cultures in operatic orchestration has been mainly supportive, such as the following remarks:

> Because the 'gang of four' carried out sabotage in theatre reform, there are some comrades who have engendered doubts on the first kind of composition of opera orchestras [i.e. a mix of European and Chinese instruments] and have even advocated doing away with it. This is incorrect. When we perform operas on modern revolutionary themes, to add Western instruments to the opera orchestra has already been proven to be feasible by many years of practice, and it has a future. But only if we take more time, do more research and gradually accumulate experience, can we definitely do it well. Since the overthrow of the 'gang of four', quite a few types of opera have achieved very great successes in the use of this kind of orchestra.[5]

It appears that there is still uncertainty about how to develop the music of the traditional forms of local theatre. Some people are still attracted to the types of innovations that were introduced in the decade of the Cultural Revolution, although of course nobody will say that they favour anything that the gang did. Overall actual practice appears to be greater use of Western instrumentation in regional styles since 1976 than before the Cultural Revolution. Other people, by contrast, are seeking a more or less total return to tradition and are suggesting that whatever the gang did must *ipso facto* be wrong. This last group includes the musicians of the *quyi* forms.

The burden of Wei Zhou's statement, the essence of his third point, is surely that, however one develops the music of Chinese traditional theatre forms, one must at all costs avoid artificial Westernisation by imposing on them badly fitting frameworks such as 'overtures' which are nowadays but rarely heard for traditional operas. It is essential to retain the original atmosphere and nature of each style by choosing appropriate topics and 'creating melodies according to its intrinsic language or libretto rules'. Wei Zhou is calling for that delicate path which allows for originality without distortion. This third point in a sense subsumes the other two on the size and composition of opera orchestras, and is the main one of the three.

To cast a general judgment on whether Wei Zhou's ideal narrow path is being successfully implemented is not possible because the new post-1976 culture is still in its infancy. I have heard operas in the traditional forms composed since 1976 which appeared admirable in feeling and structure. In the *Shaoju Exchange of the Heir-Apparent for a Leopard Cat* (see Chapter 3), the music of which was composed especially for a production first given in mid-October 1979, there were twelve players in the orchestra, the size which Wei requires, and all the instruments were traditional, the Chinese flute *dizi*, the three-stringed *sanxian*, the dulcimer *yangqin*, and clappers and drums. The emotion in the music was more tightly fitted to the action on the stage than was demanded in dynastic times and the composer Gao Zuyin, whom I met after the performance, told me that this was quite deliberate. The singing of the wronged Concubine Li, apart from the fact that the actress had a particularly beautiful voice, created a feeling of great pathos through legato passages dominated by the *dizi*. Although not a nationally famous figure, Gao appears to me to have succeeded in achieving some originality within a firm traditional framework. This is a typical but not universally valid example. A less brilliant one is a northern *Kunqu* scene from *The White Snake*, also mentioned in Chapter 3. There, the use of the cello in the orchestra detracted from the feel of the story. A member of the orchestra told me that its aim was 'to give more bass'. In a sense this is a valid point, but totally against the tradition of *Kunqu*, which does not really need a bass.

There is considerable irony in the fact that the 'gang of four', above all Jiang Qing, should come under attack, at least from some quarters, for having caused China's music to lose its national flavour, especially in the traditional local opera forms. In political and economic terms, after all, China appeared a good deal more nationalistic during the Cultural Revolution days than since the smashing of the 'gang of four', when it seems to be very keen on cultural and economic ties with Western countries, even those affecting its own society. Already in this chapter there has been occasion to mention the increased Western musical influence in China since the death of Mao. In so far as a new type of cultural nationalism has emerged, it appears to be a conservative one which takes its major expression in a hankering after and return to tradition; and directs its spearhead not against foreign powers, let alone those of the West, but against internal enemies.

Music is an essential element of traditional Chinese theatre, just as it is of Western opera. The spoken play, on the other hand, depends on communication through words, not song, so music is not strictly necessary. In China, however, music is a frequent, although certainly not invariable, companion to spoken plays, and is produced mostly by tape but occasionally by an orchestra sitting in the pit. Of course the musicians are heard only at strategic moments. They do not play continuously or compete with the actors speaking on the stage. It is the director of the play, not the composer, who decides whether there should be music, what kind and at what points it should be heard.

166

One Chinese specialist, writing on the practice of music in spoken plays, has observed that to insist on adding it to items with 'very tightly packed' dialogue is bad theatre because 'it makes people feel that the music is superfluous'. On the other hand, pieces where music is particularly effective include 'poetic and fairy-tale dramas, and those with mythical flavour, in fact generally dramas where lyricism is comparatively strong'. There are several functions for music in plays. The basic one is simply to create atmosphere, but others include 'revealing what is going on in the minds of the characters', helping to show 'the changes in the inner feelings of the characters', and 'supplementing inadequacies in things which words cannot express'. A final, more concrete, function is to provide a prologue, entr'actes, or conclusion.[6] Entr'actes may be too Western a notion for traditional operas, but they are not so for an originally foreign form like the spoken play. The nature of the music played must 'be co-ordinated, as an organic component, with the words spoken on the stage, the form, structure, and lights, etc.'.[7]

With the single exception of Cao Yu's *Leiyu* (*Thunderstorm*), a long work the dialogue of which is certainly 'very tightly packed', all plays I have seen in China include some music, especially in the form of entr'actes or prologue. The music does indeed add atmosphere. For instance, in *Save Her* (see Chapter 4), there is a lyrical scene where Li Xiaoxia discusses love with her friend Xu Zhiwei, who is a violinist. The musical accompaniment is a section from the violin concerto *Liang Shanbo and Zhu Yingtai*, a most romantic piece. The tendency is for Western instruments to dominate strongly in that majority of plays on modern or contemporary topics but for more traditional flavour and instruments to emerge in *huaju* on historical or mythical themes.

There has been some press discussion also about the writing of film music. A typical article comes from the pen of Lei Zhenbang, who wrote the musical background for a number of films. His technique is to visit the area where the film takes place and examine thoroughly the folk music and folk dances of that area. This way the music reflects the feeling of the people who dominate the content of the film. Such sensitivity, he argues, is even more important for film than for opera, because 'cinema art requires an even closer approach to the actualities of life than stage performances'.[8]

Lei's secret is to know as much, to feel as great an understanding and love as possible, for the people of the relevant area. One must never lord it over the masses, or regard oneself as a specialist. Lei is here closely following the dictates which Mao put forward in the 'Talks at the Yan'an Forum'.[9] He also graciously acknowledges

> after the showing of the abovementioned films, I received encouragement from the broad masses of audiences and a few comrades, but this was not at all an achievement which I personally made, but credit must go to the undying creation over thousands of years of the broad labouring people.[10]

Lei shows himself throughout to be particularly sensitive to the question of the music of the National Minorities who dominate a number of the films for which he has written music.

Sentiments of this sort appear to find expression in films such as the one about Abing, *Second Springs*, mentioned in the last chapter. Since its hero is a musician, its music can be regarded as important especially since the title music was written by the historical Abing. Solo music for the *erhu* and *pipa*, beautifully played and in a very traditional vein, occupies quite a bit of time in the film, as do duets with Abing's beloved Qinmei singing while he accompanies, the words of the songs being shown in subtitles. Dialogue sections are mainly silent of music, but where the action demands it, accompaniment is by traditional instruments with melodies very much in the national style. One reader of *Cinema for the Masses* summed up the music of the film as its first special feature and 'the crystallisation of Abing's bitter life and artistic creation, having very strong artistic enchantment'.[11] On the other hand, Lei's ideals are not always reality. Apart from opera films and those set in the distant past, most Chinese films use music of the Western idiom and tend to be somewhat imitative of Western film-music, though that does not prevent their being effective. In *After the*

Blue Light Flashed, the music, entirely in the Western idiom, reflects well the grim nature of the film. The music of *Little Flower*, however, is too sentimental for the theme and too strongly dominated by the quavering sounds of the theatre-organ. The national feeling, so important to the Chinese, could have come over much better with Chinese instrumentation. Still, the fact that the music was largely two major themes or leitmotifs, common in Chinese motion pictures as in those of other countries, did contribute to the overall impact of the film.

Music as education

Music helps to create an atmosphere as well as any art form, hence its use in film. It is for the same reason, and the resultant impact on the human mind, that music occupies so important a role in the Chinese education system.

No visitor to the PRC, at almost any time of its existence, can fail to have witnessed demonstrations by school children, even very young ones, playing musical instruments and singing songs. Of course, there is nothing peculiar to China about this phenomenon, yet the lack of self-consciousness of Chinese children and the enjoyment which they appear to derive from performing cannot fail to impress the visitor. To lay charges against the 'gang of four' for having suppressed music in the education system would be quite unfair. I have myself seen numerous enthusiastic displays by children, on both Chinese and Western musical instruments, during the decade of Cultural Revolution from 1966 to 1976. Yet it is quite possible to argue that the particular emphasis on music as part of a child's education has grown still stronger in recent years since the smashing of the 'gang of four'. In previous chapters there was discussion of children's theatre, which meant dramas written specifically for the enjoyment and edification of children. However, we are here concerned with children educated to be active participants in performing, not merely passive onlookers.

On 10 May 1979, Zhang Chengxian, a Deputy Minister for Education, gave an interview to a reporter from the magazine *People's Music*, in which he appealed for a more organised, systematic and consolidated approach to the instruction of music in primary and secondary schools throughout China. He said that the Ministry was preparing a three-stage initiative. First, it proposed to draft an outline for the teaching of music, which would be printed and given to the schools for discussion and implementation. Second, the Ministry would arrange for music teaching material to be edited and written. He claimed that this task had already been given to the Education Bureau of Shanghai City. Third,

> Educational departments and schools must raise
> knowledge, and strengthen leadership towards musical and
> fine arts education. They must foster teachers, improve
> teaching methods and raise the quality of teaching,
> according to the teaching outline.[12]

This final stage also calls for an expansion of extracurricular musical activities of various kinds.

It is worth emphasising that Zhang is talking about systematising and expanding, not beginning. When he made his statement music was already one of only half a dozen or so subjects taught in primary schools all over China; the curriculum included singing, and playing on Chinese or Western instruments, but not normally traditional opera. Already books of songs designed for teaching in schools had been published, not only in Beijing or Shanghai designed for the whole country but in individual provinces as well. In a primary school I visited in Guilin in December 1979 I was shown teaching material which the teachers there had developed themselves. It included detailed information on the Chinese, as well as the staff, systems of notation, the rules of harmonic progression and other material quite advanced for primary school.

Another point to remember *a propos* of Zhang's interview is that the systematisation of the education system in general was in progress at that time. It was a further stage in the process, mentioned in Chapter 2, of tightening discipline and standards in the schools to make up for the ground lost during the decade 1966 to 1976 and to push forward the four modernisations.

So music, like other subjects, can assist in economic and social development and thus carries a propaganda function. If this aspect of theatre for children was obvious when the latter were taking a passive role as onlookers, it is even more so in the case of music when the children are the active participants. Zhang makes this quite clear in another part of the interview he gave. 'Practice proves', he stated, 'that through music teaching and music education activities, one can carry out education in patriotism, internationalism and the revolutionary tradition for the students, and foster their communist morals and behaviour.'

Exactly how this should be done was under fairly wide discussion at the time. As far as the vital area of singing was concerned a series of children's songbooks had already been published since the smashing of the 'gang of four', but with most unoriginal content. There were songs about the four great leaders Mao Zedong, Zhou Enlai, Zhu De and Hua Guofeng; other topics were 'singing the praises of the Party and the motherland, criticism of the "gang of four" by little friends, love of the collective, love of labour, honouring teachers and elders, earnest study, mutual help and respect for discipline'.[13]

Then, in January 1979, a conference was held in Beijing to discuss the creation of children's songs, and individual articles were written on the topic. One of them, acknowledging that such songs must serve proletarian politics, nevertheless demands that 'we must emancipate the mind and break through into forbidden territory'. The content of the songs must, above all, avoid political slogans; the topics and style must be varied, and take special account of the tastes and the age of children. Some of the themes he suggests are not too different from what the 'gang of four' might have advocated or are identical with the immediate post-'gang' period: love of the country, of the people, of labour, and of science, and fostering the revolution tradition in order to promote the unity of the people. He then goes on:

> Children like styles of writing which are in the manner of fairytales, are personified, or rich in fancy or with stories. From flowers, birds, fishes and insects with which children are familiar to the motherland's imposing rivers and mountains, from ordinary everyday life to the vast and

exalted world of politics, all can become suitable material
for songs. We must go deeply into life, become familiar
with life, and seize rich nourishment from it. . . . At
present children's lyrical and descriptive songs are very
few, question and answer songs rich in the characteristics
of folk songs, or children's song and dance tunes in 3/4 or
6/8 time are even rarer. These are all waiting for us to find
time to forge into.[14]

It is noteworthy that the writer here takes up two quite distinct aspects of the writing of children's music and songs. One
is the old question of content. It is true that specifically children's songs from before the Cultural Revolution dealt frequently with fancy and animals. Yet he does break new ground in
that topics of this kind were not considered at all suitable during
the Cultural Revolution. The other aspect is the purely musical
one. He asks songwriters to approach new rhythms and new
styles of music. The triple waltz or minuet rhythm is very rare
indeed, if not unknown, in traditional Chinese music, and even
now, as the writer says, is not very common.

Overall this statement is rather similar in some respects to
what a Western commentator on children's songs might have
said. Despite his genuflection to the revolutionary tradition, the
writer is really calling for a downgrading of ideas reminiscent
of the Cultural Revolution. On the other hand, political content
remains vital; but the less direct politics of Deng Xiaoping, not
the more overt brand of Mao Zedong. The 'emancipation of the
mind' can be interpreted as in the more general discussion of
the topic in Chapter 2.

Indirect political content is evident also in the encouragement
given to children to sing some foreign songs. Five small books
of children's songs published in 1979 as part of the movement
to expand the variety of their content and style include several
from Japan, the United States, Kampuchea and other countries.
Just as interesting is commentary there on musicians, not only
well-known Chinese revolutionary composers like Nie Er, but
also the masters of Europe. The following comments on Schubert, written for children by Liu Jingshu, are worth comparing
with Zhao Hua's 1974 judgment on him (see p. 29):

Owing to petty bourgeois weakness of will, Schubert could escape cruel social realities only through the beautiful life of fantasy. The appearance of this spirit is embodied in his works. When Schubert was alive, his works were very rarely given public performance. An enthusiastic friend held a successful concert for him, but in the same year, 19 November 1829, he bade farewell to the world. Many of his best works were arranged by others after he died, and became famous concert items. This remarkable composer of only thirty-one years left the world of men carrying the unfair treatment given to him by a dark society, but the music he left behind will be an eternal dazzling and brilliant jewel in the treasury of the arts of human kind.[15]

Both Zhao Hua and Liu Jingshu can agree that Schubert was petty bourgeois, but the damning tone of the former could in all other respects hardly be more different from the glowing sentimentality of the latter. It is not too far-fetched to relate this change in value judgment on a composer like Schubert with the spectacular change in attitude towards foreign, and especially Western social values and culture.

Although Liu Jingshu's comments were aimed at children, their content would not have been too different had they been intended for a wider audience. Undoubtedly music remains a means of education and hence an organ of social and political propaganda, not only for children but for the general community as well. The content of the concerts discussed earlier suggests clearly a deliberate attempt to strengthen the less directly but still definitely politicised line of Deng Xiaoping in domestic affairs, and the opening up to the non-socialist world in foreign affairs.

An interesting case-study to illustrate the propaganda aspect of music emerges when the famous Communist martyr Zhang Zhixin, who had been persecuted and killed by the 'gang of four' in 1975 (see Chapter 2), turns out to be a keen and active musician. Three songs of hers, dated 10 October, 6 November and 25 December 1969, were published in the press;[16] all castigated the bad Party leadership of the late 1960s. According to the claims of the Chinese media one of them, entitled 'Shei zhi zui?' ('Whose Crime?'), became quite famous in China. After the revelations in May 1979 of what had happened to Zhang Zhixin, the people pressed for art works about her; one response was a programme broadcast by the Central People's Radio Station, of musical and other works on learning from this heroine. Among its items were performances by some very well known people including two mentioned previously in these pages, the film actor Zhao Dan and the singer Wang Yuzhen, the latter of whom took part in singing Zhang Zhixin's three published songs.

My own spot survey, admittedly not very thorough, carried out at random in December 1979 among some people on the streets, suggested that the claimed fame of Zhang's song had been real but ephemeral. Comments included 'boring political song' and 'yes, I like it very much but cannot sing it'. All respondents were very much aware both of Zhang and her connection with music.

The younger sister of Zhang Zhixin, called Zhang Zhiqin, recalls that they had come from a very musical family and that their father had engaged in musical education work. Before liberation, Zhixin and two of her sisters had formed themselves into a band which was called 'The Three Zhang Sisters'. On one occasion in 1947, they had accepted an invitation to play at a Guomindang gathering in honour of Chiang Kaishek. Zhang Zhiqin claims that the intention was 'through our performance, to express our dissatisfied feelings towards the Guomindang rule'.[17] On the other hand, it is easy to imagine that the followers of the 'gang of four' would have regarded this little incident as an expression of the family's uncertain loyalty to the CCP. Clearly the whole exercise, the association of the Zhang family with music and the content of the martyr's three little songs, is aimed at strengthening hostility to the gang and instilling the new line of Deng Xiaoping and his colleagues into the people through the medium of the arts, and in particular, music.

The type of music used most directly for propaganda purposes, whether in connection with Zhang Zhixin or in schools, is likely to be easy to perform. Probably it will show strong elements both of traditional tunes and instruments but also the influence of the West in terms of rhythm, mood and instrumentation. I have found that one kind of music specifically not taught in ordinary schools is pure traditional operatic music.

In fact, more than other branches of the performing arts music illustrates a dichotomy in contemporary Chinese society: that between growing Western influence and the return of interest in tradition. On the one hand men like Schubert can be admired again, but so can the music of the ancient Sichuan opera. Nationalism might want the tradition kept pure, but modernisation is likely to bring ever greater cultural and musical influence from overseas, especially the West. Already the music of traditional forms has adopted far more from the West than before the Cultural Revolution and foreign songs are broadcast far more over the radio than at that time.

Of course the two types of music can coexist, possibly even indefinitely. But modernisation has a way of swamping traditional cultures, at least in urban regions. The Chinese have a mixed past record in coping with foreign cultural influences. They may well again be able to solve the dichotomy between overseas influence and return to tradition by blending the two together while retaining much that is essentially their own. But their success in so doing will depend on how strong their society remains or becomes, and that in turn depends principally on the success of the four modernisations. They are a critical factor, not only from an economic, but also a cultural, point of view.

7

Bringing performances to fruition

To mount performances on a scale necessary for 1,000,000,000 people is a complex business requiring an enormous amount of organisation and effort. This chapter looks at the processes leading up to the performances and some of the social factors which the performing arts require or produce.

The recruitment and training of actors

The first and most immediate necessity to put on a theatrical performance of any kind is actors and actresses. So we begin by considering how performers are chosen and trained.

There are several ways of entering the acting profession. One is by excelling as an amateur. There are some outstanding examples of people who use this route, such as the heroine in the film *Little Flower*. At amateur festivals, specialist trainers watch out for good performers and choose particularly good ones. But to move from amateur to professional is nevertheless an unreliable path which few successfully traverse.

A much less prestigious route is the traditional one whereby a master adopts a disciple or a father trains his son, or, nowadays, his daughter, outside the control of any school or troupe. For *quyi* performers this is a common way of training, especially in the countryside where more formal methods may be unavailable. The system does not guarantee comprehensive social welfare. However, it is not necessarily easy of access and, like all others in China, it requires that the student secure a formal qualification at the end before he or she can take up a job as a performer.

For actors or actresses of opera, spoken plays, or dance, the master–disciple or father–son system just described is nearly extinct. Several different informants in various parts of China told me: 'there may be individual cases, but essentially this system no longer exists.' However, it is still common for an old or distinguished actor to adopt disciples, even among his own sons or daughters, who are already formally qualified or are attached to a formal training-school or troupe.

A third path into the ranks of performers is training-schools attached to particular troupes. In both Xi'an and Chengdu cultural authorities told me that most or nearly all companies owned their own small training-schools, and this is probably fairly typical. When I visited the Pingju Opera Troupe of China, a national-level body, I learned that it supported its own training-school which had been founded late in 1978. Entry into it is by examination and competition is extremely keen. In 1978 there were 4,000 applicants of whom only 60 were accepted. Training lasts five years and is highly rigorous, including not only the arts of the Pingju opera, but also music, politics and culture. Social welfare conditions are those of formal state-run schools or institutes described below.

Training-schools attached to troupes in the countryside may be much less standardised. Of course there are full-time schools like that of the Pingju Opera Troupe. But many potential actors or actresses continue to attend ordinary village classes and go to a training-school in their spare time. This means that the latter will not necessarily teach the student cultural subjects like reading, writing, arithmetic, history or politics, but illiteracy among actors is avoided all the same. Another result is that the training-school does not always take care of the students' social welfare.

The fourth and last route into the performing profession is also the most prestigious. Though it may not be the broadest in the sense of training the largest number of potential actors and actresses, it is the one about which most material is available

177

and I therefore treat it in the greatest detail. It is the formal state-run theatre school or institute.

There are six central or national-level art institutes in Beijing under the control of the Ministry of Culture. They are (i) the Central Drama Institute, which teaches the skills of the *huaju*, (ii) the Theatre School of China, catering for Beijing Opera, (iii) the Central Film School, (iv) the Central Philharmonic Conservatorium, (v) the Central Dance School, and (vi) the Central Fine Arts Institute. All but the last focus their attention on the performing arts.

It is striking that none of these trains actors for the local opera forms except the second, which deals with only one. Other styles are taught in state-run schools in different cities and provincial capitals. Typical examples are the Sichuan Provincial Sichuan Opera School in its capital Chengdu, which teaches Sichuan opera only, and the Jiangsu Provincial Theatre School in the capital Nanjing, where performers are trained for Beijing opera, *Kunqu*, the opera of Wuxi, Jiangsu's largest city other than Nanjing, the Yangzhou opera, the spoken play, and song and dance. In fact, the bigger provincial institutes may teach a variety of styles, not just one. In addition there are state-run schools at levels lower than provincial, especially municipal.

Formal training-schools for the *quyi* arts are far fewer than for other branches of the performing arts. Although there are formal facilities at regional level in Shanghai and Suzhou it was not until 1978 that a central-level class was set up, not in Beijing, but in Shandong province:

> In July and August we recruited new students from Ji'nan [the capital of Shandong], Qingdao, Taian and three other places and cities. The conditions were that they should be young men and women aged between sixteen and twenty years, all with a cultural level of graduation from junior middle school or above, with regular looks, a good voice and a good physique. We admitted 30 from among nearly 2,000 examinees. On 5 October of the same year [1978], the first national *quyi* class, established in the [Shandong] Arts Institute, formally began classes.[1]

There are several points of interest in this passage. The first is that even this national class is but part of an institute, not one in itself. The others relate to a number of features which I have found to be absolutely typical of formal training institutes in China.

Everywhere competition is extraordinarily keen. The acting profession is certainly no longer one to enter as a last resort. In 1978 the Shanghai Conservatorium of Music took in 300 out of 7,000 candidates, while the Central Drama Institute admitted 30 out of 6,000 applicants. Again, admission is now everywhere by examination. This is the same with all institutes of post-junior secondary level in China. Third, good looks, voice and physique are everywhere demanded. This is not surprising in view of the nature and work of the acting profession.

There are also points which may not be totally consistent. Thus the *quyi* class appears to be senior secondary and tertiary level. This and the ages of the students are also the same at the Theatre School of China, but the leadership of the Central Drama Institute told me in January 1980 that the level was tertiary, that most students had finished secondary school when they entered, and that their age was about eighteen. Institutes of lower levels, that is province, country, etc., are generally equivalent to secondary schools.

There are two aspects which are not mentioned in the quote on the *quyi* class but are nevertheless important. One is health, the other, politics. Those schools I have visited are specific that a student in poor health is unlikely to make the grade as an actor and should not be admitted. As for political commitment, this appears to have declined in importance since the 'gang of four' days. No longer is it absolutely central. 'Political level counts', I was told in one institute, 'but only in the sense that an outright reactionary cannot get in. If a student makes a good account of himself at the lower level, then it's all right.'

There appears still to be a definite bias in favour of men over women. In the Central Drama Institute and Sichuan Provincial Sichuan Opera School I was told of a quota by which male students outnumber female by two to one. The rationale in both cases is that plays and operas require more men performers than women. Even in a major *Yueju* (Shaoxing opera) school in

179

Shanghai, the ratio of students at the time of my visit in January 1980 was twenty-six to fifteen in favour of boys. The reason for the discrepancy in this case was the desire to build up a supply of actors for the male roles. In the past all parts in the Shaoxing opera were played by women. Even today this custom persists to a certain extent, but appears to be declining.

In Chinese dramas and plays it is true that male roles tend to outnumber female. This is especially so because of the emphasis on dramas about rebellion and military matters. Even those which feature women, such as *Women Generals of the Yang Family*, tend to include overall more men in the cast than women, if the minor parts are taken into account. The likelihood therefore of radical change in favour of admitting girls and boys into drama schools on the basis of absolute equality seems remote.

Whether male or female, students generally persist to the end of the course once they have gained admission. Retention rates are high. Not long after they enter, students will go through a test to ensure their suitability for acting. But even if they do not come off well, they can be transferred to another type of activity, such as costume design and maintenance or playing a musical instrument. Only if they have no aptitude is alternative education or employment found for them.

Social welfare practices in general follow those of other state-run institutes in China, which of course includes training-schools attached to state troupes. Students live on the spot, with about seven or eight to a room. In the Central Drama Institute they sleep five to a very large room, but this is certainly well above average. Tuition and medical services are free in all theatre schools. There are vacations both in summer and winter, normally four weeks in summer and three in winter, but these periods can be somewhat less in particularly demanding schools. In addition Sundays and national holidays are free. Living expenses are subjected to a means test. At the Central Drama Institute I was told that in fact 70 per cent of students are given money. The standard rate is 16 *yuan* per month which covers various kinds of expenses, but principally food. At the Shaoxing Opera School in Shanghai and Sichuan Provincial Sichuan Opera School, I learned that clothing, shoes and food were provided entirely without charge there. Free food, however, is not the norm in institutes or drama schools in China.

The length of time of a course varies according to the art being learned. The *quyi* class in Shandong was planned to be three years and Hou Baolin told me this was a normal period. On the other hand, the course at the Central Drama School to learn *huaju* acting or directing is four years, at the Shaoxing Opera School in Shanghai and Sichuan Opera School five years, and at the Jiangsu Provincial Theatre School, seven years for Beijing opera or *Kunqu* actors. These two styles appear to demand the lengthiest and toughest training. The Theatre School of China takes up to eight years fully to train a performer of the Beijing opera.

The courses themselves include a considerable amount of general cultural material. This is to ensure that actors do not grow up illiterate as they used to in the past. The planned non-specialist course for the *quyi* class in Shandong may again be cited because it is absolutely typical. There are two parts. The first is 'political classes', which include 'the history of the CCP, philosophy and political economy', all of which aims 'to give the students a basic knowledge of Marxism-Leninism, a warm love for the Party and socialism and a proper attitude towards study'. The second part is called 'basic classes on culture' and it covers general Chinese literature right from the beginning to the present, as well as the history of China.[2]

The other sections of the course are the professional ones, and they will of course depend entirely on what the institute is designed to teach. At the Shanghai Conservatorium of Music there are national music, orchestral and vocal departments, and students can learn to play both Chinese or Western instruments. At the Central Drama School there are four departments, one each for performing, directing, theatre literature, and stage arts. Each student majors in one of them but the institute encourages them to integrate their study in all four. Theatre literature includes the history of both Chinese and foreign drama, with emphasis on the former, while stage arts include painting, scenery design, and the theory of art. At the Theatre School of China, one-third of the time is devoted to general knowledge, two-thirds to basic singing, acrobatics and other skills of the

Beijing opera, as well as to learning and mastering specific roles in particular operas.

Students live highly regulated lives at theatre institutes, as they do in those of other kinds. A typical timetable includes rising at 6.30, doing exercises, both general and acting, breakfast at 8.15, followed by four classes of forty-five minutes each with fifteen-minute breaks in between. After lunch at 12.00, they rest till 2.15, and then go for further classes or rehearsals. Dinner is at 6.00 and the evening is free, but private study is the commonest activity. Lights out is at 10.00.

One of the factors which makes so regular a timetable possible is that in China staff–student ratios tend to be high. This is especially the case in theatre institutes. For instance, in the Sichuan Provincial Sichuan Opera School in January 1980 there were 75 teachers for only 145 students. The extraordinarily demanding skills of the Beijing opera, or indeed other performing arts, requires a great deal of private instruction.

There is a close relationship between students and teachers, who even take an active interest in the personal lives of those under their tutelage. They strongly discourage any sign of romance between students. In the Shaoxing Opera School in Shanghai the leadership considers that late marriage is desirable, that is after thirty, because 'the arts require a spirit of self-sacrifice', and it is probably typical.

The close relationship between staff and students also allows for intensive 'education' for delinquents. In contrast with the pre-liberation period, there is no corporal punishment of any kind. Really serious cases will be expelled, but these are rare in the extreme.

The only really important way to leave training centres is through graduation. After that event, the newly qualified actor, director, costume designer, musician, etc., is assigned a job. The process is for the leadership of the relevant state-run institute or school to consult the wishes of the graduate. Meanwhile the State Planning Committee of the State Council draws up a general plan, and responsible cadres of the Ministries of Culture and Education visit the institutes. In the light of state needs, and the wishes and capacity of each individual, they discuss with the leadership where to send each graduate and in what role.

Although the list of national arts institutes includes one for cinema, so that film actors, actresses and directors are being trained, one area where demand has greatly outstripped supply is cinema projectionists. On 14 September 1979 a forum in Beijing revealed quite serious problems in screening techniques and management in the city and its surrounding countryside, especially in the training of projectionists. One delegate bemoaned that although 'in the last few years the development of cinema screening units has not been slow, nobody has taken care of the training and raising of the skills of projectionists. There are no assessable criteria in the technical standards of projectionists', he went on, 'so that it is quite enough to check the projectionist's permit', which may in fact prove nothing of his capacities. Other delegates, broaching on the social side of the projectionists' training and hence competence, noted with dissatisfaction that 'internal reference films', that is those for restricted audiences only, 'are screened confusedly everywhere'; and that there was no uniformity in the levels of 'ideology, education and skills'. The forum called upon the leadership of cultural departments everywhere to take more notice of projectionists and help improve their training and work.[3]

By way of conclusion to this material on the bringing up of the new generation of the performing profession and its assistants, it may be interposed that if there are serious deficiencies in the preparation of projectionists, there is one type of training which conspicuously does *not* take place, either at the Theatre School of China or, as far as I know, any other training centre of traditional Chinese opera. This is that required to bring up a new generation of male *dan*, that is men who play female roles. Before liberation most troupes were unmixed, mainly exclusively male, and a special art attached to men's acting the parts of women. The only male *dan* left now are those of the old generation, the most famous being the Beijing opera actor Zhang Junqiu, who began performing again in October 1978 as part of the rehabilitation of old actors and of the reputations of dead ones (see Chapter 2). He told me, when I met him in

January 1980, that in 1951 Zhou Enlai had said: 'up to Zhang the male *dan*, and that's the end.' Except Zhang himself and his wife, who told me they regarded the passing of this art as a great pity, none of the many Chinese with whom I have discussed the matter diagrees with present policy,. which is to encourage the present male *dan*, but not to train any more. He Jingzhi, Deputy Minister of Culture, gave me three reasons for the present view. First, 'People act better if portraying those of their own sex'; second, it is unnatural for men to play the roles of women; and third, the custom of the male *dan* arose in a feudal society and reflects conditions no longer applicable to China.

It is true that the recruitment of the little boys who became the *dan* in the past was carried out in a cruel way which nobody would wish to persist.[4] But all three of He's arguments can be countered. It is, after all, possible to train under good conditions; it may be that some actors perform just as well, if not better, when playing the parts of women; and it is striking that the stricture of unnaturalness does not prevent the training of some actresses to portray men. But whatever the rights and wrongs of the matter, the likelihood is for the art of the male *dan* to die out completely in the People's Republic of China by the end of this century.

The performing profession

One brand of performing art faces extinction; acting companies as a whole are recovering from the Cultural Revolution, as explained in Chapter 3. The troupes fall into two categories: state-run and 'collectively owned' (*jiti suoyouzhi*). The former predominate in the cities, the latter in the countryside. Overall more than 60 per cent of all China's theatre troupes are 'collectively owned', while all its cinema studios are state bodies. The collectively owned companies generally perform only the traditional forms such as regional theatre and not the spoken play, *geju*, dance-drama or ballet.

Those theatre or cinema actors and directors who belong to state-run troupes come under the heading of 'state cadres' and this gives them a more than usually large influence in society and favourable working conditions. All 'literature and art workers' in state organisations are classified into sixteen grades and the size of their salaries depends upon where they belong in the scale. As of January 1980, when He Jingzhi and others explained the system to me, those of the first grade get just over RMB 330 *yuan*, of the second just under 300 *yuan*, and the lowest or sixteenth just over 40 *yuan*, all figures being monthly salaries. Only the most famous actors of all are in the first grade. Zhang Junqiu told me that he earned just over 330 *yuan* per month. The highest paid *geju* performers are in the second grade, including Guo Lanying. Provincial actors belong to lower flights. In September 1978 Zhejiang cultural authorities told me that the most famous actor in the province was the *Shaoju* actor Zhou Quanying, at that time sixty-six years old, who was paid about 240 *yuan*. In Hubei also at about that time the highest paid actor was on the same salary and was in the third grade. The sixteenth-grade artists are mainly students who have just graduated and begun work. Factors determining promotion from one grade to another include experience, talent, achievement, seniority, success, and popularity with the masses. Situ Huimin told me that, at least for film performers, there was 'collective discussion' on who should belong to which grade, but the final decision required approval by the leadership.

He said also that the average salary among film performers was between 70 and 80 *yuan* per month, and of directors about 100. Since there are only eighteen film studios in China it is reasonable to determine a mean. It is more difficult to ascertain averages among theatre personnel because of the large number throughout China. He Jingzhi did inform me, however, of his belief that in general performers of the traditional forms, because of the greater training necessary, earned a higher average salary than those of the spoken play, who in turn were on average better off than those of the dance-drama.

To give some scale of comparison for these figures it may be added that the salaries of doctors under state awards in China varies from a maximum of 360 *yuan* per month to a minimum of about 50. Secondary school teachers range from a minimum of 40 *yuan* to a maximum of about 150. In a big factory the technicians and other highly skilled people will rarely earn more than 200 *yuan* per month, and the minimum for young apprentice workers is 30. Average salaries for workers are in the order of 60 to 70 *yuan*. In January 1980 the exchange rate made three Chinese *yuan* approximately equal to two US dollars. All this means that actors and other 'literature and art workers' in state-run organisations are paid as professionals a little lower but of a similar order to doctors. They are a little better off than teachers or workers, and include a more pronounced elite at the higher end. It hardly needs adding that they are much richer than the peasantry, but earn incomparably less than counterparts in developed Western countries. Actually, the comparisons with the other urban Chinese groups are much the most meaningful of those offered here.

One group not included in the sixteen 'literature and art' grades, because they are not formal professionals, is the children. The reader will recall from Chapter 3's discussion of *Qin Xianglian* that children played the parts of the heroine's son and daughter in that opera. Actually normal practice for operas, plays and dance-dramas is for women to play the parts of children, especially if the roles are substantial, such as in the play *Indigo Flower* noted in Chapter 4. On the other hand in the more realistic medium of the motion picture children often need to play quite large and important, even highly emotional parts. Prime examples are *After the Blue Light Flashed* and *Ah! Cradle* (see Chapter 5). According to Ding Qiao, Deputy Director of the Cinema Bureau in the Central Ministry of Culture, film directors go round kindergartens or schools seeking child performers for particular films. Both the child and the parents must agree to the former's participation in this film, 'and mother often comes to rehearsals'. The child actor or actress, not the parents, receives a set sum of money the size of which will depend on a number of circumstances, including how important the role is, and how much rehearsal is necessary.

As is apparent from the treatment of child performers, the national awards cover not only salaries but a reasonably well developed system of social welfare. It includes free medical services, labour insurance and, for pregnant women, fifty-six days off on full pay for the birth of a child. These factors of social welfare apply to all workers and professional groups in China.

Also broadly consistent with other urban groups is the age of retirement, 55 for women, and 60 for men. However, it is not compulsory and in fact many actors work on long after these ages. Zhang Junqiu, who was already past retiring age when I met him in January 1980, told me that he not only still performs, but also teaches, makes records, arranges material, and administers. Many old actors research or provide data to those studying theatre history. I encountered serious resentment against the 'gang of four' on this as on so many other scores. 'They forced us to leave the stage and waste our talents' was a virtually universal complaint from older actors I met in China. It is undoubtedly true that in the period 1966–76 actors of banned forms, like traditional opera and *geju*, and all considered reactionary, were prevented from performing, whatever their age. So such people naturally wish to make up for lost time as best they may. Retirement is not their first aim in life.

Those who do retire continue to receive all their salary if they joined the ranks of 'revolutionary theatre workers' in 1938 or before, and about four-fifths if at the time of liberation or before. Otherwise some 70 per cent of their salary persists as superannuation.

In theory those performers and directors still on the job work eight hours a day for six days a week. I was told by members of the *Zhongguo Pingju yuan* (Pingju Troupe of China) in Beijing that a normal day included an hour's throat training from 8–9 a.m., rehearsals from 9–12 and again for three hours in the afternoon and sometimes in the evening as well. If there is a performance in the evening, then everyone rests in the afternoon.

The fact stresses the point that the theatre profession has to be flexible in its hours of daily work. Sometimes it may be more than eight, sometimes less. If the troupe is on tour or learning a new play against a strict deadline for imminent performance, it may need to work harder than usual. At other times schedules may be rather loose. These comments apply even more to film workers than to those in theatre. The Shanghai Film Studio leadership, for instance, told me in October 1978 that it employed about 150 performers, about 30 directors, and 14 permanent script-writers, as well as technicians, designers, administrators, and others, in all 1,700 people. The actors, actresses and directors work most intensely when a particular film involving them is being rehearsed or shot. This could be well in excess of ten hours per day. On the other hand, there may be long periods when they are not taking a direct part in the manufacture of a film, and in that case they 'go into society with a letter of introduction to learn about how the people live' in order to gain ideas and experience for the general improvement of their work and future films.

The flexibility of working times clearly applies also to holidays. Like other urban groups, 'literature and art workers' get Sundays and national holidays off, but no annual vacation. However, except for those in the cinema, other people's holiday periods are precisely when the services of theatrical entertainers are most necessary. The National Day holiday, 1–3 October, which celebrates the founding of the People's Republic, the Spring Festival, or lunar new year, and May Day, are the days for the year's main theatrical highlights. The system is to make up for work on such days by changing the holidays to other more appropriate periods, in which case there is loading or similar compensation.

The major point about the salaries and social welfare of 'literature and art workers' in state-run troupes or studios is that, since they come under national award, they are decided by a government rule and must be uniform throughout the whole country. This is not the case, however, with the troupes of the second category, those which are 'collectively owned'. As their name implies, they simply share out the income from their work among their members.

The 'collectively owned' troupes are those left over from before liberation which the government did not take over during the process of nationalisation of theatre troupes in 1956. Before the Cultural Revolution, they included not only most of the rural or small-city companies but also a few of the most famous in China. It was well known in Beijing at that time that some of the big stars like Ma Lianliang and Zhou Xinfang drew incomes well above 1,000 *yuan* per month, far higher than any state leader including Mao Zedong himself. Zhang Junqiu told me that he had secured about 1,500 *yuan* per month at that time. There were those less fortunate, however. In 1956, a spate of articles appeared in *Xiju bao (Theatre News)* and other journals complaining of desperate conditions among certain actors.[5] The government reacted by injecting subsidies into those troupes which could not ensure a reasonable living for their members.

During the Cultural Revolution, the collectively owned troupes were abolished altogether, and their members assigned to different jobs. From the viewpoint of the radical line at that time, collectively owned troups could be regarded as anti-socialist, very unegalitarian, and a feudal remnant. Just as important was the fact that they were very difficult to control and the content of the dramas they performed was not always in accordance with what the government of the time required. If they had done well on traditional operas, but fallen on bad times when forced to perform exclusively those with modern and revolutionary content, they were a living proof of the impracticability of Jiang Qing's ideas on theatre.

With the fall of Jiang and the 'gang of four' in October 1976, the problem of what to do about collectively owned troupes became a pressing one, which He Jingzhi told me had been and was being given high priority. He divided the former members into four categories. The first is simply those who have gone back into revived collectively owned troupes, which remain large in number in small cities and the countryside, but not elsewhere. The second category is those who have been reassigned to state-run troupes. The third is those old actors who may be better off teaching, researching, or providing material for study undertaken by others. This last is a singularly important point because in the old days actors were a lowly class in society and their art similarly eschewed by most educated people, so research on drama outside the biggest cities was limited. Although much work was done on the popular theatre after liberation through using 'old artists', they can still provide an immense amount of oral information and insight which will be lost forever if not quickly collected. He Jingzhi's fourth category of actors in former collectively owned troupes is those people 'whose problems are still unsolved', that is, on whom no decision has yet been reached.

It follows from this material on the four categories that the number of collectively owned troupes, though still substantial, is very much smaller than before the Cultural Revolution, but that it is quite deliberate government policy to revive at least some of them.

A few of their features remain unchanged since before 1966. Incomes still vary enormously. Probably the immensely large salaries of people like Ma Lianliang are a thing of the past. Yet some famous members of the collectively owned troupes earn a good deal more than first-grade members of state-run companies. At the other end of the scale, the subsidies persist, according to He Jingzhi provided by provincial government agencies. But, many performers certainly receive incomes rather lower than the 40 *yuan* per month minimum of their state counterparts. I heard that in parts of Zhejiang, a rich province, some troupes average only 30 *yuan* as monthly income for their performers.

Welfare is also much less secure in the collectively owned troupes and depends upon local conditions and how the company as a whole distributes its income. There is no guaranteed free medical service or insurance, and no set retirement age. Actresses who give birth should be given fifty-six days off on full pay at the expense of their rural brigade, but there is no certainty. General guarantees are still provided by state subsidy in desperate cases, so that no performers will starve or suffer too seriously, but the system is much looser than for state 'literature and art workers'; it consequently provides much less security and is more open to abuse from dishonest troupe leaders.

When I talked with him, He Jingzhi said he did not think the welfare problems in the collectively owned troupes were currently too serious. He was more concerned with another question which goes back to before the Cultural Revolution, namely that of the content of the dramas they perform. Ironically, the worry is now not that the operas will be revisionist, but will reflect influence from the 'gang of four'. One might have expected that, having been abolished during the Cultural Revolution, these troupes would be the last place to find 'gang' remnants. Possibly 'influence from the "gang of four" ' covers anything hostile to or reluctant about the current government line.

Just as before the Cultural Revolution, the government needs and wants the support of performers of all kinds because it knows they are influential. The logical follow-on is to enquire about the social status of performers. This becomes all the more interesting in the light of the desperately low position which they suffered before liberation, even though it did improve radically after 1949.

Unfortunately it is not possible to undertake a complete social survey in China. Printed material invariably stresses the mutual appreciation and help between the Party, government and people on the one hand, and actors on the other, and the consequent good social status of the latter. Of course one needs to exclude the period of the 'gang of four' from these observations. The following statement, made during a speech on 24 May 1979 by one of China's Deputy Ministers of Culture, applies to one group of actors only but is nevertheless absolutely typical:

In the old society, *quyi* was a branch of the arts which suffered total discrimination. . . . Even though the standard of quite a few *quyi* artists was high, their social status was low, their income small and their livelihood poor. The treatment they received at that time was very unjust. After liberation, the emancipation of quite a few *quyi* artists was extremely intense, they felt valued by the Party and the people's government, their social status rose and they became glorious literature and arts fighters serving the people. . . . When Lin Biao and the 'gang of four' were on the rampage, quite a few *quyi* workers also did well [by opposing them]. In the struggle to expose the 'gang of four', the *quyi* battalions have given rein to their special artistic strengths . . . have expressed their scorn and hatred for the 'gang of four', have fully exercised the function of pioneers and given play to dagger-sharp artistic effectiveness, for which they have been commended by the broad masses.[6]

My own mini-survey among ordinary people, government cadres and actors and actresses themselves, that is, asking the question how they view the social status of performers, has produced three main answers. These are: first, 'in our country everybody has the same status, actors are neither lower nor higher than anybody else'; second, actors are state cadres, and they have representatives in the National People's Congress; if anything they are even higher than workers and get more money; and third, performers vary in status, of all groups film workers are the highest because they wield the greatest influence.

The sort of touchstone of social status that comes through answers of this kind is interesting. Prestige appears to derive from being a state cadre, access to the National People's Congress, earning a good salary, and, above all, the ability to influence people. There are doubtless numerous other factors which might unconsciously help determine an individual's perception of a group's status in society. One which might have been omitted by those with whom I spoke for reasons of propriety is Party membership.

I cannot possibly guarantee that my random, but mainly urban, sample was typical. It is, however, striking that not a single respondent showed any sign of the old view that actors should be regarded as a lowly and despised class. The days when such a view prevailed are indubitably gone, probably for ever.

The statement that there are no differences in social status between groups may result from a past official doctrine. The myth of equality is found in many countries, not merely China, and is belied by reality in all of them. The view that performers are higher in society than workers can apply only to those in the state-run troupes and reflects ignorance of the existence of the collectively owned.

The most striking of the three responses is the one which claims that one can no longer regard performers as a single group. They are in fact many groups, some with higher education, income and influence than others. It makes sense to me that film performers should rank highest. They are the most famous and influential because their art reaches the largest audience. They are also the smallest of the major acting groups and, perhaps more important, the most remote. There is no tradition which dictates contempt for film performers but only admiration for their glamour and fame.

A question which cannot fail to arise in considering those performers at the top of the tree is to what extent they form an elite from a property as well as status point of view. It is not possible to answer this question fully because information cannot be gathered systematically. I have heard that at least some performers live in great luxury. However, I have visited two famous performers in their homes. One of them is Zhang Junqiu, the best known of the old-style male *dan* of the Beijing opera, and the other is Chen Shufang, certainly the most famous actress in Sichuan and distinguished by being one of those members of the National People's Congress who, in the eyes of some people at least, raise the social status of actors as a profession. Both Zhang and Chen live comfortably in simply furnished flats, but neither in anything that could be remotely described as luxury. Chen's is in the block of flats in Chengdu which houses the members and their families for her particular unit, the Sichuan Provincial Sichuan Opera Company. She does not give the impression of living in any way above the other members of her troupe.

At the other end of the profession, probably the lowest status of the major performing groups are the members of not very successful collectively owned troupes. They are certainly the poorest, least influential and least famous. It is not their members who belong to the National People's Congress. If there is any survival of the feudal contempt for actors, it will apply to those in this category more than any others. On the other hand, their status may be more appropriately seen alongside those of the peasants and lower ranks of workers, teachers and other rural or small-town people who live around them; and may not come off too badly from the comparison.

Theatres, theatre-going, audiences

Apart from actors and the 'literature and art workers' who help or guide them, the other essential ingredient of theatre is a venue.

In the countryside the problem is often solved by simply using any free space, or putting up a temporary stage, just as in the past. Open-air performances remain common there. As a matter of fact, the music of popular regional opera was originally designed primarily to be played in the open, hence its percussive nature, and some people, including the great Lu Xun, have considered it far more appropriate and charming there than in a theatre.[7] The major drawback is susceptibility to the weather which in China is frequently inclement, making it impossible to predict with certainty when a comfortable performance will take place. So rural clubs have come to be provided with indoor theatres, complete with stages.

In the cities by far the most important venue is a theatre.[8] Street drama does exist but it is rare nowadays except on special occasions. The nature of theatres has changed utterly since liberation. Whereas before they were also teahouses, now their function is solely to make dramatic performances possible.

The interior structure is very similar to a Western cinema, and many alternate between films and opera, plays or acrobatics. The seats are set out in tiered rows, and the stage faces the seats directly so that the audience sits on one side of the stage only. This point is worth making for two reasons. One is the contrast with the past, when to sit around the stage on three sides was the normal practice. The other is the lack of experimentation in China as regards interior theatre and stage structure. There is no such thing as a round stage, for instance. Considering that China was formerly among the most inventive countries in the world in this area, it seems to me a pity that its theatre architects are not more daring. Apart from *quyi*, the only variation I have seen in the interior structure of a Chinese theatre is in the Yisu Theatre in Xi'an. There, the gallery lies not only opposite the stage but at right angles to it on both sides, similar but not identical to seating the audience on three sides of the stage. However, this theatre was built in 1912, and is thus representative of old-style theatre architecture.

Contemporary theatres vary in size and comfort, if not in structure. Some contain both a gallery and stalls, but the majority the latter only, especially in local cinemas. In very few, except the newest and grandest, are the seats padded. There is in some larger theatres a special room with comfortable chairs to usher particularly important or high-ranking patrons during the interval, should there be one.

A branch of the performing arts with particular theatre needs and possibilities is the *quyi*. Items are short, so individual people may wish to attend for a short time only, not necessarily a whole evening. Before the Cultural Revolution there was a *quyi* theatre in Beijing where one went in or out at any time and paid according to the length of time one stayed, but it is no longer used in this way. There is such a theatre in Tianjin and there may be others in other cities, but not very many. Hou Baolin told me that *quyi* performers do not like this system because it means there is a constant shuffling in and out among the audience. They prefer the audience to concentrate for a whole evening.

Another characteristic of *quyi* is the low number of performers at any one time, so a smaller than usual stage is preferable. Special theatres are often set aside for *quyi* for this reason.

Quyi entertainment is clearly more feasible with a simple stage or none at all than other theatrical forms, because of its small scale. For this reason the notion of the teahouse-theatre has survived for *quyi* where it has died for operas and plays. Hou Baolin told me that in small towns and villages in Jiangsu and Zhejiang, the two rich provinces of the Yangzi Valley, it was still common to find teahouses where *quyi* performances regularly take place.

On 28 January 1980 I went to a performance in a small teahouse-theatre in a Chengdu backstreet. The first of its kind to function in the city since well before the Cultural Revolution, it had recommenced performances on 12 December 1979. There was a small curtainless platform upon which the five performers sat, to the right and left of which were billboards showing respectively the day's and the morrow's programmes. The audience sat on comfortable bamboo chairs in rows, and faced the mini-stage from any side except the rear. The chairs were interspersed by tables or stools for the teabowls which were regularly replenished by a young man with a kettle of boiling water which he poured out with singular aplomb.

The teahouse-theatre is returning not only in southern but also northern China. An article in the *Jilin Daily* recorded with approval that a teahouse with 120 seats had been set up in a small town in Jilin province, in China's northeast, at the end of September 1977. In the daytime tea is sold there, and in the evening *quyi* performances given in addition. The reporter describing this establishment continues:

> The responsible people of the *quyi* theatre (*shuchang*) told us that, every evening after 6 o'clock, the teahouse is filled to capacity. If it's the peasants' free period or the time for handing over grain to the state after autumn, then the peasants and herdsmen from round about all like to come here to listen to *quyi* performances. The theatre is always absolutely full with no empty seats. By the time the teahouse had been open one year, it had already received over 10,000 people as audience and netted a profit of over 1,000 *yuan*.[9]

The reporter's and the apparent mass enthusiasm for this type of institution opens the possibility of further revival of the traditional teahouse-theatre, at least in rural Jilin.

Having settled the general question of venue, the next stage is to co-ordinate the troupe with the theatre. There are two aspects to the problem. One is to determine what drama company will perform on which day in what theatre in the area of the troupe's normal residence, and the other is to reach the same decisions for a company on tour.

It is the aim of major companies to own their own theatre. Apart from the prestige, this saves them the necessity of arranging where they must perform and they can accustom themselves to consistent vagaries. One troupe I visited in Beijing was rather sore at having lost its theatre some time earlier and was making plans for its recovery. However, only a very few troupes are in the fortunate position of access to their own special theatre.

The vast majority must negotiate with the Bureau of Culture in their own particular area. A theatre may be owned by one of a number of different organisations and the relevant one must approve its theatre's use. But it is the Bureau of Culture which carries out the actual work of co-ordinating the timetables of the various troupes and theatres. The Bureaux are local subsidiaries of the Ministry of Culture.

There is also a Performance Company in some provinces, subordinate to the Ministry, and it is this which deals with the co-ordination of troupes on tour. Beginning in 1980, when the pre-Cultural Revolution system was restored, there is a central meeting each year which determines the general layout of which groups will go on tour to which city. Contracts are drawn up to settle the dates and number of the company's performances. It is also possible for any troupe to negotiate with a provincial Performance Company to visit any area within its control, provided that such a tour does not conflict with the general plan already worked out. Agreements reached, either as a result of the central plan or individual negotiations, may include reference to which unit will receive what proportion of the takings. The details depend on a variety of factors, such as who has issued the invitation to tour in the first place.

The circulation of films is somewhat simpler than of operas, plays or *quyi* items, because a motion picture needs no performers once the shooting is complete. A state Distribution Company makes the arrangements. It sends copies of each film to provincial Distribution Companies which ensure its circulation to the various cinemas in the relevant province. In general, the Distribution Companies receive half the takings, the cinemas the other half.

When the timetabling arrangements have been made, it becomes necessary to inform the people what is on show where, either currently or in the near future. There are two main ways. One is the newspaper. Cinema, opera, plays, all are given together. The advertisement states when and where the item will take place and sometimes when the sale of tickets begins. If tickets are already sold out the character *man* (full) is added.

197

National newspapers do not generally carry information on performance timetables so theatre- and cinema-goers buy local dailies.

Provincial newspapers give details of the provincial capital only, not the other cities. Many towns, let alone the rural areas, do not run to their own newspaper. Even in big cities it is not always convenient to buy the paper. For these reasons there are also advertisements for cinema or drama attractions displayed in the streets. They can be found everywhere in China, not only at the theatres themselves, but stuck on special billboards, in long glass-cased rows or in any free space. It thus becomes easy for the masses to find out what is going on.

Theatre performances usually take place in the evening, almost invariably beginning at 7.00 or 7.15 in the colder months or a little later in the warmer; matinées generally start at 2.00. The times of cinema shows, on the other hand, may vary enormously. It is not at all uncommon for the first session of the day to begin at 7.00 a.m. or even earlier, and to be followed by six or seven, with the final one commencing at 10.00 or later still. Cinemas are on the whole structurally small by Western standards but the Chinese compensate through a large number of daily sessions.

Plays and full-length operas generally last for about three hours, and in my experience it is completely unpredictable whether there is an interval or not. This means that 10.00 or a little after is a standard conclusion time. Another common practice is to give several short operas, scenes from longer works, together in one evening. This was the normal method of presentation in the heyday of the Beijing opera in nineteenth-century Beijing and many other times and places in China. Cinema shows run for about two hours and do not include an interval except if the film is an enormously long one in two parts.

Whether for shorter or longer performances, with or without interval, capacity audiences are, in my experience, a completely normal phenomenon in China. Good shows tend to be booked out or nearly so. On the other hand, the greater variety which has been so strong a theme in the 'new period' of Hua Guofeng has brought with it many run-of-the-mill items which do not necessarily exercise particularly great powers of attraction. One Shanghai opera I attended in Shanghai in January 1980 played to a more than half empty house and this is not at all uncommon.

In Western countries, where television viewing is almost universal, films screen to nearly empty cinemas more often than to full houses. In China the people are experiencing the excitement of a reviving and rapidly expanding film industry, so demand still outstrips supply far more and tickets are frequently unobtainable. Yet it would be quite wrong to suppose that all is well for the film distribution companies. In Beijing early in 1980 a new popular newspaper complained of 'blindness' in their operations. One colour film which was originally planned to run for eleven days in seventeen cinemas 'was in fact screened only once'; a coloured Sichuan opera film which was to have been shown for fifteen days in fifteen cinemas 'did not sell out for even a single session'; a third item lost its distribution department over RMB 20,000 *yuan* through poor attendances. The author's suggestion to solve the problem was as follows:

> Before the Cultural Revolution, Beijing's cinemas, theatres and clubs were divided into first and second grades, news cinemas and children's cinemas, so one looked at the standard of equipment and other circumstances and determined the price according to quality. Now, because there is no distinction into grades, specialist cinemas 'cannot eat enough', while documentary and scientific and educational films have no solid position for screening; this makes for a great deal of copy waste and dissatisfies the masses. To solve this problem it is absolutely necessary to set up specialist companies and implement unified management.[10]

The clear implication that one ought to restore the grading of pre-1966 days is in accordance with the elitist trends in other areas of society.

The failure to sell out in some cases is due, at least in part, to the expansion of the system whereby individuals buy theatre or cinema tickets over the counter. This point might appear too obvious to make except that the method of sale differed under the 'gang of four'. At that time block booking was more prevalent than at present. Roger Howard, a foreign observer of the Chinese performing arts at that time, writes that tickets for seats in Beijing theatres 'are supplied first to factories through the trade unions and then to other organizations, offices, schools and universities. Only rarely are any tickets kept back for sale at the box office.'[11] Informants in various parts of China told me in January 1980 that in most places individual ticket-buying had been a good deal commoner than the word 'rarely' would suggest. However, according to them the first sentence of the statement applied universally throughout the country and the people particularly resented the fact that it was the local Bureau of Culture, not the buying organisation, which determined the allocation of block tickets.

After the accession of the new leadership, it was soon pointed out that the system carried an implication: that people had gone to the theatre because they felt they ought to, not because they wanted to. Beijing was the first to change the method of ticket sale:

> Not long ago the Ministry of Culture of the State Council . . . decided, in common with the Beijing Municipal Committee, that from 19 December last year [1977], all cinemas and theatres in Beijing City should abolish the so-called 'organised distribution' method of selling tickets; and should uniformly implement public ticket sales at the doors. . . . To implement the public sale of tickets has been a first step towards solving the problems of the city's people's going to the theatre and the masses of the capital have shown strong and enthusiastic welcome.[12]

Other cities and places followed Beijing's example. By January 1980 most ticket purchase everywhere was by individuals, though block booking, as determined by the buyer, had by no means disappeared.

However sold, the price of theatre and cinema tickets is cheap in China, and limits placed by state rule. Except for foreigners, who can pay 4 *yuan*, the maximum is 1 *yuan* for theatre or *quyi*, if the troupe is of national level, the actors famous and the seat well placed. Prices then vary downwards according to the item, troupe, actors and position. A normal price is 60 *fen* (Chinese cents) for a national level troupe, and 40 *fen* for a provincial, 30–35 *fen* for a prefectural, and 25–30 *fen* for a county level company. In the *quyi* teahouse-theatre I visited in Chengdu the standard price was 20 *fen* per evening, including the tea. Amateur shows are sometimes free. Cinema tickets are naturally cheaper than theatre. Except for very long films in two parts, the maximum is about 30 *fen* and the normal price in urban cinemas 20 *fen*. Students, that is those of secondary level or above, pay 10 *fen*, and children, who include primary school pupils or younger, 5 *fen*. In the villages also 5 *fen* is a common price for a ticket.

Once at the theatre Chinese audiences demonstrate several features which are striking to foreigners. One is that, despite explicit notices and rules forbidding it, spitting is normal during all kinds of show. On the other hand, the equally clear rule not to smoke inside the theatre is almost invariably followed.

Another feature is that many people talk during the performance. Several comments may be made about this practice. First, it is possible to relate it to pre-liberation times when theatres functioned also as teahouses, so that to sip tea together with friends was simply a part of going to the opera. One did not expect to attend to all the drama but to alternate between chatting and watching the actors. Second, my impression comparing fairly extensive theatre going in autumn 1978 and the winter of 1979–80 was that the general hum was somewhat more muted in the latter period. The third point is that talking during the performance appears mainly to take place during Chinese opera forms or concerts. Audiences are more or less or even completely silent during spoken plays or films.

Actors naturally prefer the audience not to talk because they want full attention. In 1978 several actors with whom I spoke considered the constant hum offensive and a token of the lack of discipline which they associated with the influence of the 'gang of four'. Early in 1980 I heard a slightly different approach, which was to ascribe the talking to general discussion of the action on the stage. 'Young people nowadays', I was told, 'do

201

not really understand traditional opera, because it was not performed for so long. They comment on the content to one another. It does not mean a lack of concentration.' There may be some truth in this explanation. What little conversation I have heard and followed during theatre shows has been commentary on the plot of the drama under performance. The argument would also explain why talking takes place during traditional opera forms but not spoken plays or films.

Another habit of Chinese audiences is their very parsimonious attitude towards applause. It is very rare to hear more than a patter at the end of a drama. The performers will take a bow but quite often they applaud the audience as much as vice versa. I have found the same pattern in all parts of China and for all forms of theatre (of course there is no applause at the cinema). There is occasionally wild or even brief stormy applause at special moments during the show, such as when an actor performs a particularly brilliant acrobatics section or holds a note exceptionally long. Shouting approval, once a standard way of showing appreciation, is but rarely heard nowadays.

This chapter concerns the basis of the performing arts, training, performers, theatres, audiences, society, without which a cinema or drama show is impossible. Here the theme of revival is as strong or even stronger than elsewhere. Everywhere I heard the complaint 'the gang of four prevented the training of actors and thus tried to kill the arts'. Of course it was particular types of actor the 'gang of four' tried to stifle, but the very kinds now most in need. As far as concerns traditional opera, *geju* and *wuju*, or the types of plays and films now in vogue, a generation of performers is missing. The variety of performer the 'gang of four' trained is now useless because nobody likes their style any more.

Traditional theatre, especially, requires great care and long years of training before its actors can be called qualified. Moreover, once the spark and skill are interrupted they are not easy to bring back.

The Chinese are also trying to revive the customs of the pre-Cultural Revolution period, such as methods of selling tickets, distribution of artistic performances and even the *quyi* teahouse-theatre. They know that a thriving theatre rests on a particular set of social customs.

On the other hand, novelty as opposed to restoration is very weak in the area of the social base of theatre. I heard of no completely new methods of training, very few new attempts to break into new modes of theatre architecture. There is constant talk of 'moving into forbidden areas' and 'emancipating the mind'. But so far it seems to be the areas forbidden by the 'gang of four' that should be encouraged, and from the influence of the same quartet that one should free the mind.

Having turned from rejection to restoration, the Chinese may well in due course move on to novelty in the bases on which they rest their theatre. It seems to be the logical next step. In my opinion it would be desirable.

8

Conclusion

Chinese society has seen extensive changes in almost all sectors since the 'gang of four' fell in October 1976. These have been accompanied by major transformations in the performing arts, which have influenced, and been affected by, the rest of society.

Restoration and novelty

The overwhelming impression which emerges from a consideration of the Chinese performing arts since 1976 is of an attempt to revive a lost culture. During visits to China, one of the commonest terms I came across among performing arts circles was *huifu*, to restore, recover. Failure to restore was always regarded as a pity, success was the highest good.

This applied above all to the traditional forms of the performing arts. In a sense, this is too obvious to state, since to bring back a tradition which has been banned for a decade is by its very nature a restoration. However, there is more to it than that. What the Chinese are really trying to revive is not so much tradition, as the kind of traditional culture which prevailed before the Cultural Revolution. Virtually all the classical operas are actually arrangements made under the Communists, either before or after liberation. The extent of arrangement varies, but it would be true to say that a classical opera performed in a way exactly the same as would have prevailed a century ago could not be found in today's China at all.

This is not necessarily to cast a value judgment, because no culture remains static nor should aim to do so. The worry about the traditional performing arts in contemporary China, however, is that bringing back a culture defunct only a decade or so requires no more ingenuity or creativity, indeed may even require less, than restoring one dead many decades or centuries.

The resurrection of the pre-1966 culture is also an important theme for the modern branches of the performing arts. Many of the most popular *geju*, plays or dance-dramas enjoyed a strong following before the Cultural Revolution. In the early months after the 'smashing of the gang of four' restoration was probably most pronounced of all in the field of cinema since it is much easier and quicker to take an old film out of the store than to reproduce and rerehearse an old play. With the progress of time, however, new films have tended to replace the pre-1966 ones, even though the latter have not lost their importance and continue to occupy a popular place in the repertoire.

This leads on to the other major theme in the post-1976 Chinese performing arts, which is novelty. Not surprisingly, the modern forms have led the way here. Topics considered unsuitable for a decade now find their way into new works, both plays and films. An accelerating number of new plays and motion pictures are being produced. Some of them represent the contemporary post-1976 years of China.

There is a degree of novelty also in the traditional forms of the performing arts. This is found not only in the continuing adaptation of already existing operas and in the use of post-1976 themes in old opera forms, but also in the attempts to break into historical stories never before used. A prime example is the Beijing opera *Sima Qian* about the famous Chinese historian of that name who lived in the second and first centuries BC. Its subject matter is ancient, yet never before had a Beijing opera used Sima as material. Moreover the approach to the subject, with its emphasis on struggle, is very modern.

Actually the novelty in the contemporary Chinese performing arts has a ring about it which is not so new. The technical innovations in plays and films are more copies from the West or from before the Cultural Revolution than real novelty. The same goes for the traditional forms. Thus, some of the magnificently colourful types of scenery in 'ancient costume operas' and spectacular methods of rapid changes in it were common before 1966. The *style* of theatre in China today brings us back basically to the category of restoration, not of novelty.

There are several artistic characteristics both of the revived and the newly written works which illustrate this point. One is that both include familiar dramatic themes alien to the Cultural Revolution, including humour, tragedy and love. One can of course distinguish the extent to which these features are found in the various genres. Humour and comedy, so traditionally central in the local opera and the *quyi*, has reoccupied its former place there, while expanding also in other forms by comparison with the 'gang of four' decade.

Possibly more important from the point of view of world theatre, but rather less so from that of Chinese, is tragedy. Reference was made in Chapter 4 to the tragic endings not only of 'wound' plays like *Red Hearts*, but also dance-dramas such as *The Small Sword Society*. In each case the sense of tragedy is diluted by the implication that the real end follows the conclusion of the drama and that the revolution or the smashing of the 'gang of four' has put an end to the type or scale of misery or defeat shown on the stage. Sometimes the brief end of a tragedy may offer a slightly different perspective, as when their reunion as butterflies softens the blow created by the deaths of the lovers Liang Shanbo and Zhu Yingtai. Real tragedy – real in the sense that no mitigating circumstances are offered – does exist. In Chapter 3 the example of *Beating the God* was cited. Certainly the tragic ending was much more common in drama of the pre-1966 period than during the decade 1966–76, when it was virtually unknown, but at no period does it compare in importance with humour.

The broad theme of love has also returned in all forms of the performing arts. From 1966 to 1976 it was never allowed to play a central role and about the most one could expect to see was a snatch or two of 'proletarian love' in scenes lasting a few minutes. Now, however, the snatches have become veritable floods, especially in the traditional 'ancient costume' operas, but also in films and other modern forms.

Another aspect of the restoration of the pre-1966 period applying equally to revived and newly written works is in characterisation. In this field Jiang Qing's 'models' have come under particularly savage and largely justified attacks for their stereotyped portrayal of characters. The pre-1966 and more subtle methods are now again much preferred. Actually the irony is that the portrayal of characters is also still quite direct. Nobody can have any difficulty in discerning who is good and who is bad in the revived or new plays or films or traditional operas. On the other hand, it is true that the range of emotions which the characters feel is much broader than in the 'models' and, for the average onlooker, whether Chinese or foreign, very much more interesting.

Enchantment, magic and fantasy are further artistic devices which have returned for the first time since 1966. In these cases the change is virtually absolute. In other words, whereas comedy and elements of love and tragedy did exist in the theatre of the 'gang of four' decade, even if to a minimal extent by comparison with since 1976, one would search the drama of those years in vain for any magical event, or even a positive mention of enchantment or fantasy. Since October 1976, however, it has become quite common, not only in children's theatre but in general as well. Monkey dramas are most certainly not intended only for children. Adults love them just as much.

Children's theatre is yet another aspect of the restoration existing both in revived works and those written since October 1976. Actually, the difference in the importance of items especially for children is quite marked as among the various branches of the performing arts. The traditional forms have never made a point of setting children apart from adults. There is no such thing as a 'children's regional opera' or 'children's Beijing opera'. The only branch of the traditional performing arts which comes near a specific children's theatre is puppetry. On the other hand, a children's cinema is growing and children's plays are already well advanced.

Conclusion

Continuity, propaganda and cinema

Up to this point the discussion has focused on the contrasts between the theatre of the post-1976 and pre-1966 periods on the one hand and the 'gang of four' decade on the other. But there are also similarities and continuities.

The adaptability of items of the Chinese performing arts from one form to another is very much a stylistic feature of all periods. The lack of children's theatre in some genres is one of the few exceptions to this rule. Plays can be made readily into films and vice versa, or provide the material for modern operas. Operas can also be made into motion pictures. Of course adaptation is necessary to suit the medium. Films and especially operas can tolerate long periods without any dialogue much more readily than plays, and there are other differences. But they are not such as to impede seriously the transfer of an item in one form to the other. Jiang Qing had her 'models' made into films, and all kinds of traditional operas have become 'theatre films', or even ordinary feature films. *Lord Qiao's Adventure*, initially a Sichuan opera but later made into a comedy without operatic singing with the title *Qiao laoye shangjiao* (*Lord Qiao Gets in a Sedan Chair*), is a good example of the last category. The tradition by which the Chinese adapted a single plot from one regional style of theatre to another has been carried over to the more modern forms as well.

But a far more important stylistic continuity is the predominance of the political connection, the directness of the propaganda. It is true that I have drawn attention in these pages to specific examples of works where the political content is so low as to be in effect non-existent. But they are very much the exception, not the rule. Even in the 'ancient costume' operas set in the dynastic period long before the beginnings of the revolutionary movement, political or social propaganda of one sort or another is usually present.

The propaganda function of the theatre in its modern forms also remains as strong as ever. In fact, it is marginally more direct and intense than in the traditional forms, and not much weaker than during the decade of the 'gang of four'. What has changed is the targets of the propaganda. Whereas no theatrical

208

work of the late 1960s or early 1970s could possibly attack the Cultural Revolution, nowadays none could praise it. Yet there is a certain consistency in direction. It would still be impossible for a Chinese play to present the Guomindang or Japanese of the pre-Liberation period in a favourable light.

No matter how many gangs of whatever number may be smashed, the likelihood is that the CCP will continue to use the performing arts for political purposes. During the Cultural Revolution, the Red Guards and Maoist factions argued that if they themselves did not seize power in the cultural sphere and use it for propaganda purposes, then somebody else most certainly would. Despite the general backtracking from the Cultural Revolution, the Chinese leaders still appear to believe in this Maoist doctrine. Probably there will be no time in the foreseeable future when the idea's validity will be seriously challenged.

For a number of reasons cinema is of all performing arts forms considered here the best suited to political propaganda. One is that films are not necessarily fictional. However true to life it may be, one would normally expect a play or ballet to be fictional or a reflection of reality, but not fact itself. Cinema, on the other hand, is the perfect medium for the treatment of actual historical and contemporary events. For this reason, it exercises an instructional function both broader than and different from that of other forms of the performing arts. In a society where emulating models is so important, the cinema has a very great role to fulfil in telling people in one part of the country or in one profession what those elsewhere or in other walks of life are doing, in expanding detailed and factual knowledge. The ease with which films can be transported from one place to another and reach enormous audiences adds to the significance and directness of the part they can play in helping to achieve the four modernisations.

Cinema is also by far the most popular of the performing arts. The editor of *Renmin xiju* (*People's Theatre*) told me early in 1980 that his magazine had some 200,000 subscribers, but that *Dazhong dianying* (*Cinema for the Masses*) had five or six times as many. Far more people see films than plays or operas. According to figures given by the Minister of Culture, Huang Zhen, to a reporter on 27 September 1979 and given to me by the Ministry's Bureau of Arts through the Union of Chinese Dramatists, in 1979 there were 110,000 cinemas, including rural film projection troupes, in the whole country giving shows to audiences totalling 20,000,000,000 in 1978.[1] Given that their population was about 1,000,000,000, this means that the Chinese went to the cinema, on average, just under twice per month in 1978. Although comparable statistics for the various forms of theatre and *quyi* are unfortunately not available, they are most unlikely to exceed the above figures.

It is arguable then that cinema is now the premier branch of the performing arts in China. This adds point to the question of whether there is an identifiably Chinese cinema, especially since the motion picture was initially so foreign an art-form. Reference was made in Chapter 5 to the concern of some Chinese actors and producers about the development of a national style of acting. But even to create such a style is not enough. Any great nation which determines to build its own film industry must be able to devise a distinctive style of cinema as a whole.

During my interview with Situ Huimin and his deputy Ding Qiao they said that, although much further work was necessary, they believed that 'there is indeed a Chinese tradition, there is a national style'. The points they raised to identify this style included the structure of the stories, which owes as much or more to Chinese literature than to foreign ideas, the manner of relating the story, the music and the camera work. They raised the example of *Moon Reflected on the Second Springs* in which they saw a completely Chinese scenery and manner of presentation impossible in any other country. Many of the elements of this national style are more the results of tradition than contemporary initiative and originality. It is true also that many film techniques, including ways of introducing the credits and the characters, and some methods of flashback and of changing scene are foreign imports, not to mention the idea of the motion picture itself. On the other hand, total originality is in no sense necessary for a national style, and I believe the points which Situ and Ding put forward to be fair, and a valid judgment on China's cinema art.

There is no question that the Chinese as a whole appreciate

their own cinema and presumably regard it as a form properly integrated into their own national way of life. I was struck by the number of people in China, both those involved in theatre and those in other walks of life, who said that 'young people are not interested in traditional theatre any more because they cannot understand it. They much prefer plays and especially films.' Although one can confirm simply by looking at audiences that there are indeed some members of the young generation who still like those classical operas, no observer can fail to note that by and large there is a lower average of ages at cinema or spoken play shows than at traditional operas. The statistics quoted earlier appear to confirm that it is cinema which attracts the largest and hence most varied audiences.

The future of the traditional theatre forms

There is a very important implication here. If the young are currently tending to stay away from traditional operas and if these draw most of their patronage from middle-aged or old people, what will happen in twenty or thirty years' time? By then the present audiences will largely have vanished and, unless the young move towards classical theatre as they grow older, there will be relatively fewer people coming forward in replacement. In that case traditional theatre forms are likely to decline in popularity to an ever greater degree.

Chinese involved in the theatre, especially in its traditional forms, are of course aware of the problem and very concerned about it. On 13 December 1979, the editorial department of the magazine *People's Theatre* held a forum in Beijing to discuss it. Although the focus was on Beijing opera, in fact the issues are the same for all traditional forms.

Those taking part included quite a few of the most distinguished names in Beijing opera, and they brought forward a number of central points.

They agreed that the young were losing interest. One member, probably reflecting general opinion, suggested that 'the greatest problem with traditional theatre is that people do not understand it. There are many reasons why they do not un-

211

derstand, there is the problem of scripts and also the problem of formulas in performance', the latter of which 'have definite limitations in expressing the thoughts and feelings of the people of today'.[2]

No real way of solving these problems is suggested. If one gives up the formulas altogether one sacrifices much of the beauty of Beijing opera. If the young do not understand them, it is necessary to introduce them into the education system. This was not suggested at the forum and would be a very artificial way of keeping a tradition alive.

Another reason why 'Beijing opera audiences are getting less and less' is because 'the quality of the art is falling'. 'Some young performers are very deficient in the basic skills; once they know their lines and have rehearsed a bit they go straight on the stage; of course the quality of performance cannot be good that way.'[3] This brings us back to the lost generation of actors noted in Chapter 7, and to the deficiencies in the training system. One speaker called for more attention to be given to the skills of the old artists, but it is doubtful if this can solve the problem. While I am in no position to question what so many people say, that standards of acting have fallen, the young people will not remember what performances were like before the Cultural Revolution and are therefore unlikely to make the comparisons. I am doubtful if the 'quality of performance' is as bad as suggested in the above quotation; and, even if it is, whether it is really a critical factor in the overall problem of the survival of the traditional performing arts.

Other speakers moved on from acting styles more to content.

Now we must develop Beijing opera art and dare to create something new, dare to reform. There are things we should learn from former people, but also we need things which former people did not have. Also there is the problem of modern opera. Jiang Qing gave modern opera a bad reputation, but it is after all created by the masses and there are sung sections in some operas I like very much, their vocal music is good. Just because some counter-revolutionaries meddled in them, we cannot say these operas are of themselves counter-revolutionary.[4]

The same theme was taken up by a number of other speakers. It is a valid argument and suggests that people are most interested in identifying themselves with those they see on the stage. Although it is now ritually necessary to divorce oneself from the 'gang of four' by calling them counter-revolutionary, the principle is very similar to what Jiang Qing and her followers were propounding in the 1960s and early 1970s.

The supporters of the Cultural Revolution found that this reform of the traditional theatre led to changes in it so basic that they came near to destruction of an art. It is doubtful if anybody would be prepared to go so far again.

The arguments put forward at the forum on Beijing opera are not without force. But they appear to me to overlook a basic dilemma which is that no matter how far one modernises a traditional form of art to make it relevant to the younger generation, it is unlikely to be able to compete with the modern genres, especially the cinema. This has become so highly developed and is so agile and versatile in what it can portray and represent that few young people are likely to make the effort to understand and appreciate a traditional form if a modern is easily available.

Experience in other societies suggests that it is modernisation itself which is the principal enemy of the traditional arts. By embarking so thoroughly on the four modernisations the Chinese have, in my opinion, made the decline of the traditional opera inevitable. What is striking to me at present is not the poverty of the classical theatre in China, but its richness. Despite the views put forward at forums such as the one described, the theatres at classical performances are currently full. As modernisation progresses this is likely to change, whatever theatre workers do, because society will be transformed. The problems of classical theatre are not the fault of theatre activists or actors but of society itself.

All this is not to say that the classical forms of theatre are on the verge of extinction. It is likely that they will survive indefinitely but not in the vitally important place they occupy at present. They may well become the kind of beautiful sideshow or museum piece they already seem to be in some countries more advanced than China. A select but substantial audience may well continue to admire the magnificence of such ancient arts. The old actors of a future generation may become regarded as 'national treasures', just as in Japan.

But no matter what value judgment may be cast, successful modernisation cannot fail to bring a deleterious effect on traditional theatre forms. Correspondingly, it will benefit the modern forms greatly, especially the cinema. Its present preponderance is likely to become ever more pronounced, just as in the world's advanced countries, and the Chinese success in developing a 'national cinema' cannot help but accentuate the cinema's dominance. It was noted earlier that many items of its traditional performing arts had been filmed; and this process will certainly continue. Modern techniques can make the sound of a filmed opera as good as an actual performance. It will be ironical indeed if the cinema thus turns out to be the saviour and preserver of the traditional performing arts.

Appendix
Musical notation

The notation system in almost universal use among the Chinese is based upon the designation of notes through numbers. At the beginning a particular note is associated with the number 1. The tonic of the major scale is represented by 1, the supertonic by 2, the median by 3, the subdominant by 4 and so on. A sharp or flat is shown just before the note affected. The octave above the tonic is shown through a dot above the number 1, or 2 if the supertonic etc., and the octave below through a dot below the number.

The time signature and tempo are shown at the beginning, just as in the staff notation. A number with no line underneath represents a simple crotchet, a single line means a quaver, two lines a semiquaver and so on. A dot after the number shows that it is held on half as long again. Rests, barlines, double bars and ties are the same as in staff notation.

The following passage, shown both in the Chinese and staff notations, will enable the reader to compare the way the two systems operate. The tune is a short section from a children's song, an Indonesian folk-song called 'Xiao mutong' ('Little Herdsboy'), taken from *Shaonian ertong gequ, diwuji (Young Children's Songs, Fifth Collection)* (People's Music Press, Beijing, 1979), p. 37.

For a mass audience the Chinese system has the great advantage of simplicity which makes it easy to understand. It is much less satisfactory for the expression of complicated harmony, but this tends to be lacking in Chinese music of the traditional style. Music in the Western idiom is usually written in staff notation, especially if designed to be read by specialists.

I = C $\frac{4}{4}$

Light and quick

0 3 4 | 5 3̇ 5 3̇ 5 0 5♯5 | 6 4̇⌢4 3̇ 5̇. 3 4 |
5 3̇ 5 ♯4 ♮4 2̇. | 1̇ – – ‖

Allegro

Notes

1 Historical background

1 Mao Zedong, 'Jieshao yige hezuoshe', *Hongqi* (*Red Flag*) 1 (1 June 1958), p. 3. I have followed the translation in Stuart R. Schram, *The Political Thought of Mao Tse-tung* (Praeger, New York, 1963), p. 253.
2 'Report on an Investigation of the Peasant Movement in Hunan', *Selected Works of Mao Tse-tung*, I (Foreign Languages Press, Peking, 1965), p. 28.
3 *Ibid*.
4 'China's Two Possible Destinies', *Selected Works of Mao Tse-tung*, III (Foreign Languages Press, Peking, 1965), p. 252. This was Mao's speech opening the 7th National Congress of the CCP on 23 April 1945.
5 See 'Press Communique of the 11th National Congress of the Communist Party of China', dated 18 August 1977, *Peking Review* 35 (26 August 1977), p. 6.
6 I have considered this topic in some detail in 'Theater and the Masses', in Colin Mackerras, ed., *Chinese Theater: History and Practice* which will be published by the University Press of Hawaii in Honolulu.
7 The rural and urban movements noted here are clearly in a Maoist image. In one of his first works Mao wrote that 'the landlord class and the comprador class are wholly appendages of the international bourgeoisie, depending upon imperialism for their survival and growth'. See 'Analysis of the Classes in Chinese Society', *Selected Works*, I, p. 13.
8 This section of the directive is quoted in Wang Du, 'Huanying kaifang jinxi', *Xiju bao* 11 (11 June 1957), p. 14.
9 See 'Yi xiandai jumu wei gang', *Xiju bao* 15 (17 August 1958), p. 15.
10 See *Renmin ribao*, 26 May 1967, p. 4.

217

11 Jack Chen, *Inside the Cultural Revolution* (Macmillan, New York, 1975), pp. 163–4.
12 'Report to the Ninth National Congress of the Communist Party of China', *Peking Review* 18 (30 April 1969), p. 28.
13 The most complete account of Chinese theatre in this period is Lois Wheeler Snow's *China on Stage, An American Actress in the People's Republic* (Random House, New York, 1972), which includes the texts of the three items named.
14 See an article by Zhao Hua translated from *Renmin ribao*, 14 January 1974, under the title 'Has Absolute Music No Class Character?' in *Peking Review* 9 (1 March 1974), p. 16.
15 See *Hongqi* 5 (23 April 1976), p. 6, translated *Peking Review* 15 (9 April 1976), p. 3.
16 *Mingshi* (Zhonghua shuju, Beijing, 1974 ed.), chap. 30, p. 500.
17 'Chronicle', in *Chinese Literature* 5 (1976), p. 113.
18 *Ibid.* 9 (1976), p. 132.
19 Mass Criticism Group of Beijing and Qinghua Universities, 'Negating the Revolution in Literature and Art Aims at Restoring Capitalism', *Peking Review* 22 (28 May 1976), p. 7.
20 'Spring Comes to China's Stage', *Peking Review* 14 (2 April 1976), p. 10.

2 Performing arts policy in the history of China since Mao Zedong

1 'Speech at the Second National Conference on Learning from Tachai [Dazhai] in Agriculture', *Peking Review* 1 (1 January 1977), p. 42; 'Zhongguo Gongchandang zhongyang weiyuanhui zhuxi Hua Guofeng tongzhi zai dierci quanguo nongye xue Dazhai huiyi shang de jianghua', *Hongqi* 1 (7 January 1977), p. 38.
2 The translation, under the title 'A Brilliant Historic Document', comes from *Peking Review* 47 (19 November 1976), p. 13.
3 Translated *ibid.* 17 (22 April 1977), p. 27; original in *Hongqi* 5 (3 May 1977), p. 33.
4 See *Renmin ribao* editorial of 23 May 1977, p. 1, translated *Peking Review* 23 (3 June 1977), p. 9.
5 'Zai Zhongguo Gongchandang di shiyici quanguo daibiao dahui shang de zhengzhi baogao', *Hongqi* 9 (4 September 1977), p. 26, translated as 'Political Report to the Eleventh National Congress of the Communist Party of China', *Peking Review* 35 (26 August 1977), p. 50.
6 Lin Kehuan, 'Xiezai "Baozi wan zhandou" chongxin shangyan de shihou', *Renmin xiju* 3 (25 March 1977), p. 62.
7 See *Peking Review* 1 (1 January 1977), p. 25; *Hongqi* 1 (1 January 1977), p. 23.
8 *Renmin ribao*, 4 June 1977, p. 4.

9 Xue Yuan, 'Gengduodi wei shaonian ertong xiexi', *Renmin xiju* 6 (25 June 1977), p. 56.

10 'Communique of the Third Plenary Session of the Eleventh Central Committee of the Communist Party of China', *Peking Review* 52 (29 December 1978), p. 10.

11 *Ibid.*, p. 11.

12 *Ibid.*, p. 15.

13 ' "Heixian zhuanzheng" lun moshabuliao Mao zhuxi, Zhou zongli de fenggong weiji', *Renmin xiju* 12 (25 December 1977), p. 4.

14 *Renmin ribao*, 6 February 1978, p. 1.

15 *Ibid.*, 11 April 1978, p. 3.

16 *Ibid.*, 13 July 1978, p. 3.

17 'Tuanjieqilai, wei jianshe shehuizhuyi de xiandaihua qiangguo er fendou', *Hongqi* 3 (12 March 1978), p. 20, translated in 'Unite and Strive to Build a Modern, Powerful Socialist Country', *Peking Review* 10 (10 March 1978), pp. 28, 29.

18 Mu Qing, 'Rang guangda qunzhong kandeshang xi', *Renmin xiju* 3 (18 March 1978), p. 29.

19 *Peking Review* 10 (10 March 1978), p. 29; *Hongqi* 3 (12 March 1978), p. 20.

20 *Renmin ribao*, 22 July 1978, p. 4. See also the letters to the editor in *Guangming ribao*, 7 October 1978, p. 3 in which two apparently ordinary citizens call for more and better Chinese and foreign films.

21 Summary of the note's proposal in *Beijing Review* 14 (6 April 1979), p. 4.

22 See *Beijing Review* 4 (28 January 1980), p. 8.

23 Shi Zhengwen, 'Readjusting the National Economy: Why and How?', *Beijing Review* 26 (29 June 1979), p. 17.

24 'The Third Movement to Emancipate the Mind', *Beijing Review* 21 (25 May 1979), p. 11.

25 'Explanation on Seven Laws', *Beijing Review* 28 (13 July 1979), p. 11.

26 'Wei Jingzheng Sentenced', *Beijing Review* 43 (26 October 1979), p. 6.

27 Quoted in Gerald Chen, 'The Tragic Story of Zhang Zhixin', *Eastern Horizon* XVIII, 8 (August 1979), p. 40.

28 See the article by Su Shuangbi in *Guangming ribao*, 15 November 1978, p. 3.

29 'Shi "Wenhua da geming de xumu" haishi cuandang duoquan de xumu?, *Renmin xiju* 1 (18 January 1979), p. 4.

30 Li Shu, 'Jiang Qing pohuai Wenhua da geming de yige yinmou', *Renmin xiju* 1 (18 January 1979), p. 6.

31 The full text of the speech can be found in *Guangming ribao*, 6 February 1979, pp. 1–3 among a number of other places. The official abridged translation of the speech entitled 'Zhou Enlai on Literature and Art' is carried in *Beijing Review* 13 (30 March 1979), pp. 9–16.

32 *Guangming ribao*, 6 February 1979, p. 2; *Beijing Review* 13 (30 March 1979), p. 13.
33 *Renmin ribao*, 27 October 1970, p. 2.
34 *Guangming ribao*, 6 February 1979, p. 3; *Beijing Review* 13 (30 March 1979), p. 13.
35 *Guangming ribao*, 6 February 1979, p. 3; *Beijing Review* 13 (30 March 1979), p. 14.
36 *Renmin ribao*, 4 June 1979, p. 3.
37 See the Chinese original in *Guangming ribao*, 9 September 1979, p. 1. I have used the official translation in 'A Talk to Music Workers', *Beijing Review* 37 (14 September 1979), pp. 13, 14.
38 *Guangming ribao*, 9 September 1979, p. 1; *Beijing Review* 37 (14 September 1979), p. 12.
39 'Our Lessons and Tasks Ahead', *Beijing Review* 50 (14 December 1979), p. 13.
40 *Ibid.*, pp. 12–13.
41 *Ibid.*, p. 15.

3 The traditional forms of the performing arts since 1976

1 Zhang Zichen, *Minjian wenxue jiben zhishi* (Shanghai Literature and Arts Press, Shanghai, 1979), pp. 137–8.
2 Tian Han's report to the Second Congress of the Union of Chinese Dramatists in *Renmin ribao*, 9 September 1960, p. 7.
3 Xiao Jia, 'Tan lishi ju', *Renmin xiju* 1 (18 January 1978), p. 38.
4 Zhang Zhen, 'Lishi ticai, da you kewei', *Juben* 7 (28 July 1979), p. 56.
5 *Ibid.*
6 Xiao Jia, *op. cit.*, p. 37.
7 'On Contradiction', *Selected Works of Mao Tse-tung*, I (Foreign Languages Press, Beijing, 1965), p. 324.
8 Ren Guilin, Wei Zhenxu, Li Lun, 'Yi Liu Zhiming tongzhi lingdao bianyan *Sanda Zhujiazhuang*', *Renmin xiju* 8 (18 August 1979), p. 16.
9 Xu Jinzhong, 'Zhi you tuichen chuxin cai neng baoliu chuantong jumu', *Renmin xiju* 5 (18 May 1979), p. 25.
10 'Yuemu cizi de tuichen chuxin', *Renmin xiju* 7 (18 July 1979), p. 31.
11 See the complete text of the drama in *Renmin xiju* 12 (25 December 1977), pp. 59–80.
12 Guo Liang, 'Chongkan *Yangmen nüjiang* yougan', *Renmin xiju* 12 (25 December 1977), pp. 18, 19.
13 *Beijing ribao*, 1 June 1979, as translated in *Ta Kung Pao*, 21 June 1979, p. 18.
14 David Bonavia, 'Monkey Subdues the Left-Wing Demons', *Far Eastern Economic Review*, vol. 108, no. 18 (25 April 1980), p. 17.

15 Perry Link, 'Hou Baolin: An Appreciation', *Chinese Literature* 2 (February 1980), pp. 85–6.
16 Hou Baolin, Xue Baokun, Wang Jingshou and Li Wanpeng, 'Xiangsheng yu xiaohua, shang', *Quyi* 1 (15 January 1980), p. 7.
17 *Guangming ribao*, 27 May 1979, p. 3.
18 Shi Chengming, 'Daxing xiandai Pingju "Shei zhi zui" gongyan', *Shaanxi xiju* 6 (25 November 1979), p. 16.

4 Theatre in its modern forms

1 Xing Yuan, 'Kan geju "Baimao nü" chongxin shangyan de ganxiang', *Renmin xiju* 4 (25 April 1977), p. 62.
2 See 'Zaiban qianyan', the introduction to the republication of *Honghu chiwei dui* (Hubei People's Press, Hubei, 1977).
3 Raymond L. Whitehead, 'The Small Sword Society', *Eastern Horizon* XVI, 11 (November 1977), p. 29.
4 See Wang Qingcheng, 'Recent Developments in the Study of the Taiping Heavenly Kingdom – A Review of the 1979 Academic Symposium in Nanjing', *Social Services in China* vol. 1, no. 1 (March 1980), pp. 156–67.
5 Li Ling, 'Balei wuju yu yinyue suitan', *Wudao* 1 (30 January 1979), p. 17.
6 *Ta Kung Pao*, 14 September 1978, p. 4.
7 See the text of the drama in *Renmin xiju* 7 (18 July 1978), pp. 49–89.
8 'Xiju chuangzuo de zhongyao keti', *Renmin xiju* 10 (18 October 1978), p. 9.
9 The official translation of the story is in *Chinese Literature* 3 (1979), pp. 25–38.
10 Su Shuyang, 'How I came to Write "Loyal Hearts" ', *Chinese Literature* 10 (1978), p. 107.
11 The Chinese text of the play, including the epilogue, may be found in *Renmin xiju* 5 (18 May 1978), pp. 16–54. The official translation, without epilogue, is in *Chinese Literature* 10 (1978), pp. 23–105, under the title 'Loyal Hearts'.
12 'New Play "Red Hearts" ', *Peking Review* 23 (9 June 1978), p. 28.
13 Su Shuyang, 'Cong shiji shenghuo chufa suzao renwu', *Renmin xiju* 5 (18 May 1978), p. 62.
14 *Huaju Tong Xin* (Shanghai Literature and Arts Press, Shanghai, 1979), p. 91.
15 *Ibid.*, p. 94.
16 Ding Haipeng, '*Tong Xin*', *Wenyi bao* 1 (12 January 1979), p. 55.
17 *Renmin ribao*, 16 January 1980, p. 5.
18 *Ta Kung Pao*, 13 September 1979, p. 17.
19 First printed in the magazine *Renmin wenxue (People's Literature)*, the play was published as a separate book in Chengdu by the Sichuan

People's Press in February 1979 under the title *Wang Zhaojun (Wumu lishi ju)*.

20 Yishan, 'Zuotan Cao Yu tongzhi xinzuo "Wang Zhaojun" ', *Juben* 9 (28 September 1979), p. 37.
21 This is the phrase Miao Junjie of the *People's Daily* used, during my discussion with him in January 1980, in categorising all Chinese *huaju* performed since October 1976. Apart from plays with contemporary content, his classifications were: (i) historical plays, e.g. *Wang Zhaojun*; (ii) 'plays which sing the praises of the old generation of revolutionaries', e.g. *Yang Kaihui*, *The Xi'an Incident*; and (iii) children's plays, e.g. *Indigo Flower*.

5 The cinema

1 Zhu Ma, *Dianying yishu yu dianying wenxue jichu* (Sichuan People's Press, Chengdu, 1979), p. 61.
2 *Ibid.*, p. 18.
3 Quoted in Jay Leyda, *Dianying, An Account of Films and the Film Audience in China* (Massachusetts Institute of Technology, Cambridge, Mass., 1972), p. 25.
4 Mei Lanfang, *Wode dianying shenghuo* (China Cinema Press, Beijing, 1962), p. 4.
5 *Guangming ribao*, 5 May 1979, p. 3.
6 Liang Hsiao, 'Keep on Criticizing the Bourgeoisie', *Peking Review* 21 (23 May 1975), p. 15.
7 Sun Hua, 'China Popularises Science and Technology Through Films', *New China News* XVI, 27 (26 July 1978), p. 3.
8 See *Dazhong dianying* 5 (20 May 1979), between pp. 16, 17.
9 'Xiwang zai yinmu shang kandao women de laoshi', *Renmin dianying* 8 (22 August 1978), p. 14.
10 'Why so few Good Films?', *Beijing Review* 14 (6 April 1979), p. 8.
11 *Beijing ribao*, 20 January 1980, p. 4.
12 'How Is a Studio Run?', *China Reconstructs* XXVIII, 8 (August 1979), p. 7.
13 'Dianying wenxue juben xiezuo zatan', *Renmin dianying* 10, 11 (22 November 1978), p. 23.
14 *Ibid.*, p. 21.
15 *Ibid.*, p. 22.
16 'In Search of a Chinese Style of Acting', *China Reconstructs* XXVIII, 8 (August 1979), p. 14.
17 'Renzhen jiuzheng cuoan, fanrong dianying chuangzuo', *Dazhong dianying* 1 (20 January 1979), p. 17. The film-script *Zaochun eryue*, arranged by Xie Tieli, was published by the Chinese Cinema Press in Beijing in August 1979.

18 Bo Zhi, ' "Zhaochun eryue" guanhou suibi', *Dazhong dianying* 3 (20 March 1979), p. 19.
19 Luo Li, 'Juyou yishu tese de "Erquan yingyue" ', *Dazhong dianying* 12 (20 December 1979), p. 12.
20 He Cangling, 'Zhunque lijie yu shenke jieshi', *Renmin yinyue* 2 (28 February 1979), p. 28.
21 See Peng Chengliang, 'A Bing, the Blind Folk Musician', *Chinese Literature* no. 5 (May 1980), p. 99.
22 Lu Qixin, 'Zhenqie, shuqing, youmei de "Xiaohua" ', *Dazhong dianying* 12 (20 December 1979), p. 13.
23 *Beijing ribao*, 15 January 1980, p. 2.
24 *Renmin ribao*, 30 January 1980, p. 5.
25 Jia Hua, 'Yiqu Huanghe ernü de songge', *Dazhong dianying* 1 (20 January 1979), p. 5.
26 Wu Datang, 'Guanyu Mao zhuxi yishu xingxiang de suzao', *Dazhong dianying* 4 (20 April 1979), p. 11.
27 Tang Baogen, 'Yingpian pinglun yao shishi qiushi', *Dazhong dianying* 4 (20 April 1979), p. 11.
28 Ding Zhaoguo, 'Youxie changjing bu zhenshi', *Dazhong dianying* 4 (20 April 1979), p. 11.
29 'Acting with Confidence Again', *China Reconstructs* XXVIII, 8 (August 1979), p. 13.
30 *Guangming ribao*, 5 May 1979, p. 3.
31 *Ibid.*

6 Music in the performing arts

1 'Jicheng minzu yinyue yichan de zhongyao cuoshi', *Renmin yinyue* 7 (30 July 1979), p. 36.
2 *Ta Kung Pao*, 15 June 1978, p. 17.
3 'Chongshi chuantong, boluan fanzheng', *Renmin yinyue* 5 (30 September 1978), p. 16.
4 Zhang Zelun, 'Ye tan xiqu yuedui de bianzhi wenti', *Renmin yinyue* 1 (30 January 1979), p. 37.
5 Zhang Wenli, 'Xiqu yuedui ye ying baihua qifang', *Renmin yinyue* 1 (30 January 1979), p. 36.
6 Jiang Hongsheng, 'Qiantan huaju yinyue', *Xiju xuexi* 10 (December 1978), p. 120.
7 *Ibid.*, p. 121.
8 Lei Zhenbang, 'Wo chuangzuo dianying yinyue de yixie tihui', *Renmin yinyue* 1 (30 January 1979), p. 15.
9 Mao says of the specialist, 'If he regards himself as their master, as an aristocrat who lords it over the "lower orders", then, no matter how talented he may be, he will not be needed by the masses and his work will have no future.' See 'Talks at the Yenan [Yan'an]

Forum on Literature and Art', *Selected Works of Mao Tse-tung [Zedong]*, III (Foreign Languages Press, Beijing, 1965), p. 85.

10 Lei Zhenbang, 'Wo chuangzuo dianying yinyue de yixie tihui', *Renmin yinyue* 1 (30 January 1979), p. 15.

11 Luo Li, 'Juyou yishu tese de "Erquan yingyue"', *Dazhong dianying* 12 (20 December 1979), p. 12.

12 'Guanyu zhongxiaoxue yinyue jiaoyu wenti', *Renmin yinyue* 6 (30 June 1979), p. 3; *Guangming ribao*, 29 May 1979, p. 3.

13 *Youer gequ xuan disanji* (Shanghai People's Press, Shanghai, 1977), p. 75 (inside back cover).

14 Gong Yuenian, 'Mantan shaonian ertong gequ chuangzuo', *Renmin yinyue* 3 (30 March 1979), p. 40.

15 ' "Gequ zhi wang" – Shubote', in *Shaonian ertong gequ, disiji* (People's Music Press, Beijing, 1979), p. 42.

16 *Guangming ribao*, 24 June 1979, p. 3.

17 Zhang Zhiqin, 'Yao ha qin dang qiang shi', *Renmin yinyue* 8 (30 August 1979), p. 3.

7 Bringing performances to fruition

1 Zhang Jun, 'Yingzhe kunnan chuang xinlu', *Quyi* 1 (15 January 1980), p. 34.

2 *Ibid.*

3 'Dianying fangying yishu he guanli gongzuo zuotanhui', *Dianying jishu* 6 (10 November 1979), pp. 4–5. The quotations are the (unnamed) reporter's summary of the proceedings.

4 I have treated this subject in some detail in *The Rise of the Peking Opera 1770–1870* (Clarendon, Oxford, 1972), pp. 145–53 and elsewhere.

5 I have discussed this problem in *The Chinese Theatre in Modern Times* (Thames & Hudson, London, 1975), pp. 185–6, 192.

6 Zhou Weizhi, 'Jin yibu jiaqiang quyi gongzuo', *Quyi* 7 (15 July 1979), p. 11.

7 See 'Village Opera' in Gladys Yang and Yang Hsien-i trs. *Selected Stories of Lu Hsun* (Foreign Languages Press, Peking, 1954), p. 84.

8 Detail on particular theatres in Beijing is given by Roger Howard in *Contemporary Chinese Theatre* (Heinemann, London, 1978), pp. 40–1.

9 Zheng Lun, 'Chaguan tingshu jishi', *Quyi* 4 (15 April 1979), p. 47, reprinted from *Jilin ribao*.

10 *Shichang*, 10 January 1980, p. 13.

11 *Contemporary Chinese Theatre, op. cit.*, pp. 41–2.

12 Mu Qing, 'Rang guangda qunzhong kandeshang xi', *Renmin xiju* 3 (18 March 1978), p. 28.

8 Conclusion

1 See also *Ta Kung Pao*, 4 October 1979, p. 8. According to the same newspaper, 19 June 1980, p. 13, China's 'estimated total number of filmgoers in 1979 was 'a staggering 70 million a day', which comes to 25,550,000,000.
2 Yang Yumin, in 'Jingju xiang hechu qu?', *Renmin xiju* 1 (18 January 1980), p. 4.
3 Wang Mengyun in *ibid.*
4 Zheng Yiqiu in *ibid.*, p. 8.

Selected further English-language reading on Chinese performing arts since 1949

Bi Hua, 'Some Conjectures on the Future of Arts in China', in Chi Hsin, *The Case of the Gang of Four* (Cosmos Books, Hong Kong, 1977), pp. 184–93.

Chu, Godwin C., *Radical Change Through Communication in Mao's China* (University Press of Hawaii, Honolulu, 1977).

Chu, Godwin C., ed., *Popular Media in China Shaping New Cultural Patterns* (University Press of Hawaii, Honolulu, 1978).

Chung, Hua-min and Miller, Arthur C., *Madame Mao, A Profile of Chiang Ch'ing* (Union Research Institute, Hong Kong, 1968).

Fletcher, M. D., 'Springtime for Chinese Culture', *World Review* XVIII, 2 (June 1979), pp. 46–60.

Howard, Roger, *Contemporary Chinese Theatre* (Heinemann, London, 1978).

Kartomi, Margaret J., 'Some Changes in China's Performing Arts', *Eastern Horizon* XVI, 11 (November 1977), pp. 31–42.

Leyda, Jay, *Dianying, An Account of Films and the Film Audience in China* (MIT Press, Cambridge, Mass., 1972).

Liu, Alan P. L., *Communications and National Integration in Communist China* (University of California Press, Berkeley, 1975).

Mackerras, Colin, *Amateur Theatre in China 1949–1966* (Australian National University Press, Canberra, 1973).

Mackerras, Colin, 'Chinese Opera after the Cultural Revolution (1970–72)', *China Quarterly* 55 (July/September 1973), pp. 478–510.

Mackerras, Colin, *The Chinese Theatre in Modern Times From 1840 to the Present Day* (Thames & Hudson, London, 1975).

Mackerras, Colin, 'The Taming of the Shrew: Chinese Theatre and Social Change Since Mao', *Australian Journal of Chinese Affairs* 1 (January 1979), pp. 1–18.

Meserve, Walter J. and Meserve, Ruth I., comp., *Modern Drama from Communist China* (New York University Press, New York, 1970).

Meserve, Walter J. and Meserve, Ruth I., 'Theatre for Assimilation:

China's National Minorities', *Journal of Asian History* XIII, 2 (1979), pp. 95-120.

Mowry, Hua-yuan Li, *Yang-pan Hsi – New Theater in China* (Center for Chinese Studies, University of California, Berkeley, 1973).

Snow, Lois Wheeler, *China on Stage: An American Actress in the People's Republic* (Random House, New York, 1972).

Yang, Richard F. S., 'The Reform of Peking Opera Under the Communists', *China Quarterly* 11 (July/September 1962), pp. 124–39.

Yang, Richard F. S., 'The Performing and Visual Arts and Music', in Yuan-li Wu, *China: A Handbook* (Encyclopaedia Britannica, USA, 1973), pp. 737–58.

Selection of journals useful for the Chinese performing arts since 1976

Dates given refer to the time either of inauguration or revival after the Cultural Revolution.

Beijing Review, Beijing Review, Beijing, March 1958 (Originally entitled *Peking Review*, this journal was renamed in January 1979).

Chinese Literature, Foreign Languages Press, Beijing, Autumn, 1951.

Dazhong dianying (*Cinema for the Masses*), China Cinema Press, Beijing, January 1979.

Juben (*Scripts*), People's Literary Press, later People's Theatre Press, Beijing, January 1979.

Quyi (*Quyi*), People's Literary Press, Beijing, January 1979.

Renmin dianying (*People's Cinema*), People's Literary Press, Beijing, March 1976.

Renmin ribao (*People's Daily*), People's Daily, Beijing, June 1948.

Renmin xiju (*People's Drama*), People's Literary Press, later People's Theatre Press, Beijing, March 1976.

Renmin yinyue (*People's Music*), People's Music Press, Beijing, March 1976.

Shaanxi xiju (*Shaanxi Drama*), Shaanxi People's Press, Xi'an, January 1979.

Wudao (*Dance*), People's Music Press, Beijing, March 1976.

Yanyuan shenghuo (*Performers' Life*), The Pingju Troupe of China, Beijing, September 1979.

Yilin (*Forest of Translations*), Jiangsu People's Press, Nanjing, November 1979.

Index

A! Yaolan (film), *see Ah! Cradle*
Abing (Hua Yanjun) (musician), 140–3, 168
acrobats, acrobatics, 202; in Beijing opera, 81, 84, 104, 159; in dance-drama, 112; in Monkey dramas, 99, 100; as separate performing arts type, 74, 77, 104, 194; training in, 181
acting style, Chinese national, 138, 210
actors, actresses, 185–94, 201, 202, 210, 212–14; the profession, 184–202; social status of, 191–3; training of, 176–84
Actress Places an Accusation (Chuigushou gaozhuang) (*Pingju*), 105
advertisements, for performances, 197, 198
Afghanistan, 61
After the Blue Light Flashed (Languang shanguo zhihou) (film), 134, 146, 147, 148, 168–9, 186
Agrarian Reform Law, 10
agriculture, 11, 13, 16, 17, 39, 40, 133
Ah! Cradle (A! Yaolan) (film), 143–7, 186
Ai yu hen (Shanghai opera), *see Love and Hate*
Albania, 48
All-China Federation of Literature and Art Circles, 55
American(s), 13, 27, 59, 145

Andersen, Hans (author), story 'The Wild Swans', 105
Anti-Rightist Campaign, 14, 15, 16
army, 24
audiences, 81, 86–7, 90, 201–2
August 1st Storm (Bayi fengbao) (spoken play), 116, 117
Autumn River (Qiujiang) (Sichuanese opera), 95, 96, 102, 163

Baimao nü (geju), *see White-haired Girl*
Baishe zhuan (opera), *see Story of the White Snake*
ballet, 112, 113–14, 115, 209; as imported form, 76, 107, 158, 159, 161, 184; *see also* Jiang Qing and individual ballets
Ballet Troupe of the Central *Geju* and Dance-Drama Company, 158
Bao Zheng (judge 999–1069), 88–91
Bayi fengbao (spoken play), *see August 1st Storm*
Beating the God (Dashen) (Sichuanese opera), 97, 206
Beijing, 24, 111, 134, 170, 188, 198; cinema, cinema studios in, 129, 133, 139, 146, 199; concerts, orchestras in, 159, 160; conferences, congresses, festivals in, 21, 28, 33, 39, 41, 50, 55, 171, 183, 211; 'Democracy Walls' in, 14, 61, *see also* 'Democracy Walls'; drama performances in, 45, 58, 99, 105, 109, 124; Mayor of, 19, 22, 23;

229

Index

Municipal CCP Committee, 51, 59, 200; national institutes in, 178; opera companies in, 20, 187, 196; and Tangshan earthquake, 146; theatres in, 195, 199, 200; Tiananmen Incident in, *see* Tiananmen Square, Incident; University, 30; visited by Kissinger, 27

Beijing Film Studio, 136–7

Beijing opera: actors of, 56, 193; adaptation to other forms, 78, 95, 162; companies, 15, 20, 82, 86, 163; Festival of Beijing Operas on Contemporary Themes, 21, 83; future of, 211–14; history of, pre-1949, 75, 198; model, modern, 28, 34, 36, 76, 77; music of, 83, 84, 154, 161, *see also* under opera; revival of after 1976, 46, 79, 105; training in, 178, 181, 182, 183; *see also* acrobats, opera, individual Beijing operas

Beijing Opera Company of China, 15

Beijing Review, 219, 220, 222, 228

Beijing ribao, 222, 223

Bhutto, Z. A. (Prime Minister of Pakistan), 31

Bi Hua (author), 226

Bishang Liangshan (Beijing opera), *see Forced Up Mt Liang*

Bizhi (Sichuanese opera), *see Compelling a Nephew*

Bo Zhi, 223

Bonavia, David (journalist), 220

Boulder Bay (*Panshi wan*) (revolutionary opera), 34

Boulder Bay, 35

bourgeois(ie), 10, 19, 27, 29, 34, 70, 148, 173, 217

Brecht, Bertolt (playwright), 71

British, 112, 143

Burma, 56

cadre(s): and the arts, 68, 182; in fiction, 111, 118, 120; of newspapers as informants, 126, 143, 144, 145, 151; privileges of, 103; and revolutionary committees, 24; rural, 19; state, 184, 192; suppression by 'gang of four', 59, 63, 71, 119; *see also* 'gang of four'

Calcutta earthquake, 32

Campaign to Criticise Lin Biao and Confucius, 26, 28, 29, 122

Canada, 27

Cantonese opera, theatre (*Yueju*), 76, 78, 111, 163

Cao Yu (playwright), 53–6, 115, 125, 167

caravan troupes, 57, 58

cartoons, 134

CCP, *see* Chinese Communist Party

Changsha, 76

Chao Gai (drama character), 81, 82

chaotou wenxue (new wave literature), 118

characterisation, model operas, 83–4, 207; *see also* cinema

Chen Chong (film-star), 145

Chen Gang (musician), 160

Chen, Gerald (author), 219

Chen, Jack (author), 217

Chen Miaochang (drama character), 95, 96, 102

Chen Shimei (drama character), 88, 89

Chen Shufang (actress), 193

Chen Yi (minister), 136

Chengdu, 95, 102, 163, 177, 178, 193, 195, 201; Municipal Opera Company, 97

Cheng Zhanggeng (actor), 75

Chi Hsin (author), 226

Chiang Kaishek (head of Guomindang China), 34, 83, 118, 149, 150, 174

children's theatre, 46, 95, 124, 125, 207, 208; Arts Theatre, 121, 124; films, 131–5; performers, 186; play (*ertong huaju*), 121; *see also* Cultural Revolution

China Drama School (*Zhongguo xiqu xuexiao*), 84

China on Stage, An American Actress in the People's Republic, Lois Wheeler Snow, 218

China Reconstructs, 222, 223

Chinese Communist Party (CCP), 6, 151, 209; campaign against the 'gang of four', 39, 41, 44, 51–2; cultural bureaux of, 20; Eighth Route Army, 109; in fiction, 103, 108, 116, 149; founding of, 5; and

Great Leap Forward, 16; heroes, heroines honoured by, 63, 85, 174; laws and land reform by, 9–13; in period after 1966, 26, 28, 31; revisionism in, 21, 23; size of, 6; and social change, 2, 77; study of, by trainee performers, 181; victory of, 9, 76, 130; view of the Taipings, 113; in Yan'an, 82; *see also* Cultural Revolution, Hua Guofeng, Mao Zedong, National Congress, Plenary Session, *and* Zhou Enlai

Chinese Federation of Literary and Art Circles, 71

Chinese Literature, 218, 221, 223, 228

Chinese Theatre in Modern Times, Colin Mackerras, 224

chou (clown), 90

Chu, Godwin C. (author), 226

Chuangye (film), *see* Pioneers

Chuigushou gaozhuang (Pingju), *see* *Actress Places an Accusation*

Chung Hua-min (author), 226

cinema, the, 128, 209–11; advertisements for screening, 197, 198; audiences, 201, 202; characters in, 7, 207, *see also* individual characters; and children, 133–5, 147, 207; Cinema Bureau, distribution, 133; and Cultural Revolution, 25, 36, 140; as entertainment, 69; foreign, 70–1, 134, 152; as foreign import, 107, 129; history of, pre-1949, 129–30; as means of communication, 12, 13, 209; and music, 129, 141, 142, 155, 167–9, 210; performers of, salary, conditions and status, 184, 185, 187, 188, 192, 193, 202; and politics, 143, 149, 209; popularity of, 58, 199, 209–10, 211, 213; in the PRC, pre-1966, 13, 15, 18, 21, 53, 130–1, 205; projectionists, 183; revival since 1976, 37, 53, 58; suppression of, 42, 130; techniques in, 141, 146, 147, 152, 205; technology of, 128, 214; themes of, 2, 13, 21, 136, 139, 140, 142, 143; violence in, 144–5; *see also* 'gang of four', model opera, opera, traditional opera

Cinema for the Masses (Dazhong dianying), 145, 168, 209, 222, 223, 224, 228

cinemas, 194, 195, 199; tickets to, 201; *see also* Western

Ciwei bei xigua (film), *see* Hedgehog Carries a Watermelon

class(es), 5, 19, 88; exploited, ruled, 4, 80; exploiting, ruling, 4, 9, 17, 26, 80, 132; struggle, 28, 51, 52, 72, 132

coal, producing area, Tangshan, 32

collectively owned (*jiti suoyouzhi*) performing troupes, 184, 188, 189, 190, 192, 193

communes, 3, 16, 17, 24, 28, 50

communication(s), 7, 8, 9

Compelling a Nephew (Bizhi) (*Sichuanese opera*), 95

concubinage, 11

Confucius (551–479 BC) (philosopher), 26, 120

Conservatorium: Central Philharmonic, in Beijing, 178; of Music, Shanghai, 179, 181

Contemporary Chinese Theatre, Roger Howard, 224

control of the arts, 8, 15–16; *see also* Cultural Revolution, opera

co-operatives, co-operativisation, 13, 15, 16

Criminal Law, 64

Cultural Revolution: attacked in literature and the performing arts, 91, 118, 119, 122, 123; and ballet, 113, 114; and children's theatre, 46, 124; and fancy, magic, 95, 172; impact on artists, 56, 105, 110, 111, 125–6; impact on the CCP, 5–6, 62; impact on troupes, 189, 190–1, 197, 202; influence on the arts, 21, 22, 24–6, 28, 33, 35–6, 37, 54, 130, 139, 162, 209, 213; influence on China in general, 22–4, 26, 30, 37, 49–51, 166; items and forms banned during, 86, 94, 104, 108, 135, 205; and law, 64, 71; and Lin Biao, 24–8; and music, 156, 160, 163, 165, 169, 172, 175; negation of, in the arts, 53–9 *passim*, 66, 69, 76, 112, 126, 130, 140, 160, 204, 206; negation of, in China in general, 38, 40, 52–3, 63, 65, 67, 72–3, 209;

as period in China's history, 9, 35,
44, 77, 212; preparation for, 19;
and theatres, 195, 199, 202–3; and
tragedy, 97, 206; view of history
during, 85; *see also* Deng Xiaoping,
'gang of four', Mao Zedong, *and*
spoken play
Culture: Ministry of, Minister of, 12,
15, 17, 69, 77, 135, 139, 151, 178,
182, 191, 197, 200, 209–10; Bureau
of, 197, 200; Cinema Bureau, 186;
Deputy Minister of, He Jingzhi,
108, 184; Deputy Minister of, Situ
Huimin, 133, 136; Minister of,
Huang Zhen, 209
curtain(s), 87, 91

Dahe benliu (film), *see Great River
Flows On*
dan, male, 183, 184, 193
Dance (Wudao), 221, 228
dance, dancing, 22, 33, 77, 84, 120,
157, 158, 161, 177, 178
dance-drama, 112–14, 125, 184, 185,
186, 205, 206; *see also* acrobats,
'gang of four'
Dance School, Central, in Beijing,
178
Danxin pu (spoken play), *see Red
Hearts*
Daqing oilfield, 42
Dashen (Beating the God) (Sichuanese
opera), 97
*Dazhong dianying, see Cinema for the
Masses*
Death on the Nile (film), 152
'Democracy Walls', 14, 51, 61
Deng Xiaoping (Vice-Premier):
attacked by radical faction, 23, 30–
4, 36, 41, 43, 51, 52, 63, 148; in
power (since 1977), 48, 50, 51, 62,
64, 104, 172, 173, 174; reinstated,
41, 42, 43, 45, 47, 72, 100, 123; and
the US, 59, 60; *see also* model
opera, traditional opera
*Dianying, An Account of Films and the
Film Audience in China*, Jay Leyda,
222
Dianying jishu (Cinema Technique), 224
'dictatorship of the sinister line in
literature and art' (*wenyi heixian

zhuanzheng), 53, 54, 55; *see also*
Jiang Qing
Ding Haipeng (reviewer), 221
Ding Qiao (Deputy Director of the
Cinema Bureau), 186, 210
Ding Zhaoguo, 223
Dismissal of Hai Rui (Hai Rui baguan)
(historical drama), 22, 66, 67, 68
dizi (Chinese flute), 75, 155, 164, 165,
166
documentary films, 130, 131–5
Dongfang hong (music and dance
pageant), *see The East is Red*
drama, *see* drama troupes, opera,
spoken plays, theatres, *et passim*
drama troupes, children in, 186;
conditions in, 186–90;
nationalisation of, 15, 189; salaries
of members of, 185, 187; training
of, 176–83; types of, 184; *see also*
actors, actresses, Jiang Qing, *and*
individual drama troupes
Drama Institute, Central, in Beijing,
178, 179, 180, 181
Drama Reform Committee, 12
Dream of Red Mansions (Honglou meng)
(film), 18, 131, 132
drought, 3

earthquake, Tangshan, 32
East China Drama Festival, 20
East is Red, The (Dongfang hong)
(music and dance pageant), 22, 131
Eastern Horizon, 219, 221
economic conditions, change:
influence on art, 1; and law, 11;
model of development, 16, 17, 22;
nationalisation, 15; primacy since
1976, 39, 40, 41, 49, 61, 72, 73;
soviet influence, 13, 16; and the
Tangshan earthquake, 32; as theme
in the arts, 2
education(al), 9, 16, 41, 46, 56, 61,
69, 72, 133, 148, 212; Deputy
Minister of, Zhang Chengxian,
169, 170; Ministry, Minister of,
169, 170, 182; music as education,
169–74
Eighth Route Army, 109
elite, 6, 8, 23, 75, 186, 193
Empress Dowager Cixi, 75
erhu, 140, 141, 168

Index

Erquan yingyue (film), see Moon Reflected on the Second Springs
ertong huaju (children's play), 121
Eryue (February) (novel), 21
Exchange of the Heir-Apparent for a Leopard Cat (Limao huan taizi) (Shaoju), 89–92, 104, 165

Fahai (drama character), 94, 96
family life, 10–11, 95, 144
famine, 3
Fan Zhonghua (drama character), 90
Fang Ai (drama character), 122, 123
Fang Lingxuan (drama character), 118
Far Eastern Economic Review, 220
feature films (gushi pian), 130–51, 208
February (Eryue) (novel), 21
February in Early Spring (Zaochun eryue) (film), 21, 139, 140
Festival of Beijing Operas on Contemporary Themes, see Beijing opera
fiddle (huqin), 154
film(s): Distribution Company, 197; industry, see cinema, documentary films, feature films, and individual films
Film School, Central, in Beijing, 178
Five Year Plan, first, 1953–57, 13, 15, 16
Fletcher, M. D. (author), 226
Flood in Sizhou (Shuiyan Sizhou) (Shaanxi opera), 99, 100
flute, Chinese (dizi), 75, 154
folk, music, songs, dances, 156, 157, 160, 167
Forced Up Mt Liang (Bishang Liangshan) (Beijing opera), 45, 78, 81, 82, 162; praised by Mao Zedong, 82
foreign: art, attitude to, 29, 45, 70, 156, 172–3, 175; capital in China, 64; enterprises, takeover of, 12; friendships with, peoples, 136; harmful connections with China, 2, 10, 39; influences on Chinese arts, 18, 166, 210; theatre, 46, 66, 70–1, 114, 181; see also cinema, foreign affairs, Western, and individual foreign countries

foreign affairs: policy, 12, 19, 27, 31, 47, 48, 59, 173; Ministry of, 61
Forest of Translations (Yilin), 228
four modernisations, 72; continued in 1979–80, 61, 62; and culture, 170, 175, 209, 213; emphasised by Plenum, 52; and foreign relations, 49; introduced by Hua Guofeng, 30, 119; and science and technology, 50; see also modern, and modernisation
Fu Zhifang (wife of Mei Lanfang), 56
Fujian Provincial Art School, 104

'gang of four': attacked in films, 136; attacked in literature or songs, 103, 118–23, 171; and ballet, 114; and Cultural Revolution, 38, 53, 58, 67, 123; and Deng Xiaoping, 51; and education, 41, 120, 122, 123, 169; fall of, impact on the arts in general, 22, 42–3, 44, 53, 55, 66, 72, 203, 207, 208, impact on China in general, 39, 47, 59, 72, 166, impact on cinema, 130–7, 149, 150, 205, impact on dance-drama, 112, impact on geju, 108, 109, impact on ideology, 62, impact on music, 156, 159, 160, 162, 164, 165, 169, impact on quyi, 101–2, 103, 164, impact on spoken plays, 59, 118–23, 126, impact on traditional styles of opera, 77, 81, 162, 164, 165, 189; and humour, satire, 104, 206; influence on literature and art, 35, 36, 111, 112, 155, 159, 162, 163, 201, 213; and law, 63, 92; and reservation of tickets, 200; and Taipings, 113; and Tangshan earthquake, 148; treatment of artists, 54, 55, 56, 110, 179, 187, 190, 191, 202; treatment of cadres, 59, 71; trial of, 64–5; and Zhang Zhixin, 63, 66, 105, 173, 174; see also Jiang Qing, Wang Hongwen, Yao Wenynam, and Zhang Chunqiao
Gansu, 3
Gao Lian (dramatist), 95
Gao Zhanxiang (reviewer), 122
Gao Zuyin (musician), 165, 166
geju, 77, 107–12, 184, 185, 187, 202,

233

205; Central *Geju* and Dance-Drama Company, 158

Genü Hong Mudan (film), *see Singing Girl Red Peony*

gestures, 75, 83

Giselle (ballet), 114

Going up Peach Peak Three Times (Sanshang Taofeng) (Shanxi opera), 28

Gong Yuenian (author), 224

Great Leap Forward, 16, 17, 18, 22, 41, 68; *see also* Mao Zedong, traditional opera

Great River Flows On (Dahe benliu) (film), 148, 149, 150, 152

Guan Zhengming (actor), 81

Guangdong, 111; Provincial Opera Company, 78

Guangming Daily (Guangming ribao), 143–6 *passim*, 151, 220–4 *passim*

Guangxi, 123; *Huaju* Troupe, 123

Guanyin (goddess), 99, 100

Guangzhou, 18, 158, 161

guanzi, 155

Guilin, 123, 140, 170

Guizhou, 3

Guo Lanying (actress), 111, 185

Guo Liang (reviewer), 220

Guomindang (Nationalist Party): censorship against films, 130; civil war with CCP, 9, 28; in dramas, 28, 83–4, 109, 116, 209; and marriage regulations, 11; personalities executed by, 21, 116; on the screen, 149, 151; threat of return by, 13; and Zhang Zhixin, 174

Guoyu, 130, 132

Hai Rui (Ming official), 67, 140

Hai Rui baguan (historical drama), *see Dismissal of Hai Rui*

Han, 126

Han Ying (drama character), 109, 110

Hangzhou, 5, 77, 86, 87, 89, 90, 94

Havoc in Heaven (Nao tiangong) (Kunqu), 99, 100

He Cangling (author), 223

He Jian (warlord), 116

He Jingzhi (Deputy Minister of Culture and playwright), 108, 184, 185, 189, 190

He Long (revolutionary), 110, 136

He Zhanhao (musician), 160

Hebei, 32, 105

Hedgehog Carries a Watermelon (Ciwei bei xigua) (film), 134

Henan, 78, 149, 163

Hong Kong, films, 145

Hongdeng ji (Beijing opera), *see Story of the Red Lantern*

Honghu chiwei dui (geju), *see Red Guards of Honghu Lake*

Honglou meng (film), *see A Dream of Red Mansions*

Hongqi (Red Flag), 217, 218, 219

Hongse niangzi jun (ballet), *see Red Detachment of Women*

Hongzhu nü (Shaoxing opera), *see Red Pearl Girl*

Hou Baolin (*xiangsheng* artist), 102, 103, 164, 181, 195, 221

Howard, Roger (author), 200, 224, 226

Hua Guofeng (Chairman of the CCP): and the arts, 36, 42, 44, 57, 58, 66, 171, 198; as Chairman of the CCP, 32–3, 39; and Deng Xiaoping, 41, 51, 62, 104, 123; establishes policies, 39–40, 47; in foreign affairs, 31–2, 132; Premier of the State Council, 31–2, 65; smashes the 'gang of four', 35, 38, 39; and the Tangshan earthquake, 32, 148; and Zhou Enlai, 40

Hua Yanjun (Abing) (musician 1893–1950), 140

huagu xi (flower and drum theatre), 76

huaju, *see* spoken play

hualian (painted face), warrior or heroic official, 75

Huang Yanjun (soldier), 55

Huang Zhen (Minister of Culture), 209

Hubei, 23, 78, 109, 110, 133, 185; Provincial *Geju* Troupe, 109

Hunan, 76, 116

Hunanese opera, 78

Hundred Flowers Movement, 14, 15, 16, 18, 34, 43, 44, 47

huposzu, Mongolian musical instrument, 156

huqin (fiddle), 154, 164

images in the performing arts, 7–8, 43, 117, 136, 150

Indigo Flower (*Malan Hua*) (spoken play), 124, 186, 222

individual, role in history, 4–5, 6

industry, 11, 13, 16, 17, 39, 40, 133

injustices, righted, 88, 91, 92

Inner Mongolia, 57, 156

Inside the Cultural Revolution, Jack Chen, 218

Italy, 27

Japan, Japanese, 214; occupation of China by, 12, 118, 149, 209; relations with, before 1972, 13, 28, 49; relations with, since 1976, 48, 49, 72; songs from, for children, 172; visit of prime minister to China, 27; War against, 9, 76, 108, 115

Jia Hua (reviewer), 223

Jiang Hongshen (author), 223

Jiang Qing (leader of 'gang of four'): adversary of Peng Zhen, 23, 63, 83; attacked in drama, 91; attacks individual artists, 56, 110; and ballet, 109, 114; changes opera orchestras, 161, 166; and the 'dictatorship of the sinister line', 53, 54, 55, 139; influence on the arts, 25, 33, 36, 42, 46, 66, 95, 189, 212, 213; influences opera troupes, 20, 28; leader of move against traditional opera, 20–1, 76; leader of radical faction, 23, 31, 32, 38, 77; and models, 22, 28, 34, 44, 66, 106, 113, 114, 137, 207, 208; suppresses individual forms or works, 67, 86, 108, 109, 116; wife of Mao Zedong, 20, 31, 38, 117; *see also* 'gang of four'

Jiangsu, 3, 133, 140, 195; Provincial Theatre School, 178, 181

Jiangxi, 109, 156

Jiao Guiying (drama character), 97, 98

Jilin, 196

Jilin ribao, 196, 224

Jin, 84

Ji'nan, 178

Jing Hua (actress), 97, 98

jinzhong baoguo, 84, 85

Jiujiu ta (spoken play), *see Save Her*

Journey to the West (*Xiyou ji*) (novel), 98

Juben (*Scripts*), 220, 228

Kampuchean, 60, 172

Kaifeng, 149

Kang Zhilin (actor, 1870–1931), 96

Kartomi, Margaret J. (author), 226

Ke Qingshi (Mayor of Shanghai), 20

Kissinger, Dr Henry (politician), 27

Korea, Korean War, 12, 13, 22, 132

Kunming, 55

Kunqu, 75, 95, 99, 155, 166, 178, 181

Kuomintang, *see* Guomindang

land reform, 10, 12, 13

landlords, 5, 10, 108

Languang shanguo zhihou (film), *see After the Blue Light Flashed*

laosheng, 75

law, 63–5; *see also* Cultural Revolution, 'gang of four', *and* legal system

Leben des Galilei (*Life of Galileo*) (play), 71

Lee Kuan Yew (Prime Minister of Singapore), 31

legal system, 63, 64, 65, 73, 91

Lei Zhenbang (film musician), 167, 168, 224

Leiyu (spoken play), *see Thunderstorm*

Leninism, *see* Marxism-Leninism-Mao Zedong thought

Leyda, Jay (author), 222, 226

Li, Concubine (drama character), 90, 91, 165

Li Jinhui (*geju* writer), 108

Li Ling (author), 221

Li Lun (opera-arranger), 220

Li Mai (film character), 149, 150

Li Shisan (dramatist), 94

Li Shu (author), 219

Li Wanpeng (author), 221

Li Xiaoxia (drama character), 122, 123, 167

Li Xifan (cultural journalist), 161, 162

Li Zhenmin (actor), 100

Li Zhun (film scriptwriter), 149

Liang Changdong (example of bad husband), 89

Liang Hsiao (penname of radical author), 222
Liang Shanbo (drama character), 206
Liang Shanbo and Zhu Yingtai (Liang Shanbo yu Zhu Yingtai) (Shaoxing opera, film), 15, 96, 131, 160, 163, 167
Life of Galileo (Leben des Galilei) (play), 71
Limao huan taizi (Shaoju), *see Exchange of the Heir-Apparent for a Leopard Cat*
Lin Biao (CCP leader), 23–7, 54, 62, 63, 92, 105, 191; *see also* Cultural Revolution, Mao Zedong
Lin Kehuan (reviewer), 218
Link, Perry (author), 221
literature of the wound *(shanghen wenxue)*, 118, 119
Little Flower (Xiaohua) (film), 143, 144, 145, 146, 169, 176
Little Red Book (Quotations from Chairman Mao Zedong), 23
Liu, Alan P. L. (author), 226
Liu, Concubine (drama character), 90, 91
Liu Jingshu (author), 172, 173
Liu Shaoqi (PRC President), 16, 17, 19, 23, 24, 63, 65, 67
Lord Qiao Gets in a Sedan Chair (Qiao laoye shangjiao) (film), 208
Lord Qiao's Adventure (Qiao laoye qiyu) (Sichuanese opera), 93, 208
Love and Hate (Ai yu hen) (Shanghai opera), 164
love dramas, 92–8
Lu Dingyi (Director CCP Central Committee Propaganda Department), 21, 23, 79
Lu Qixin, 223
Lü Ruiming (opera-writer), 86
Lu Xinhua (author), 118
Lu Xun (author), 36, 131, 194
Lu Xun zhandou de yisheng (film), *see Militant Life of Lu Xun*
Lun shida guanxi (On the Ten Major Relationships), 40
Luo Li, 223, 224
lute *(pipa)*, 154

Ma Lianliang (actor), 188, 190
Mahler (film), 143
Mahler, Gustav (musician), 143;

Mahler, Alma (wife of Gustav Mahler), 143
Malan Hua (play), *see Indigo Flower*
Manchu dynasty, 112
Mao Zedong (CCP Chairman): China since, 38, 47, 128, 166; and the Cultural Revolution, 23, 24, 41, 51, 65, 70; death of, 1, 6, 30, 32; and the 'gang of four', 51; and the Great Leap Forward, 16, 18, 41; and Hua Guofeng, 39; influence on the arts, 20, 172; influence within the CCP, 6, 16, 18–19, 52, 104; and Lin Biao, 26; and Mei Lanfang, 56; portrayed on stage or screen, 116, 117, 136, 150; salary of, 189; speech 'On the Ten Major Relationships', 40; as topic of songs, 171; view on the arts, 25, 28, 42, 43, 44, 54, 69, 70, 71; view of China's poverty, 3, 217; and Zhou Enlai, 67, 68, 151; *see also Forced up Mt Liang*, Jiang Qing, Maoism, revolution, 'Talks at the Yan'an Forum on Literature and Art'
Mao Zedong xuanji, *see Selected works of Mao Zedong*
Maoism, Maoist, Mao Zedong thought: on classes, 217; dialectics in, 5; era of, 35; model of development, 16; on the performing arts, 28, 46, 70, 79, 81, 109, 209; since 1976, 40, 47, 62, 151; on war, 86; *see also* Mao Zedong
Marriage, reform, Law, 11, 12–13, 13, 89, 93, 95
Marxism, Marxist, 4, 5, 6, 7, 43, 53
Marxism-Leninism-Mao Zedong thought, 4, 5, 43, 79, 181
masses, the: as creators of art, 29, 212; education of, through the arts, 9, 56, 69, 80; equality with cadres, 19; exploitation or suppression of, 59, 67, 111; as heroes of history, 81; mobilisation of, 16, 17, 26; model opera heroes' disdain for, 45; and the performing arts, 8, 43, 57–8, 69, 75, 115, 161, 198, 200; and the PRC state constitution, 14; and revolutionary committees, 24, 50; service to, 23, 26, 43, 56, 57–8,

192, 199, 200; as theme in the arts, 111, 118
materialism, 4, 7
May Fourth Movement, 115
media, 8, 14, 21, 35, 39, 63
Mei Lanfang (actor), 15, 56, 222
Meihu xi (Meihu opera), 94
Meserve, Walter J. and Meserve, Ruth I. (authors), 226
Miao Junjie (journalist), 78, 114, 115, 222
Militant Life of Lu Xun (Lu Xun zhandou de yisheng) (film), 36
Miller, Arthur C. (author), 226
Ming dynasty (1368–1644), 95, 162; earthquake, 32; opera and story telling, 74
Mingshi, 218
model operas, dramas, 22, 25, 35; attitude to, after 1976, 44, 45, 66, 121, 137; characterisation in, 25, 45, 150, 162, 207; and cinema, 28, 150, 208; and forms other than Beijing opera, 36, 76, 106, 113, 114; ideology of, 25, 28; opposition to, by Deng Xiaoping, 34; performances of, 111; *see also* Beijing opera *and* Jiang Qing
modern: conventions in drama, 91; culture, 70; drama, 17, 18, 19, 20, 59, 107–27, 160, 212; forms in the theatre, 107–27, 205, 206, 208, 213; themes in theatre, 12, 28, 105, 106, 107–27, 189; *see also* four modernisations, modernisation
modernisation, 100, 137, 175, 214; economic, 26, 40, 50, 52; *see also* four modernisations *and* modern
Monkey (Sun Wukong), 98–100, 207; *see also* acrobats
Moon Reflected on the Second Springs (Erquan yingyue) (film), 140, 142, 143, 146, 168, 210
'Moon Reflected on the Second Springs' (tune), 140
Moscow, 60
Mowry, Hua-yuan Li (author), 227
Mu Qing (author), 224
Much Ado about Nothing (Wushi shengfei) (play), 71
Muldoon, Robert (Prime Minister of New Zealand), 31

music, 22, 37, 113, 128, 142, 154–75, 177; attitude to foreign, 29, 70, 156, 172–3, 175; in dance-drama, 112; notation, 215–16; *see also* Beijing opera, cinema, Cultural Revolution, opera, propaganda, *quyi*, Shanghai, spoken play, tradition, traditional opera, *and* Western
Musicians, Association of, 70, 156

Nanchang Uprising, 116
Nangzai (Wanwanqiang), 93, 94
Nanjing, 89, 116, 178
Nao tiangong (Kunqu), *see Havoc in Heaven*
National Conference for the Creation of Spoken Plays and Operas, March 1962 in Guangzhou, 18
National Conference on Learning from Dazhai in Agriculture, 39
National Congress of the CCP: Seventh, 108; Eighth, 14; Ninth, 24, 26; Eleventh, 41, 44, 47, 53
National Congress of Chinese Trade Unions, 50
National Congress of Chinese Writers and Artists, 71
National Congress of Communist Youth League of China, 50
National Day, 9, 188
National People's Congress: actors, actresses represented in, 192, 193; First, 13, 14; Second, 16; Fifth, 49, 57, 58; Second Session of the Fifth, 61, 63–4
National Science Conference, 50
National Women's Congress, 50
nationalism, national identity, 1, 2, 108, 166, 168, 169, 175
Nationalist Party, *see* Guomindang
Nepal, 56
New China News, 222
New China News Agency, 23, 40
New Democratic revolution, culture, 79
New Zealand, 31
new wave literature (*chaotou wenxue*), 118
Nie Er (musician), 108, 172
Nixon, Richard (President of United States), 27

North China Theatrical Festival, Beijing (1974), 28

opera: actions, conventions of, 74–5, 100, 138; adaptation of forms, 76, 78, 205; and cinema, 15, 128, 129, 131–2, 136, 137; civil, 99; and comedy, 97, 206; control of, 15–16, 18, 66; future of, 211–14; length of performance, 198; and love, 92–8, 206; military, 99; and music, 155, 157, 160–8, 170; performance of banned, 110–11; and politics, 91, 208–9; sites of performance, *see* theatres; and tragedy, 97, 206; *see also* Beijing opera, Cantonese opera, *geju*, *huagu xi*, Hunanese opera, *Kunqu*, models, *Pingju*, regional, Shaanxi opera, *Shaoju*, Shaoxing opera, Sichuanese opera, traditional, *and* individual operas
orchestra(s), 87, 107, 112, 154, 157, 161, 163–6
Ouyang Qianshu (musician), 109

Pakistan, 31
Panshi wan (revolutionary opera), *see* Boulder Bay
Party Propaganda Department, *see* propaganda
patriotism, patriotic, 1, 17, 57, 84, 86
peasantry, peasants, 26; co-operativisation of agriculture, 13; drama in service of, 18, 20, 35, 43, 57; and entertainment, 69; exploitation of, 20, 29; and land reform, 10; level of culture, 70; in PRC state constitution, 14; and revolution, 5; support for the CCP, 9; as themes in art, 3
Peking Review, 217, 218, 219, 221
Peng Chengliang (author), 223
Peng Zhen (politician), 19, 20, 23, 63, 64, 83
People's Cinema (*Renmin dianying*), 35, 222, 228
People's Daily, 14, 42, 44, 46, 54, 55, 56, 67, 69, 78, 89, 98, 114, 122, 126, 148, 161, 217–20, 222, 223, 228
People's Liberation Army (PLA), 20, 54, 110

People's Literature (*Renmin wenxue*), 221
People's Music (*Renmin yinyue*), 169, 223, 224, 228
People's Press, 67
People's Theatre (*Renmin xiju*), 35, 53, 66, 117, 209, 211, 219, 220, 221, 224, 225, 228
Performers' Life (*Yanyuan shenghuo*), 228
Phnom Penh, 60
Pingju, Hebei regional style, 105, 177
Pingju Opera Troupe of China, 177, 187
Pioneers (*Chuangye*) (film), 42
pipa (lute), 140, 141, 154, 164, 168
plays, *see* spoken plays
Plenary Session (Plenum) of CCP Central Committee: of September 1962, 18; of October 1968, 24; of July 1977, 41; of December 1978, 47, 51–3, 59, 61, 63; of February 1980, 65, 73
Pol Pot (Kampuchean leader), 60
political, politics, 13; influence on the performing arts, 1, 68, 72, 73, 151; and Marriage Law, 11; since 1976, 38, 50, 64, 72, 73, 127; as theme in the performing arts, 115, 116, 143, 148, 149; *see also* cinema
Political Thought of Mao Tse-tung, Stuart R. Schram, 217
polygamy, 11
poverty, 3, 5
projectionists, cinema, film, 183
propaganda, 135; in cinema, 209; in modern drama, 18, 105, 108, 131; music, 171, 173, 174; in performing arts in general, 9, 47; *see also* spoken plays, traditional opera
Propaganda Department of Central Committee of CCP, 21
Puppet Art Company of China, 105
puppets, puppetry, 74, 97, 98, 104, 128, 207
Putonghua, standard Chinese, 104, 123, 124, 132

Qiao laoye qiyu (Sichuanese opera), *see* Lord Qiao's Adventure
Qiao laoye shangjiao (film), *see* Lord Qiao Gets in a Sedan Chair

Index

Qielilüe zhuan (play), *see Life of Galileo*
qin (zither), 154, 156
Qin Gui (bad minister), 84
Qin Peichun (playwright), 120, 121
Qin Xianglian (Beijing opera), 88, 89, 90, 92, 186
Qing dynasty (1644–1911), 162; court, 75; opera and story telling, 74
Qingdao, 178
Qinmei (Little Sister Qin) (wife of Abing), 140, 141, 142, 168
Qinqiang (Shaanxi opera), 94
Qiujiang (Sichuanese opera), *see Autumn River*
Quanzhou marionettes, 105
Quotations from Chairman Mao Zedong (Little Red Book), 23
quyi (ballad singing, story-telling and cross-talk), 74, 101–4, 197, 210; festival of, 33; humour in, 102, 103, 104, 206; and models, 76; music of, 101, 102, 154, 164, 165; regional, 77, 101, 102; social status, 191–2; teahouse-theatres, venues, 194, 195, 196, 201, 202–3; training of performers, 176, 178, 179, 181
Quyi, 224, 228

railways, 12
Red Detachment of Women (*Hongse niangzi jun*) (ballet), 22, 28, 113–14
Red Flag (*Hongqi*), 217
Red Guard(s), 23, 56, 85, 209
Red Guards of Honghu Lake (*Honghu chiwei dui*) (geju), 109, 110, 111, 131
Red Hearts (*Danxin pu*) (spoken·play), 118, 119, 120, 124, 126, 137, 206
Red Pearl Girl (*Hongzhu nü*) (Shaoxing opera), 94, 95, 96, 98
regional, theatrical forms, 74–8, 99, 101, 132, 154, 165, 184, 194, 208; *see also* individual regional styles, *and* opera
religion, 95, 98
Ren Guilin (opera-arranger), 220
Renmin dianying, *see People's Cinema*
Renmin ribao, *see People's Daily*
Renmin wenxue, *see People's literature*
Renmin xiju, *see People's Theatre*
Renmin yinyue, *see People's Music*
revisionism, revisionist, 52; the arts and, 21, 34, 42, 54, 79, 80, 190;

film, 22, 139; groups, 50, 55; leaders, 23, 33, 34, 42; novel, 27
revolution, revolutionary: arts in the service of, 18; cadres, 119; campaigns and, 26; dramas, 21, 22, 28, 76, 108, 189; history of, as themes in the theatre, 111, 112, 116, 117, 136, 143, 144, 208; and ideology, 40, 49; impetus for change, 2, 3, 4, 23; influence on the arts, 2, 36, 88, 98, 172; Mao's definition of, 3, 5; tradition, education in, 171; *see also* Cultural Revolution
Rise of the Peking Opera, Colin Mackerras, 224
Romance of the Yang Family Generals (*Yangmen jiang yanyi*), 86
Rou Shi (penname of Zhao Pingfu), 21
Russell, Ken (film director), 143
Russian, 113, 130; *see also* Soviet Union

Sanda Zhujiazhuang (Beijing opera), *see Three Attacks on the Zhu Family Village*
Sanshang Taofeng (Shanxi opera), *see Going up Peak Three Times*
sanxian, 154, 165
Save Her (*Jiujiu ta*) (spoken play), 105, 122, 123, 126, 167
Schubert, Franz (musician), 29, 172, 173, 175
Second Springs, *see Moon Reflected on the Second Springs*
Selected Stories of Lu Hsun, Gladys Yang and Yang Hsien-i, 224
Selected Works of Mao Zedong (*Mao Zedong xuanji*), 40, 43, 217, 220, 224
sexes, equality between, 11, 93, 95
Shaanxi, 82, 92, 94; opera (*Qinqiang*), 94, 99
Shaanxi Drama (*Shaanxi xiju*), 221, 228
shadow play, 94, 129
Shakespeare, William (playwright), 71
Shandong, 134, 178, 181
Shanghai, 75; arts education, 170; beginning of the Cultural Revolution, 66; CCP founded in, 5; dialect, 130; drama festival in, 20;

drama set in, 112; drama troupes
and schools in, 15, 96, 163, 178–81;
dramas premiered or performed
in, 59, 120, 199; film studios in,
133; first films in China in, 129;
music in, 157, 159, 160; publication
of *Little Red Book*, 23
Shanghai Conservatorium of Music,
179
Shanghai Film Studio, 135, 136, 146,
187
Shanghai Foreign Languages
Institute, 145
Shanghai opera (*Huju*), 199
shanghen wenxue (literature of the
wound), 118
Shanxi, 57, 156
Shaoju, regional style, 104, 165;
Shaoju, Troupe, 89, 138
Shaoxing 15, 90, 163; opera (*Yueju*),
78, 96, 131, 163, 180; Opera
School, 180, 181, 182
Shei zhi zui? (*Pingju*), see *Whose
Crime?*
'Shei zhi zui?' (song), see 'Whose
Crime?'
Shi Chengming (author), 221
Shi Zhengwen (author), 219
Shichang, 224
Shuihu zhuan (novel), see *Water
Margin*
Shuiyan Sizhou (Shaanxi opera), see
Flood in Sizhou
Sichuan, 56, 57, 92, 133, 193;
Provincial Sichuan Opera School,
178, 179, 180, 181, 182; Provincial
Sichuan Opera Troupe, 57, 92, 193
Sichuanese Opera, 78, 93, 95, 97,
105, 163, 175, 199, 208; *quyi*, 102
Sima Qian (Beijing opera), 205
Singapore, 31
Singing Girl Red Peony (*Genü Hong
Mudan*) (film), 129
Situ Huimin (Deputy Minister of
Culture), 133, 136, 185, 210
Slipper and the Rose (film), 152
Small Sword Society (*Xiaodao hui*)
(dance-drama), 112, 113, 206
Small Sword Society, 113
Snow, Lois Wheeler (author), 218,
227
social, conditions, change, forces, 9;

and the CCP, 2; influence on
history, 4–5, 6; and Marriage Law,
11; and the performing arts, 1, 38,
72, 73, 176; and poverty, 3; since
1976, 41, 50, 59, 64, 65, 72, 73, 151;
as theme in spoken plays, 115,
116, 119, 121, 122, 124; and USSR,
16
Social Sciences in China, 221
Socialist Education Movement, 19
soldiers, 18, 26, 35, 43, 57, 69
Song dynasty (960–1279), 81;
Southern (1125–1279), 84
Soviet Union, 12, 16–19, 27, 47, 49,
52, 60, 61, 113, 130
spoken plays, 115–25, 137, 207;
actors, actresses of, 185, 186, 202;
attacks on Cultural Revolution,
118, 206, 209; and cinema, 129,
131, 147, 208; as entertainment, 69;
as foreign import, 74, 76, 107, 167;
length of, 198; and music, 115,
155, 166, 167; popularity of, 211;
portrayal of revolutionary heroes
in, 117; as propaganda, 120, 208–9;
revival since 1976, 35–6, 53, 116,
160, 205; and technology, 128;
theatres, 194, 195; themes of, 2,
115, 116ff; tragedy in, 97, 120, 121;
troupes, 77, 177, 178, 179, 184; see
also individual spoken plays
Stalin (USSR leader), 43
state-run performing troupes, 184,
185, 186, 188, 189, 190, 192
Storm on the Yangzi River (*Yangzi jiang
de baofengyu*) (*geju*), 108
Story of the Red Lantern (*Hongdeng ji*)
(revolutionary opera), 22, 28, 76
Story of the White Snake (*Baishe zhuan*)
(opera), 94, 95
Su Shuyang (playwright), 118, 137,
139, 141, 151, 221
Sun Hua (journalist), 222
Sun Wukong (Monkey), 98
suona, 155, 157
superstructure of society, 7
Suzhou, 96, 178
Swan Lake (ballet), 105, 114, 158, 159,
161

Ta Kung Pao, 221, 223, 225
Tai, Lake, 140, 141

Taian, 178
Taiping Revolution, 112, 113
Taiwan, 35, 49
Taiyuan, 156
Taking Tiger Mountain by Strategy (Zhiqu Weihu shan) (Beijing opera), 28
Tale of the Jade Hairpin (Yuzan ji) (Ming drama), 95
'Talk to Music Workers', 70
'Talks of the Yan'an Forum on Literature and Art', 45, 46, 68, 108, 109, 168, 223–4
Tan Xinpei (actor, 1847–1917), 20
Tan Yuanshou (actor), 20
Tanaka Kakuei (Prime Minister of Japan), 27
Tang dynasty (618–907), 98
Tang Baogen, 223
Tangshan, earthquake, 32, 146, 147, 148; *see also* 'gang of four'
Tchaikovsky, Peter (musician), ballet *Swan Lake*, 105
teahouse(s), 194, 195, 196, 201, 203
Ten Major Relationships, On the (Lun shida guanxi), 40, 45
theatre films *(xiqu pian)*, 131–5
Theatre News (Xiju bao), 189
Theatre School of China, in Beijing, 178, 179, 181, 183
theatres, 194–202; *see also* Cultural Revolution
Three Attacks on the Zhu Family Village (Sanda Zhujiazhuang) (Beijing opera), 81, 83, 84
Thunderstorm (Leiyu) (spoken play), 167
Tian Han (playwright), 25, 108, 220
Tiananmen Square, Incident, 30, 31, 51, 58, 59, 62, 118
Tianjin, 15, 195
Tong Xin (spoken play), 120, 121–2, 124, 221
Tong Xin (drama character), 120, 121
tradition, 74, 210; music, 155, 157, 158, 161, 162, 174, 175; strength of, 2
traditional opera, 205; banned by 'gang of four', 25, 187; characterisation in, 207; and cinema, 15, 136, 142, 208; conventions in, 83, 85, 87, 88, 91,

96, 99, 183–4; *see also* under opera, and Deng Xiaoping, 56–7, 92; forms of, 74–106, 184, 185, *see also* regional theatrical forms; future of, 211–14; and Great Leap Forward, 17, 18; and Mei Lanfang, 56; music of, 108, 163, *see also* under opera; propaganda in, 46, 80, 91, 92, 107, 208; reform of, 12, 76, 204; revival since 1977, 45, 57, 66, 72, 79–80, 160; themes of, 57, 81, 84, 88, 92, 98; training of actors in, 176ff, 202; underground performance under 'gang of four', 111; *see also* Jiang Qing
tragedy, *see* Cultural Revolution, opera, spoken plays
training schools, 176–83
transport system, 12
troupes, *see* drama troupes

Union of Chinese Dramatists, 77, 210
United Nations, 12, 27
United States of America, 12, 13, 49, 59, 60, 61, 72, 144, 172

Vienna Philharmonic Orchestra, 29
Vietnam, 27, 47, 48, 49, 60, 61

'walking on two legs', 17
wan, 94
Wang Du (author), 217
Wang Kui (drama character), 97
Wang Hongwen (member of 'gang of four'), 38
Wang Jinghua (opera-arranger), 85
Wang Jingshou (author), 221
Wang Mengyun (author), 225
Wang Qingcheng (author), 221
Wang Yuzhen (actress), 110, 111, 174
Wang Zhaojun (spoken play), 126, 222
Wang Zhaojun (princess), 126
Wanwanqiang, 93, 94
Water Margin (Shuihu zhuan) (novel), 27, 81, 82, 83, 84
Wei Jingsheng (leader of 'democracy movement'), 65
Wei Zhenxu (opera-arranger), 220
Wei Zhou (music commentator), 162, 163, 165
Weinan, 94
wenxi (civil dramas), 99

241

Wenyi bao (*Literature and Art*), 221
wenyi heixian zhuangzheng, see
'dictatorship of the sinister line in
literature and art'
Western: arts or society, compared
with Chinese, 8, 74, 112, 134, 144,
154, 159, 167, 186, 199; cinemas,
194, 198, 199; comment on China,
47, 65, 112, 172; influence on
China, 73, 173; influence on
Chinese audiences, 115; influence
on Chinese music, theatre, 108,
157–61, 163–9, 172, 174–5, 205;
musical instruments, 25, 155, 159,
161–5, 170, 174–5, 181; nations'
relations with China, 27–8, 29, 30,
47, 48, 72; as origin of forms of the
arts, 107, 114, 127; *see also* foreign
Where Silence Reigns (*Yu wusheng chu*)
(spoken play), 58, 126
White-haired Girl (*Baimao nü*) (*geju*,
ballet), 15, 108, 109, 111, 113, 114
White Snake, Story of the (*Baishe
zhuan*), 94, 95, 98, 99, 166
Whitehead, Raymond L. (author),
221
Whose Crime? (*Shei zhi zui?*) (*Pingju*),
105
'Whose Crime?' ('Shei zhi zui?')
(song), 173–4
'Wild Swans', Hans Andersen's
story, 105
women, 11, 13, 83, 85–6, 88, 95, 96,
111, 118; *see also* Women Generals of
the Yang Family
Women Generals of the Yang Family
(*Yangmen nüjiang*) (Beijing opera),
86, 88, 180
workers, 9, 14, 18, 20, 26, 29, 35, 43,
57, 69
'Wound, The', 118, 119
Wu Datang, 223
Wu Han (historian and Deputy
Mayor of Beijing), 22, 67, 68
Wudao, see Dance
Wuhan, 23, 78, 81, 82, 87, 109, 110,
157; Municipal Beijing Opera
Troupe, 81
wuju (dance-drama), 107, 202; *see also*
'gang of four'
Wushi shengfei (play), *see Much Ado
about Nothing*

wuxi (military dramas), 99, 178
Wuxi, 140, 141, 142

Xi'an, 92, 94, 96, 99, 105, 177, 194
Xi'an Incident (*Xi'an shibian*) (spoken
play), 118, 222
Xia Yan (film producer), 25
Xiang Lin sao (film), 131
Xiang Lin sao (film character), 131
xiangsheng (form of *quyi*), 102, 103,
104
Xiao Jia (author), 220
Xiaodao hui (dance-drama), *see Small
Sword Society*
Xiaohua (film), *see Little Flower*
Xiaoshan, 89
xiaosheng, scholar-lover, 75
Xie Tieli (film director), 149, 222
Xier (White-haired Girl, *geju*, ballet
character), 108, 111
Xiju bao (*Theatre News*), 189, 217
xiju pian (theatre films), 131–5
Xiju xuexi (*Drama Studies*), 223
Xiongnu, 126
Xing Huiming (film character), 147
Xing Yuan (reviewer), 221
Xiyou ji (novel), *see Journey to the West*
Xu Jinzhong (author), 220
Xu Zhiwei (drama character), 122,
123, 167
Xuanzang (Buddhist monk), 98
Xue Baokun (author), 221
Xue Yuan (author), 219

Yan Jizhou (film director), 142
Yan'an, 14, 45, 82, 108, 109; Beiping
[Beijing] Opera Company, 82
Yandang, Mt (*Yandang shan*) (Beijing
opera), 84
Yandang shan (Beijing opera), *see Mt
Yandang*
Yang family, 86
Yang, Gladys and Hsien-i
(translators), 224
Yang Kaihui (spoken play), 116, 142,
222
Yang Kaihui (wife of Mao Zedong),
116, 117
Yang, Richard F. S. (author), 227
Yang Yumin (author), 225
Yangmen jiang yanyi (novel), *see
Romance of the Yang Family Generals*

Yangmen nüjiang (Beijing opera), *see Women Generals of the Yang Family*
yangqin (dulcimer), 164, 165
Yangzhou opera, 86, 178
Yangzi jiang de baofengyu (*geju*), *see Storm on the Yangzi River*
Yangzi Valley, 3, 195
Yannan, 146
Yanyuan shenghuo, see Performer's Life
Yao Wenyuan (member of 'gang of four'), 38, 66, 67
Yellow River, 149
Yilin, see Forest of Translations
Yishan (reviewer), 222
Yisu Theatre, Xi'an, 194
Yu Lan (film actress), 136
Yu wusheng chu (spoken play), *see Where Silence Reigns*
Yuan Mengya (film actress), 141
Yue Fei (patriotic hero), 84, 88, 89
Yueju, regional Shaoxing Opera of Zhejiang, 78, 96, 179
Yuemu cizi (Beijing opera), *see Yue's Mother Tattoos Characters*
Yue's Mother Tattoos Characters (*Yuemu cizi*) (Beijing opera), 84
Yuju, regional opera of Henan, 78
yuyan yishu ('language art'), 103
Yuzan ji (Ming drama), *see Tale of the Jade Hairpin*

Zaochun eryue (film), *see February in Early Spring*
Zhang Chengxian (Deputy Minister of Education), 169, 170, 171
Zhang Chunqiao (member of the 'gang of four'), 38, 41
Zhang Jing'an (musician), 109
Zhang Jun (author), 224
Zhang Junqiu (actor), 183, 184, 185, 187, 189, 193
Zhang Ruifang (film actress), 149, 150
Zhang Wenli (author), 223
Zhang Zelun (author), 223
Zhang Zhen (author), 220
Zhang Zhixin (CCP martyr), 63, 64, 66, 105, 114, 173, 174; 'The Three

Zhang Sisters', 174; Zhang Zhiqin (sister of Zhixin), 174, 224; *see also* 'gang of four'
Zhang Zichen (author), 220
Zhao Dan (film star), 138, 174
Zhao Hua (author), 172, 173, 218
Zhao Pingfu (author, penname Rou Shi), 21
Zhejiang, 3, 77, 78, 90, 185, 190, 195
Zheng Lun (journalist), 224
Zheng Songmao (film actor), 141
Zheng Yiqiu (author), 225
Zhengzhou, 149
Zhenzong (Emperor), 90
Zhiqu Weihu shan (Beijing opera), *see Taking Tiger Mountain by Strategy*
Zhongguo Pingju yuan, see Pingju Opera Troupe of China
Zhongguo xiqu xuexiao, see China Drama School
Zhou Enlai (Premier of the State Council): death of, 1, 6, 30; and Deng Xiaoping, 30; portrayed on the screen, 136, 149, 150, 151; reverence for, 6–7, 40; role in the Cultural Revolution, 24; role in foreign affairs, 6, 27; role in the performing arts, 44, 56, 67, 68–70, 73, 184; succeeded as Premier by Hua Guofeng, 31; as theme in drama or portrayed on stage, 116, 117–18; as theme in songs, 171
Zhou Enlai Discusses Literature and Art (*Zhou Enlai lun wenyi*), 67
Zhou Enlai lun wenyi, see Zhou Enlai Discusses Literature and Art
Zhou Quanying (actor), 185
Zhou Weizhi (Deputy Minister of Culture), 224
Zhou Xinfang (actor), 25, 56, 188
Zhou Yang (cultural leader), 23, 61, 62, 69, 71
Zhou Zishan (*geju*), 108
Zhu, family village, 81, 82
Zhu De (revolutionary), 117–18, 171
Zhu Ma (author), 222
Zhu Yingtai (drama character), 206
zither (*qin*), 154
Zorro (film), 152